Aesthetic Essays

Aesthetic Essays

Malcolm Budd

OXFORD
UNIVERSITY PRESS

OXFORD
UNIVERSITY PRESS

Great Clarendon Street, Oxford OX2 6DP

Oxford University Press is a department of the University of Oxford.
It furthers the University's objective of excellence in research, scholarship,
and education by publishing worldwide in

Oxford New York

Auckland Cape Town Dar es Salaam Hong Kong Karachi
Kuala Lumpur Madrid Melbourne Mexico City Nairobi
New Delhi Shanghai Taipei Toronto

With offices in

Argentina Austria Brazil Chile Czech Republic France Greece
Guatemala Hungary Italy Japan Poland Portugal Singapore
South Korea Switzerland Thailand Turkey Ukraine Vietnam

Oxford is a registered trade mark of Oxford University Press
in the UK and in certain other countries

Published in the United States
by Oxford University Press Inc., New York

© in this volume Malcolm Budd 2008

British Library Cataloguing in Publication Data
Data available

Library of Congress Cataloging in Publication Data
Data available

Typeset by Laserwords Private Limited, Chennai, India
Printed in Great Britain
on acid-free paper by
Biddles Ltd, King's Lynn, Norfolk

ISBN 978-0-19-955617-5

10 9 8 7 6 5 4 3 2 1

Contents

Introduction

A significant proportion of the essays collected in this volume are aimed at the abstract heart of aesthetics. This hard core of the subject is composed of a number of interconnected issues. Perhaps the principal components are these: the scope and essence of the aesthetic; the nature and proper limits of the claim to intersubjective validity which is built into aesthetic judgements and how this claim might be vindicated; whether particular aesthetic judgements can ever be proved to be true or to be false and, if so, how this might be achieved; the canonical bases of the various species of aesthetic judgement, the distinctive problems these judgements raise, and the aesthetic relevance of the kind of object at which they might be directed; the significance of metaphor in the expression of aesthetic judgements and the articulation of aesthetic experience; the nature of aesthetic pleasure and value; the vital relations between aesthetic and non-aesthetic properties; the ontological status of aesthetic properties, and in particular whether they—all or some—should be understood in a realistic or non-realistic fashion; the possibility and significance of the transmission of aesthetic knowledge by testimony; the nature of artistic understanding and appreciation; what it is for a work of art to be expressive of emotion or other psychological states; the distinctive aim of art; the incommensurability of both aesthetic and artistic value and the implications of this for comparative judgements of one or the other value; the ontological status of works of art. Some of the threads that form this complex knot of issues are easy to disentangle; others are subtly intertwined or bound together more tightly. Accordingly, those essays aimed at the abstract heart of the subject—each of which attempts to resolve one or more of the issues, and which taken together engage with all of them (except the ontological status of works of art, in which I have never had a real interest)—inevitably display a network of links, and in their course sometimes approach the same topics from different directions, give them greater or lesser consideration, and move on from them for different destinations. They were written independently of one another and I have not been concerned to ensure that they form a consistent set. I will, of course, be happy if contrary pronouncements are rare or non-existent.

To extract the pith of the conception of the subject that is embodied in these essays by removing all the supporting arguments and necessary elaborations and refinements is to strip them of what gives them their life. And no summary formulation can in itself be expected to carry conviction, even if the arguments and positions taken up in the essays are correct. Nevertheless, I shall hazard here a very broad sketch, in a series of bald, unsupported, and unqualified assertions, of the distinctive character of general aesthetics as conceived of in the essays. This will at least bring together some of the leading ideas spread across them and indicate my overall view of the terrain.

At the very centre of aesthetics is the concept of aesthetic value: the idea of an object which is intrinsically valuable to experience, with understanding of both what kind of thing it is and its specific character. This is true however widely or narrowly the scope of aesthetics is construed; in particular, whether it includes both the aesthetic appreciation of the natural world and the appreciation of art in all its forms or it has a more restricted range, perhaps excluding one or more arts or various properties of works of art relevant to their appreciation as art. All fields of aesthetics are united by this central concept: what differentiates them is the nature of the object that falls within the respective domain—a work of art, an artefact of another kind, a work of nature—this nature determining the appropriate focus of aesthetic appreciation for objects within the domain.

The various categories of the aesthetic—aesthetic value, pleasure, judgement, property, attitude, and so on—no matter how exactly they are related to one another (not everyone understanding them as being connected in the same manner), and despite disagreements about what should properly be thought of as falling within a particular category, are interdefinable, so that if any category can be defined in non-aesthetic terms, all can be, and the aesthetic is not an irreducible concept. This is indeed the case.

The aim of art is, in short, the achievement of intrinsic value in a medium. There is no aspect of a work's artistic meaning or value that cannot be experienced in a proper engagement with the work by one who has the requisite grasp of the work's place in the history of art and understands the way in which it should be perceived. A work's *specific* artistic value must be distinguished from its artistic value in the sense of how good a work of art it is. In this second sense artistic value is a matter of degree. The value of a work of art as art cannot be elucidated in terms of pleasure unless pleasure is understood in an unnaturally wide sense. Nature has no aim, but to appreciate nature aesthetically is to perceive it as the repository of intrinsically valuable perceptual experiences. Evaluative aesthetic judgements are properly applicable to both art and nature.

All aesthetic judgements, whether descriptive, evaluative, or some combination of the two, and whatever they might be about, whether works of art, artefacts of other kinds, or natural things, declare themselves to be, not mere announcements or expressions of personal responses to the objects of judgement, but claims meriting the agreement of others. This claim to intersubjective validity is in principle justifiable, however far short of meriting it any particular aesthetic judgement might fall. But the contents of aesthetic judgements are of various kinds, which dictate what their claims to intersubjective validity amount to and determine the proper limits of the claims.

One kind of aesthetic judgement—Kant's pure judgement of taste, the judgement of so-called free beauty—demands special treatment in the light of its importance in Kant's thought and his ambitious attempt to effect a deduction of such judgements by means of a certain doctrine about the free and harmonious play of the faculties of the imagination and understanding at work in this kind of judgement, the precise character of Kant's reasoning not being crystal clear, as he himself acknowledged. (The scepticism that is sometimes expressed about our ability to make judgements of this sort is unfounded.) The standard interpretations of Kant's thought about the free and harmonious play of the two faculties are unacceptable: something along the lines of the more plausible interpretation I have proposed might well achieve the vindication of the judgement's claim to intersubjective validity which Kant aspired to.

Aesthetic (or artistic) value accrues to or is withheld from an item in virtue of the qualities it possesses and the category to which it belongs. An aesthetic property is one that is a ground of aesthetic value, positive or negative, a property in virtue of which the item may be aesthetically praised or faulted, a property that is dependent on the lower-order, non-aesthetic properties of the item. Which aesthetic properties an item possesses is not derivable conceptually from its non-aesthetic properties. Particular aesthetic judgements about an object, whether about its value or its properties (or both), are justifiable in a variety of ways, ultimately by reference to its non-aesthetic properties. But although singular aesthetic judgements about an item's aesthetic properties can in principle be shown to be true or false, this is not in a manner that would be acceptable to everyone, for the only sort of proof that such aesthetic judgements are capable of is 'experiential' proof. Aesthetic value and artistic value are both incommensurable (a fact that in no way affects the possibility of showing singular judgements to be true or false). The incommensurability of artistic value derives from a number of factors: positive and negative qualities are of indefinitely many kinds, for which there is no measure of their comparative values and no order of rank; they can be possessed to different degrees, for which there is no metric; they can be possessed by works of art in numbers that might vary enormously; they contribute to a work's artistic value not individually but holistically. Although incommensurability does not preclude the possibility of true or false aesthetic judgements to the effect that one object is finer than another—there are many such comparative judgements, about both works of art and works of nature—it does impose severe limits on the range of judgements of this character that do have a determinate truth-value.

Aesthetic properties are susceptible of both realistic and non-realistic interpretations. But realism and non-realism can themselves be understood in many different ways. The most significant distinction between aesthetic realism and non-realism is captured by defining it in terms of the nature of the canonical basis on which a judgement about a particular kind of aesthetic property of an item is made. This makes precise the question of how the ontological status of aesthetic properties should be understood. There is no good reason to insist, a priori, that all aesthetic properties must have the same ontological status: whether they do is a matter for detailed investigation. According to the criterion I have proposed, some kinds of aesthetic property should be understood realistically, others non-realistically. Although the canonical basis of an aesthetic judgement about an object is acquaintance with the object, no acceptable form of realism or non-realism, whether about aesthetic value or aesthetic properties, implies that an aesthetic judgement, even one that constitutes aesthetic knowledge, must be based on acquaintance with the item judged: acquaintance is required, not for thought, belief or knowledge, but for appreciation.

Metaphor plays a significant role in the expression of aesthetic judgements and the articulation of aesthetic experience for more than one reason. Judgements that attribute aesthetic properties to objects are often expressed by metaphors. To understand what aesthetic judgement is expressed by a metaphor it is necessary to grasp the point of the metaphor, which is to say what commitment is undertaken by one who embraces it. Such commitments consist of a small number of kinds, principally concerning resemblance between different sorts of properties or an exercise of the imagination. Either the concept of the property signified by the predicate expression of the metaphor when this expression is used literally is essential to the specification of the nature of the aesthetic property, or it is not. If the use of the concept is not essential, the commitment is likely to be to some form of resemblance or correspondence between the aesthetic and the non-aesthetic property. If the commitment is to an exercise of the imagination, the use of the concept will be essential (as is typically the case with the expressive properties of works of art). For some aesthetic properties which can be characterized adequately only by means of terms that in their literal use do not signify these properties, a radical, minimalist conception of the experience of perceiving an item as possessing the property is the right one.

There will, I am sure, be a wide consensus about some of what I take to be the basic facts of general aesthetics, but sharp disagreement over others. I am optimistic about the prospects of such disagreements being settled, one way or another, in the near future. This would encourage a concentration of energies on the more concrete, and perhaps more appealing, issues in aesthetics—in the aesthetics of the various forms of art, the aesthetics of nature, and the aesthetics of the multiplicity of artefacts and activities that figure in our everyday life. However, in whatever manner these disagreements might be resolved, a vital issue, which might well be thought to be the preserve of general value theory, rather than aesthetics itself, will remain untouched: the value of aesthetic and artistic value. I hope to make a contribution to this in the coming years.

Not all of the essays in the volume are aimed at the abstract core of the subject—at least, that is not always their principal target, even when they throw light on it. Some have a more concrete focus. This is true of the two essays that are concerned with what I take to be the most fundamental issue in the aesthetics of music, the question of the correct conception of the phenomenology of the experience of listening to music with understanding, and in particular whether extra-musical concepts are integral to this experience in such a manner that an account of this phenomenology must invoke the idea of metaphor. I argue that this phenomenology does not need to be articulated by means of metaphor, either for the reason that hearing music with understanding consists in hearing music in such a manner that apt figurative descriptions would be appropriate to the experience, or because the nature of the experiences of the elements of music—tones, melody, rhythm, and harmony—can be described only by means of metaphors, the extra-musical concepts invoked being essential ingredients of the experience of music. The first of these views was put forward by Frank Sibley, whom I met just once but whose work I had long admired. As is evident in a number of the essays, I have greatly profited from his writings. The second view belongs to Roger Scruton, whom I first met when he arrived at Cambridge as an undergraduate student, one year after I had entered the university to study mathematics, and—because I had moved at the end of my first year from the Mathematics tripos to that which was then called Moral Sciences (Philosophy) and because we were both undergraduates at the same college—we at once found ourselves composing a tutorial group in which we took turns each week to write and read out essays, to which the other would respond. I remember little of the details of these tutorials, much more of the times we listened to music together, and we have remained friends ever since. It is therefore unsurprising that I have made myself thoroughly acquainted with his writings on aesthetics, especially musical aesthetics, and have engaged more than once with his pioneering attempts to articulate the phenomenology of the experience of music, an endeavour that I regard as essential to resolving the still unanswered questions about it.

The last four essays also stand somewhat apart, even though two of them have significant connections with the main body of the essays. One of the four is focused on expressive perception, by which I mean the perception of a work of art as the bearer of an emotional quality or the corresponding perception directed at a natural scene or object. Now the nature of the artistic expression of emotion has long been one of the cardinal problems of aesthetics. For while the phenomenon has received universal acknowledgement as a significant, and even on occasion as a paramount, virtue of art, it has been subjected to highly various interpretations of what it amounts to. A recurrent idea has been that the expression by works of art of emotions, which of course they cannot literally possess—or the apparent possession by natural things of emotional qualities they cannot literally possess—should be understood in terms of the *projection* of emotions onto or into insentient objects. This idea has assumed many forms. Even what might be called empathy theory—in acknowledgement of the contribution of Theodor Lipps—is chameleon-like. The basic idea of empathy theory is that it is possible for one to endow inanimate objects with expression by 'animating' them (or insentient objects by introducing sentience into them), and this is achieved by the projection of feeling into them. But there is more than one way in which it is supposed this might come about. Leaving this aside, the crucial issue is how this idea of projection is to be understood. According to empathy theory, the projection of emotion is imaginative projection: it is a matter of imagining the object to be in the emotional state projected into it. An extreme version of projection theory—the celebrated theory of George Santayana—construed the upshot of projection not as imagining but, to put it in the strongest terms, being under the illusion that the object possesses the emotion projected. But projection theory came of age only when Richard Wollheim brought the necessary sophistication to it, rejecting the idea of the perception of expression as being founded on projection understood as imagining (in some unanalysed way) or falsely believing, replacing it by the psychoanalytic notion of projection, according to which projection is a form of unconscious phantasy, introducing into psychoanalytic theory a distinction between two kinds of projection, so-called simple and complex, and redefining the upshot of projection as the perception of a distinctive kind of property, rather than the thought of the object projected upon being the locus of psychological states. My essay expounds and subjects to critical examination his theory of the nature of the expression of emotion in painting.

Two of the last four essays focus on a subject which, unlike the artistic expression of emotion, has come to the fore in philosophy only recently—the nature of pictorial representation. Here Wollheim again figures prominently, for in fact he was largely responsible for the explosion of philosophical interest in the topic that has taken place in the last fifty years. Beginning with his incisive critique of certain aspects of Ernst Gombrich's view, he went on to advance an account of depiction in terms of Wittgenstein's notion of 'seeing-as', before regarding this as too crude an idea to capture the phenomenon of depiction, since it covered very different kinds of case. As a result he proposed his initial 'seeing-in' conception, which represented pictorial perception as a combination of two different kinds of visual experience, this being itself replaced by a different conception of 'seeing-in', which conceived of it as a single experience with two aspects. In tandem with this progress of his own ideas, he criticized rival accounts, notably those of Nelson Goodman and Kendall Walton, always rejecting accounts that purported to elucidate pictorial perception in a semiotic fashion or in terms of imagined seeing or perceived resemblance, elaborating and defending his later conception a number of times throughout the rest of his life. The first of my essays on pictorial perception begins with an exposition and critique of Gombrich's illusionistic theory of the experience of realistic pictures, modulates to its main theme, a critical examination of Wollheim's view of pictorial perception as a matter of seeing one thing in another, lays down guidelines for a correct theory and scouts a number of candidates, and (as a late afterthought) concludes by articulating worries about Walton's 'make-believe seeing' conception of pictorial perception; the second essay outlines an alternative account of pictorial perception in terms of the perception of a certain kind of resemblance, a view which, I believe, had not previously been given the consideration it deserved, which now flourishes in a variety of forms, but which I have never managed to convince myself captures the phenomenology correctly.

The final essay in the collection retrieves and examines the thoughts about aesthetics, as written down by him or recorded more or less reliably by others, of the twentieth century's most brilliant philosopher, without whose inspiration I myself might not have become a philosopher. Given what is to be found in these thoughts, but also what is not, it is to be regretted that he did not apply himself to aesthetics with the same intensity he gave to the philosophy of language, or even to the philosophy of mathematics.

I have dedicated this volume to Richard Wollheim, the outstanding aesthetician of his generation, for many years a colleague, a longstanding friend, without whose influence I would certainly not have become an aesthetician.

In general, the essays stand as they were written when first published. Some needed a small amount of trimming to detach them from the contexts in which they first appeared. I have changed the text of one of the essays in two significant ways, taking out an element I was dissatisfied with—even before the paper in which it occurred was first published—and incorporating a substantial part of another piece of writing. I have added postscripts to two essays, inserted additional material into one, and elsewhere I have made a few minor alterations and added some footnotes. Further details are in Sources and Acknowledgements.

1

Aesthetic Judgements, Aesthetic Principles, and Aesthetic Properties

For any given kind of judgement, two issues of justification might arise, one concerning the type of judgement, the other an instance of it. First, there is the question of establishing the credentials of that kind of judgement to being a bona fide judgement, a judgement with a well-founded claim to intersubjective validity, instances of which can have a genuine truth-value.[1] Secondly, there is the question of how, if at all, it is possible to establish, perhaps conclusively, that a particular instance of that kind of judgement is correct (and in particular, what the canonical or most fundamental method of doing this is—for there are usually many methods of establishing the truth of a judgement). So for aesthetic judgements, or aesthetic judgements of a particular kind, there is, first, the issue of establishing the legitimacy of the claim to intersubjective validity, if such a claim is built into them, and, second, the issue of showing that, of the opposed aesthetic judgements that might be made about a certain thing, this judgement is right, that one wrong.

In the *Critique of Aesthetic Judgement* Kant's leading idea is that an aesthetic judgement about an item is a judgement the 'determining ground' of which cannot be other than the subject's pleasure or displeasure in experiencing the item.[2] In other words, the judgement must be based on the subject's

---

[1] It is clear that what aesthetic properties an item possesses—the aesthetic character of an item—is relative to a kind of sensibility: the acceptability of aesthetic judgements made by human beings must be understood as relative to a distinctively human sensibility, with distinctively human powers of perception, understanding, and emotional response, and who flourish and are vulnerable to harm in distinctively human ways. In what follows this relativizing of the truth-value of aesthetic judgements will be taken as understood.

[2] Kant regards pleasure as being indefinable. But he holds that it is integral to a representation's being pleasant that it has a causality inherent in it that tends to preserve the continuation of the state.

hedonic reaction to the item. This criterion is intended to apply to kinds of judgement: a kind or type of judgement is aesthetic if and only if any instance of that kind must be based on the pleasure or must be based on the displeasure felt by the subject in experiencing the object judged. And by judgement Kant means more than mere belief (which might be a belief based on another's opinion, for instance): he means a judgement about an item that the subject is currently aware of, the judgement being based solely on the nature of the item as it is presented to the subject in perception or some other form of awareness. He is concerned, therefore, only with judgements that might be said to ascribe a positive or negative aesthetic value to an item, and his conception of an aesthetic judgement implies that an aesthetic judgement concerns an item's capacity, disposition, or suitability to yield pleasure of the kind that grounds the judgement, either just to the subject or to some class of people who satisfy some requirement of knowledge, experience, morality or whatever. I take his conception of an aesthetic judgement to be tantamount to the idea that to experience an item as possessing a certain (value-laden) aesthetic property—to 'perceive' that property in the item—the perception of the relevant non-aesthetic property of the item—a sensory quality, the item's perceptual structure, its sheer immensity, or whatever—must be characterized by the hedonic response integral to the concept of that aesthetic property. This might be objected to on the ground that Kant denies that beauty is a property of an object (and explains why it might seem as if this is what it must be). But what his denial comes to is that beauty is not a property of the appearance of an item, considered in itself, rather than with respect to the item's suitability to yield disinterested pleasure in the contemplation of its perceptual form. A judgement that predicates beauty of an item does not characterize the intrinsic nature of the item (the item's form) in any way at all. Rather, it attributes to the item's form a relation in which this is alleged to stand to human beings. In other words, for Kant beauty is a certain kind of relational property of an item, 'beauty' being construed as an affective term, comparable in this respect to 'exciting', 'thrilling', 'interesting', 'boring', 'funny', 'disgusting', or 'saddening', the affect of beauty being pleasure. Accordingly, given Kant's understanding of a pure judgement of taste

His notion of an experience of pleasure is therefore much the same as that of an experience that is inherently rewarding.

(a judgement of free beauty), to experience an item as being beautiful the contemplation of the item's form must be experienced with disinterested pleasure in the perception of that form (independently of how the item that possesses that form is conceptualized), and such a judgement alleges the suitability of an object to yield disinterested pleasure in the object's form to any human being with normal perceptual capacities—to any human being who is capable of perceiving that form. Hence, establishing the credentials of judgements of free beauty to being bona fide judgements is a matter of showing how a judgement based on a subject's own disinterested pleasure in something's form can rightly lay claim to universal validity—in Kant's language, it is to effect a deduction of such judgements—and establishing that a particular judgement of this kind is correct is a matter of establishing the object's suitability to yield this pleasure to all relevant subjects.[3]

Now although Kant believes that it is possible to effect a deduction of pure judgements of taste, a deduction he attempts to carry out and which I do not propose here to question, he also argues that no pure judgement of taste can ever be proved to be correct. As Kant expresses it, a pure judgement of taste cannot be determined by bases of proof: there is neither an empirical nor an a priori criterion by reference to which any judgement of taste can be proved.[4] In rejecting an empirical basis of proof what Kant explicitly denies is that the agreed judgements of others can be considered to be a sufficient basis of proof for a judgement of taste (whether a judgement of free or dependent beauty). For perceptual judgements, the fact that many other people have perceived a situation in a certain way—perhaps in a way different from how it seemed to oneself—is a sufficient reason to judge as they do; but a consensus of aesthetic judgements about an item, no matter how great the number of people that form the consensus, is never a sufficient basis for an aesthetic judgement, Kant claims. In rejecting the possibility of an a priori basis of proof Kant is rejecting the idea that conformity with rules of beauty—rules that can be known a priori—can be considered to be a sufficient basis of proof. In addition, Kant claims that there cannot be an objective principle of taste, that is, a principle of the form 'If [the form of] an object is of

---

[3] Scepticism about the idea of judgements of free beauty has sometimes been expressed. In what follows I ignore the possibility that such scepticism might be well-founded.

[4] Immanuel Kant, *Critique of Judgment*, trans. W. S. Pluhar (Indianapolis: Hackett Publishing Co., 1987), §33.

kind K, then it is beautiful', where 'K' is a term that can be determined to apply to an object independently of determining whether its form is disinterestedly pleasurable—a universal formula that could be used to establish that an object is beautiful.[5] Now such a principle would specify an allegedly *sufficient* condition of an object's being beautiful. Accordingly, if there could be such a principle, judgements of taste would be susceptible of *proof*: they could be established by deductive proof from two premises, one the principle of taste, the other the proposition that the object possesses the property specified in the principle of taste—which proposition could be established by empirical means. But for (positive) judgements of taste to be susceptible of *disproof* by reference to a principle of taste, the principle would have to specify a *necessary* condition of an item's being beautiful: 'Unless the form of an object is of kind K, it is not beautiful' or 'If the form of an object is beautiful, then it is of kind K'. In the 'Antinomy of Taste', Kant represents a judgement of taste as being insusceptible of proof or disproof—as not being open to *dispute*—which implies that he also denies the possibility of this second sort of principle.

Now what in fact Kant is inclined to do, in rejecting the possibility of an empirical basis of proof, an a priori basis of proof, and an objective principle of taste, is to exploit the defining characteristic of an aesthetic judgement, namely that it must be based on the subject's own pleasurable or unpleasurable response to the object judged, in order to reach his conclusion.[6] But this is not enough to show that, say, a consensus of judgements about an item's beauty cannot be a sufficient basis for a belief *with the same content* as the assertoric content of an aesthetic judgement, so that, for example, someone who is not in a position to judge that an item is beautiful might nevertheless have a compelling reason to believe that it is. Perhaps Kant would reject an empirical proof of an item's beauty based on some consensus of judgements about its beauty on the ground that, if someone who is not part of the consensus were to experience the item and not find it beautiful, the proper reaction would be for the person to reject the consensus as mistaken. But this presupposes that the person would necessarily have better reason to consider her own hedonic response to

---

[5] Kant, *Critique of Judgment*, §34. This is the counterpart of Kant's claim that there can be no determinate rule for the production of a beautiful work of fine art (§46), i.e. a rule the following of which would ensure that the resulting work is an artistic success.

[6] Ibid., §§33–4, §57, p. 341.

be disinterested pleasure in the contemplation of the item's form than the hedonic responses of those who constitute the consensus, and, given that she has no evidence that this consensus is formed of people who are more likely than she is to be mistaken about the source of the pleasure they take in the experience of the object, the supposition would be unwarranted.

Furthermore, given that there is such a thing as a correct judgement of free beauty, as Kant believes there is, then, for any such judgement, anything with the same form as that of the object correctly judged to be beautiful will also be beautiful. Hence there will be valid principles of the form 'If the form of an object is of kind K, it is beautiful'. And if it is possible to know that one's delight in the perception of an object is disinterested delight in the contemplation of its form, so that, given the acceptability of Kant's deduction of judgements of taste, one can know that a pure judgement of taste is correct, then such principles can be known (a posteriori) to be true. Accordingly, a judgement of taste about an item with a certain form will be susceptible of empirical proof by reference to a principle of taste that asserts that the possession of this form is sufficient for an item's being beautiful.[7] I believe that Kant is unduly sceptical of one's being able to know that one's response to an object is disinterested delight in the object's form (considered independently of the kind of thing the object is). For the ever-present forces of self-interest and the desire to think better of oneself than one merits, from which his counterpart claim about the morality of an action—that one can never know that the thought of an action's being one's duty was sufficient to move one to perform the action—derives its plausibility, are unlikely to play any role in our contemplation of an object's form, and there appear to be no other difficult, let alone insuperable obstacles to a correct understanding of the nature and object of one's pleasure.

The concept of (free) beauty, as Kant understands it, allows of the possibility that beautiful forms are radically heterogeneous—that there is no empirically detectable property common and peculiar to beautiful forms in virtue of which they are beautiful, i.e. in virtue of which they are such as to induce in all human beings the pleasure distinctive of the beautiful. I believe, although I shall not here argue, that Kant thinks of

---

[7] Of course, this could not be the canonical method of establishing the truth of such a judgement. And the principle of taste is not such as to be known a priori.

this possibility as being actual.[8] Now if we were to suppose that there is no non-relational property of beautiful forms common and specific to them, it might seem that a pure judgement of taste could not be justified by reference to the intrinsic nature of the form of the object judged. But this conclusion does not follow. Perhaps Kant's identification of the disinterested pleasure in the beautiful with the free play of the imagination in accordance with the rule-governed nature of the understanding precludes disinterested pleasure in the beautiful from having degrees,[9] in which case his apparent neglect of two commonly recognized kinds of comparative judgements of beauty, one explicit, the other implicit—judgements of the comparative beauty of objects and judgements that attribute a (high or low) degree of beauty to an object—is understandable. Conforming with this restriction simplifies the task of justifying a particular judgement of some item's beauty, if it is necessary to show only that the form of the item is such as to make it *to some degree* intrinsically rewarding to perceive (independently of any concept it might be perceived to instantiate). This is especially so for visible objects if the idea of an object's perceptual form—the perceptible structure of its elements—is understood, contrary to Kant's apparent intention, to accommodate, not merely its shape and inner contours, but also relations amongst the colours displayed by, or the coloured markings of, its various parts. But it is also sometimes easy to justify a judgement of comparative beauty—that one form is better suited to capture attention and reward sustained looking than is another. For both absolute and comparative judgements of beauty, what matters is that a beautiful form must not offer too little to perceptual contemplation

---

[8] This follows at once from Kant's denial of the possibility of both kinds of objective principles of taste (one that specifies a sufficient condition and one that specifies a necessary condition of an object's being beautiful), if this denial is unqualified. It might be thought, however, that Kant's denial of the possibility of an objective principle of taste amounts to no more than the rejection of the possibility of knowing such a principle *a priori*. Perhaps. But Kant does not build this qualification into his denial. Furthermore, there are two features of his aesthetic theory that appear to commit him to the stronger conclusion that there cannot be a determinate objective principle of taste: (i) the requirement that an aesthetic judgement must be based on the subject's experience of pleasure or displeasure, and (ii) the resolution of the Antinomy of Taste—the denial that a judgement of taste is based on a determinable concept (i.e. one that can be exemplified in experience) conjoined with the affirmation that it is based on an indeterminable concept.

[9] Kant's acquiescence in the traditional idea of beautiful forms as those possessing both unity and variety (*Critique of Judgment*, §61) would enable him to attribute degrees to beauty, if not on the basis of degree of unity (unless unity is a matter of how unified a form is, and so susceptible of degree), at least on the basis of degree of variety.

or exploration (as a simple geometrical figure does),[10] or present an array of contours, shapes, volumes, and colours that appear unrelated to one another, so that it is difficult to grasp perceptually as a unified whole. Rather, it must display an appearance of some complexity that invites the eyes to play back and forth across its features in appreciation of the various relations among its aspects and that facilitates integration in an harmonious gestalt—one in which no part or feature appears out of place or unsuited to the others. Accordingly, it is not impossible to give reasons in support of the view that a certain form is beautiful or that one form is more beautiful than another (although the truth-value of judgements of comparative beauty will often be indeterminate).

In addition to the pure judgement of taste, Kant recognizes another kind of pure aesthetic judgement—the judgement of the sublime in nature. Kant claims that the exposition of judgements of the sublime is at the same time their deduction, i.e. the justification of their claim to universal validity, whereas this is not true of the exposition of pure judgements of taste. But the sublime contrasts with the beautiful not just with respect to the need for a deduction in addition to the exposition of judgements of that kind: there is also a disanalogy concerning the justification of particular instances of such judgements. A pure judgement of taste is an expression of disinterested pleasure in an object's form. But not everything with a form is suited to yield this pleasure (to the same degree), so that for each instance the question arises whether an object judged to have a beautiful form really does so. However, on Kant's understanding of the nature and generation of the emotion of the sublime there is no question of justifying a particular judgement of the sublime, given that it is produced by the failed attempt of the imagination to comprehend nature's extent or might.[11] On my own understanding of the nature and generation of the emotion, which is considerably different from Kant's,[12] and rejecting his idiosyncratic conception of the sublime as that which is 'absolutely great', again there is no question of justification, given that the emotion really is a response to something in nature that is immense—for *anything* immense is suitable to

---

[10] For Kant's own reason for denying that regular geometrical figures are beautiful, see *Critique of Judgment*, 241–2, 365–6.

[11] Kant's insistence that sublimity is improperly predicated of items in, or even of the entirety of, the natural world is irrelevant here.

[12] See Malcolm Budd, 'Delight in the Natural World: Kant on the Aesthetic Appreciation of Nature, Part III, The Sublime in Nature', *The British Journal of Aesthetics*, 38/3 (July 1998).

induce the experience. Furthermore, given that the sublime is a matter of a certain kind of reaction to sheer immensity, there is (with due allowance for the vagueness of the idea of immensity) an objective principle of the sublime: 'If (and only if) a natural object or phenomenon is immense (in extent or force), then it is sublime'.

But Kant's conception of an aesthetic judgement and the implied restriction of aesthetic properties to affective aesthetic properties is not the only or even the most widely recognized conception of an aesthetic judgement or an aesthetic property. An alternative and more accommodating conception of an aesthetic judgement is like Kant's in one respect but unlike it in two different ways. This is the conception of an aesthetic judgement as a judgement that requires and so is expressive of aesthetic sensitivity (however exactly that notion is to be understood). More precisely, according to this conception an aesthetic judgement is a judgement made about an item on the basis of the subject's experience of the item and which is expressive or reflective of that person's aesthetic sensitivity as exercised in that experience. (Correlatively, an aesthetic property is one that requires for its discernment an exercise of aesthetic sensitivity.)[13] As with Kant's conception, this requires an aesthetic judgement to be based on the subject's experience of the item judged. But whereas Kant requires an aesthetic judgement to be based on the subject's hedonic response, this conception does not (at least, explicitly), and whereas Kant's account of an aesthetic judgement does not rely on a prior understanding of the aesthetic, this conception does. Nevertheless, this definition of an aesthetic judgement, as it stands, leaves open two possibilities: first, that certain sorts of aesthetic judgement are such that they must be expressions of a particular kind of hedonic response (or an experience in some other way inherently rewarding or unappealing), and second, that an elucidation of the notion of aesthetic sensitivity will deliver the result that all aesthetic judgements must be based on the subject's hedonic response.

Leaving aside his own understanding, whatever exactly this may have been, of the notion of aesthetic sensitivity—he appears to offer nothing

---

[13] For those who distinguish aesthetic from artistic properties and aesthetic from artistic value—a work's artistic value being something other than its aesthetic value—if the class of aesthetic judgements is to accommodate judgements of artistic value and artistic but non-aesthetic properties relevant to artistic value, the notion of aesthetic sensitivity must be understood to embrace that of sensitivity to artistic properties and value. But it would, I believe, be better to restrict the class of aesthetic judgements to judgements of specifically aesthetic value and specifically aesthetic properties.

more than the unhelpful idea that normal perceptual abilities and intelligence are not sufficient for aesthetic sensitivity—this conception of an aesthetic judgement is essentially the same as Frank Sibley's.[14] But the usefulness of this conception depends on the clarity and precision of the notion of aesthetic sensitivity. A related conception of an aesthetic judgement that might be thought preferable would be this: an aesthetic judgement is a judgement, based on the nature of the subject's experience of an item, of the item's aesthetic value or its aesthetic properties (the two kinds of aesthetic judgement being linked together by the fact that a well-grounded judgement of the first kind will be founded on judgements of the second kind). But this requires elucidations of the notions of aesthetic value and aesthetic property. One suggestion would be that the idea of an aesthetic property should be introduced by a list of examples. But without an explanation of what qualifies an item to be a member of the list, uncertainty about what constitutes an exercise of aesthetic sensitivity might well be mirrored by uncertainty about extrapolation from the list. Perhaps it would be better to define the notion of an aesthetic property in terms of the idea of aesthetic value in some such manner as this: an aesthetic property of an item is one that is dependent on other properties of the item and is integral or directly relevant to the item's aesthetic value.[15] But, apart from any other considerations, this would render this proposed alternative conception of an aesthetic judgement no different from the one for which it might be substituted, if the idea of aesthetic sensitivity were to be understood, as it might well be, as sensitivity to an item's aesthetic value (and so sensitivity to those of its properties that are integral or directly relevant to its aesthetic value). So there seems to be little or no advantage in shifting from the original conception.

---

[14] See, for example, Frank Sibley, 'Aesthetic and Nonaesthetic', reprinted in his *Approach to Aesthetics*, ed. John Benson, Betty Redfern, and Jeremy Roxbee Cox (Oxford: Clarendon Press, 2001), 33–4. Sibley was always inclined to distinguish aesthetic sensitivity ('taste') as an ability to discern the aesthetic qualities of things from aesthetic sensitivity as an ability to recognize aesthetic merit and make judgements of aesthetic value. See, for example, his 'About Taste', reprinted in *Approach to Aesthetics*. His reliance on examples of aesthetic qualities, buttressed by the idea of the insufficiency of normal perceptual abilities and intelligence to discern such qualities, to give content to the correlative ideas of taste and aesthetic qualities has long been recognized as the Achilles' heel of his account.

[15] Compare M. C. Beardsley's suggestion that an aesthetic quality is one that 'can independently be cited as a ground of aesthetic value', i.e. one that 'counts without the help of any other quality' ('What is an Aesthetic Quality', reprinted in his *The Aesthetic Point of View* (Ithaca and London: Cornell University Press, 1982)).

Now this conception of an aesthetic judgement embraces a wide variety of aesthetic judgements. But it is helpful to distinguish three different kinds of judgement. First, there are (to use Sibley's terms) 'purely evaluative' judgements or 'verdicts': judgements of an item's aesthetic (or artistic) value that do not indicate the nature of the qualities of the item in virtue of which it (supposedly) possesses the aesthetic value ascribed to it. Although judgements of this kind do not attribute any particular property (other than a certain aesthetic value) to the item judged, they do indicate that the person who makes the judgement values or disvalues the item aesthetically. Secondly, there are judgements that attribute to an item a property that is, from the aesthetic point of view, inherently a merit or defect—judgements that (in Sibley's terms)[16] ascribe inherent aesthetic merit- or defect-constituting properties. Such judgements are not necessarily evaluative: while they attribute properties that, in themselves, constitute aesthetic merits or defects, it does not follow that they are expressions or reflections of an evaluative response by the person who makes the judgement. And third—if the notion of aesthetic sensitivity allows this—there are judgements that ascribe an aesthetic property to an item, but one that is not, in itself, an aesthetic merit or defect.

Given that whatever aesthetic properties an item possesses, it possesses them in virtue of its non-aesthetic properties, and that an item's aesthetic value is dependent on its aesthetic properties, whether and how aesthetic judgements of these three kinds can be justified will ultimately depend on the relations between non-aesthetic and aesthetic properties.

Quietening doubts about the distinction between aesthetic and non-aesthetic properties and so the scope of aesthetic properties—doubts engendered by reliance on the unanalysed notion of aesthetic sensitivity—I want to accept three elements of Sibley's bold, pioneering account of the conceptual relations between aesthetic and non-aesthetic properties:[17] (i) For any aesthetic property, there is no set of non-aesthetic properties such that it is a conceptual truth that the possession of the set by an item is both logically necessary and logically sufficient for the item's possession of

---

[16] Frank Sibley, 'General Criteria and Reasons in Aesthetics', reprinted in *Approach to Aesthetics*, 105.

[17] It is a common criticism to accuse Sibley of conflating claims about concepts with claims about properties. But this criticism misinterprets various loose formulations of claims about conceptual truths concerning properties as claims about properties *per se*—which is not to conflate concepts and properties.

the aesthetic property. Hence, there are no aesthetic principles, capable of being known a priori, of the form 'An item possesses aesthetic property A if and only if it possesses non-aesthetic property N'. (ii) Except, perhaps, for certain peripheral cases,[18] for any aesthetic property there is no non-aesthetic property (or set of properties) such that it is a conceptual truth that the possession of the non-aesthetic property by an item is logically sufficient for the item's possession of the aesthetic property. Hence, there are no aesthetic principles, capable of being known a priori, of the form 'If an item possesses non-aesthetic property N, it possesses aesthetic property A'. It follows that aesthetic judgements that ascribe aesthetic properties are not susceptible of *proof* by reference to an a priori aesthetic principle linking aesthetic and non-aesthetic properties. (iii) For some aesthetic properties, there is a non-aesthetic property (or set of properties) such that it is a conceptual truth that the possession of the non-aesthetic property by an item is a logically necessary condition for the item's possession of the aesthetic property. Hence, there are aesthetic principles, capable of being known a priori, of the form 'If an item possesses aesthetic property A, it possesses non-aesthetic property N'. It follows that aesthetic judgements that ascribe aesthetic properties of this kind are susceptible of *disproof* by reference to an a priori aesthetic principle linking aesthetic and non-aesthetic properties.

I also agree with Sibley that there are (numerous) inherent aesthetic merit-constituting and defect-constituting properties,[19] but I reject his explanation of why (in general) there can be no interesting aesthetic principles linking non-aesthetic properties to inherent aesthetic merit-constituting properties as sufficient conditions of them.

A positive or negative aesthetic evaluation of an item can be supported by an aesthetic judgement that attributes to the item a property that is inherently an aesthetic merit or defect. Such a property will be realized in the item in a particular manner, as, for example, gracefulness might be realized in the shape of a certain vase. Sibley argues that it is typically the case that the properties of an item in virtue of which it possesses an aesthetic merit-constituting property—those that are responsible for its possessing that merit-constituting property—are determinate, not determinable, as,

---

[18] See, for example, Frank Sibley, 'Aesthetic Concepts', reprinted in *Approach to Aesthetics*, 10.

[19] For a critique of and proposed alternative to this aspect of Sibley's account, see J. W. Bender, 'General but Defeasible Reasons in Aesthetic Evaluation: The Particularist/Generalist Dispute', *The Journal of Aesthetics and Art Criticism*, 53/4 (Fall 1995).

to take Sibley's example, being square is being a determinate shape, a shape not further determinable, whereas being triangular is not being a determinate shape, but a shape that is further determinable. He allows that there may be some determinable merit-responsible properties—if an item is symmetrical then it is balanced—but they will be peripheral cases, and in general the properties of an item that are responsible for its possessing an aesthetic merit-constituting property are determinate; that is to say, it is in virtue of the precise curvature of a line, or the exact hue, brightness, and intensity of the colours distributed across its surface, that an item is graceful or harmonious, for example. Given that this is so, if a vase is graceful in virtue of its shape, it follows that anything with exactly the same shape will have a graceful shape, but no conclusions can be drawn about the gracefulness of an item with a similar but not exactly matching shape. Hence (leaving the peripheral cases aside), if all merit-responsible properties are determinate—determinate in the sense that what is responsible for the possession by an item of a merit-constituting property is always a determinate property of that item—then, Sibley concludes, an item cannot properly be judged to possess a merit-constituting property on the basis of its possessing some determinable property: there are no acceptable principles of the form 'If something possesses determinable non-aesthetic property N, it possesses aesthetic merit-constituting property A'.

   Here it is necessary to distinguish two different understandings of the idea of an item's possession of a non-aesthetic property (or complex of properties) being responsible for its possession of an inherent merit-constituting property. The first, which identifies a weaker sense of responsibility, is this: for a non-aesthetic property of an item to be responsible for the item's possession of a certain aesthetic merit-constituting property is for the non-aesthetic property to be such that *some* change in it would result in the non-possession by the item of that merit-constituting property. In other words, it is definitive of a non-aesthetic merit-responsible property that some change in it would result in the loss of the merit-constituting property for which it is responsible. The second understanding of the responsibility relation invokes a stronger sense of responsibility: a non-aesthetic property of an item is responsible for the item's possession of a certain aesthetic merit-constituting property if and only if *any* change in that non-aesthetic property would result in the item's no longer possessing that merit-constituting property. Sibley's claim that, apart from peripheral cases, merit-responsible properties are determinate, not determinable, is a claim about the weaker notion of responsibility.[20] But this claim, which I take to be true,[21] is not sufficient to establish the thesis that there are no aesthetic principles of the form 'If something possesses determinable non-aesthetic property N, it possesses aesthetic merit-constituting property A'. What would be sufficient to establish the thesis is the proposition that merit-responsible properties are determinate, not in the weaker, but in the stronger sense of responsibility. For if any (noticeable) change of the properties of an item that realize an aesthetic merit-constituting property will result in the item's not possessing that merit-constituting property, no determinable property can be sufficient for the possession of a merit-constituting property. It is true, as Sibley says, that 'it is a commonplace in aesthetics that the slightest change, of a word in a poem, a colour or line in a painting, or a note in a musical composition may give an entirely different aesthetic character to the whole or part'.[22] But this commonplace is tantamount to the modest assertion that any noticeable change in the relevant properties of an item *may* give it a different aesthetic merit- or defect-constituting property (rendering what was, for instance, graceful, no longer graceful); and this is not equivalent to and does not imply the strong claim that any such change *will* alter the item's relevant aesthetic merit- or defect-constituting property. Furthermore, it is rarely, if ever, true that any

[20] Frank Sibley, 'Particularity, Art and Evaluation', reprinted in *Approach to Aesthetics*, 96. Sibley's concession that perhaps there are exceptional cases of determinable merit-responsible properties (being symmetrical, for example) amounts to this: whereas some change in the determinable property would remove the merit-constituting property for which it is responsible, no change from one to another determinate of that determinable would result in that loss.

[21] Sibley argues that the distinctive character of aesthetic assessment is principally due to this feature of the responsibility relation, which concerns its left-hand term, and two further features. First, that the responsibility relation that obtains between a determinate merit-responsible property and the aesthetic merit-constituting property for which it is responsible is typically *non-conceptual* in the sense that there is no conceptual connection between an item's possessing a determinate merit-responsible property and the item's possessing the merit-constituting property for which the determinate merit-responsible property is responsible. In other words, there is no conceptual guarantee that the possession of a certain determinate merit-responsible property ensures that the item possesses the relevant aesthetic merit-constituting property. Secondly, that the merit-constituting and merit-responsible properties must be co-discernible. I take both of these additional features to be correct.

[22] Frank Sibley, 'Particularity, Art and Evaluation', reprinted in *Approach to Aesthetics*, 96. Compare this earlier formulation: 'the features which make something delicate or graceful, and so on, are combined in a peculiar and unique way; ... the aesthetic quality depends on exactly this individual or unique combination of just these specific colours and shapes so that even a slight change *might* make all the difference' (Frank Sibley, 'Aesthetic Concepts', reprinted in *Approach to Aesthetics*, 11–12, my emphasis).

perceptible difference, no matter how slight, in the features that realize an aesthetic merit-constituting property, gracefulness, balance, tragic intensity, or whatever, would result in the item's no longer possessing that property (or no longer possessing it to the same degree). It follows immediately that the possession of a merit-constituting property is (typically) not dependent in the strong sense on the fully determinate nature of the properties in which it is realized.

I now return to the issue of the justification of aesthetic judgements and I begin with verdicts.

It is clear that verdicts can be supported by judgements that ascribe inherent aesthetic merit- or defect-constituting properties. But the correctness or incorrectness of a verdict about an item is not a matter of its being in accordance with or in conflict with the sum of the aesthetic values of the item's inherent aesthetic merit-constituting properties minus the sum of the aesthetic disvalues of its inherent aesthetic defect-constituting properties. Hence, there is no valid aesthetic principle of the form 'O possesses aesthetic value V if and only if M minus D = V', where M = the sum of the aesthetic values of O's inherent aesthetic merit-constituting properties, and D = the sum of the aesthetic disvalues of O's inherent aesthetic defect-constituting properties. For, first, aesthetic value is not a measurable quantity, and, second, inherent aesthetic merit- or defect-constituting properties do not have various amounts of aesthetic value or disvalue built into them (nor are they subject to an ordering of relative strength). Furthermore, even if each inherent aesthetic merit-constituting property did have a certain positive weight and each inherent defect-constituting property a certain negative weight, it would not follow that an item's aesthetic value is determined by the sum of the weights of the totality of its properties of these two kinds. For—leaving aside both the questionable idea of the totality of an item's merit- and defect-constituting properties and the fact that such properties can be of higher- and lower-orders—in the case of works of art (but not, I believe, natural objects) the presence of an inherent aesthetic merit-constituting property in an item is not necessarily an aesthetic virtue of that item: a property that is, in itself, an aesthetic merit, is not necessarily a property that always, in every item, makes a positive contribution to the item's aesthetic value. This is because, in the first place, properties that are aesthetically valuable in themselves—inherent aesthetic merit-constituting properties—can be combined together in a work of art in an incongruous manner, so that they do not enhance or support one another, but one diminishes or clashes with another, revealing a lack of clarity in the artist's aim or a mistaken conception of how to achieve that aim. This signals further agreement with Sibley, who argued that an inherently aesthetic merit-constituting property is not necessarily an aesthetic merit of any particular work of art that possesses it: whether it is so is determined, not by its inherent aesthetic 'polarity', but by whether it enhances or detracts from the other inherent aesthetic merit-constituting properties possessed by the work.[23] But there is a further reason why the presence of an inherent aesthetic merit-constituting property in an item is not necessarily an aesthetic virtue of that item: an inherent aesthetic merit-constituting property can be combined in a work with an inherent aesthetic defect-constituting property so as to strengthen the appeal or disguise the unattractiveness of that defect-constituting property, as in the case of a powerful or subtle expression of a deeply repugnant ideology that a work presents as admirable.[24]

Given the lack of aesthetic principles, capable of being known a priori, that would enable the attribution of aesthetic properties to, or the aesthetic evaluation of, an item without an exercise of aesthetic sensitivity, and given that any *a posteriori* principles would have to be founded on aesthetic judgements, it follows that the canonical method of establishing the truth of an attribution of an aesthetic property or an aesthetic evaluation, if such attributions and evaluations are susceptible of truth, is the exercise of aesthetic sensitivity, that is, the making of aesthetic judgements.[25] And the

---

[23] Frank Sibley, 'General Criteria and Reasons in Aesthetics', reprinted in *Approach to Aesthetics*. The example Sibley provides is one where the aesthetic character of certain parts of a work (their being highly comic) weakens the effect of the aesthetic character of other parts of the work (their tragic intensity), diluting the predominant aesthetic character of the work (tragic intensity).

[24] The looseness of the notion of the aesthetic (aesthetic value, aesthetic sensitivity) leaves it uncertain whether the only properties that directly determine an item's aesthetic value are the inherent aesthetic merit- and defect-constituting properties that it possesses. If this should not be so, there is a further reason why an item's aesthetic value is not the sum of the weights of the aesthetic values of the totality of its inherent aesthetic merit- and defect-constituting properties.

[25] Sibley insists 'that, broadly speaking, aesthetics deals with a kind of perception' ('Aesthetic and Nonaesthetic', reprinted in *Approach to Aesthetics*, 35), and, accordingly, represents the canonical method of establishing that an item possesses a certain aesthetic property by securing agreement in judgements as being 'perceptual proof' (p. 39). But he understands this kind of 'perception' to include feeling the power, or mood, or uncertainty of tone of a novel, for example, and counts the property of being tightly knit or moving, for instance, as an aesthetic property. Since aesthetic properties are of heterogeneous kinds, the nature of the experiences required for their discernment correspondingly

reliability of aesthetic judgements will be a function of the qualifications of the person who makes them: the better-qualified someone is—the more finely honed and better-trained his aesthetic sensitivity—the more reliable will be his aesthetic judgements in which this sensitivity is well exercised. This will, I assume, have been obvious all along. Furthermore, as Sibley insisted, the only kind of proof that, ultimately, there could be that an item possesses a certain aesthetic property is by appeal to agreement in discrimination or reactions, with a corresponding convergence of judgements about the particular case.[26] The remaining question is, then, whether attributions of aesthetic properties and aesthetic evaluations are susceptible of truth.

To make real headway with this question two different things are needed. Well-founded aesthetic evaluations rest on attributions of aesthetic properties, and so are susceptible of truth only if attributions of aesthetic properties are so susceptible. If attributions of aesthetic properties are susceptible of truth, then—given the incommensurability of aesthetic value (and so of the inherent aesthetic value of inherent aesthetic merit-constituting properties) and the interacting nature of inherent aesthetic merit-constituting properties—the main issue about aesthetic evaluations concerns the *degree* of aesthetic value attributed to an item (and so aesthetic judgements about the relative aesthetic value of two items). What is needed here is, first, a greater understanding of judgements about incommensurable values, and then, on the basis of this understanding, an account of what the limitations are of comparative judgements of aesthetic value resting securely on the attribution of inherent aesthetic merit- and defect-constituting properties. I am unable to explore these limitations here.[27] For attributions of aesthetic properties what is needed is an account of what it is for an item to possess an aesthetic property, or rather, since aesthetic properties are of various kinds, a number of accounts of what it is for an item to possess an aesthetic property, one for each of the different kinds. Without these accounts, the credentials of such attributions of aesthetic properties as lay

diverse, and the fact that these experiences are not all species of perception, it would be better to call this 'experiential proof'.

[26] Frank Sibley, 'Objectivity and Aesthetics', reprinted in *Approach to Aesthetics*, 75–6.

[27] Bruce Vermazen's 'Comparing Evaluations of Works of Art' (*The Journal of Aesthetics and Art Criticism*, 34/1 (Fall 1975)) contains some pertinent observations and offers an explanation of why the notion of aesthetic value effects only a partial ordering of works of art.

claim to universal validity and what their truth or falsity would amount to must remain uncertain.[28]

Despite the heterogeneity of what are commonly recognized as aesthetic properties, at least the great majority of them are response-dependent. One conception of aesthetic properties represents them as being, in short, dispositions to induce distinctive kinds of non-evaluative experiences (in the main, perceptual experiences) in duly qualified subjects. Another conception represents them as being dispositions to induce certain kinds of evaluative responses in duly qualified subjects. Of course, without a specification of the various natures of the non-evaluative experiences or evaluative responses, these conceptions are merely programmatic. But I shall conclude by commenting briefly on Alan Goldman's account of aesthetic properties—an account that accommodates both these conceptions—and the non-realist view of aesthetic properties he is led to embrace.

Goldman presents this form of analysis—'the Humean structure'—of the possession of aesthetic properties:

Object O has aesthetic property P = O is such as to elicit response of kind R in ideal viewers of kind V in virtue of its more basic properties B.[29]

Although intended to apply to aesthetic properties of all kinds, Goldman is primarily concerned with *evaluative* aesthetic properties (so that R will be an evaluative, positive, or negative, response),[30] because he believes that the vast majority of aesthetic properties are evaluative. He distinguishes between so-called 'broadly' and 'narrowly' evaluative aesthetic properties (or rather, since the distinction is one of degree, he indicates a continuum along which evaluative aesthetic properties lie, their relative position determining whether they are broader or narrower than other evaluative aesthetic

---

[28] A major weakness of Sibley's various writings about aesthetic concepts, it seems to me, is that, although they do not merely acknowledge, but contain, arguments for the view that aesthetic judgements are apt for truth, they fail to provide, or even see the need for, an account of what exactly the truth or falsity of attributions of aesthetic properties amounts to or consists in.

[29] Alan Goldman, *Aesthetic Value* (Oxford: Westview Press, 1995), 21. See also his 'Aesthetic Properties', in D. Cooper (ed.), *A Companion to Aesthetics* (Oxford: Basil Blackwell, 1992). Goldman claims that V will remain relatively constant across the range of aesthetic properties. But there is no reason to expect that someone who is an ideal viewer with respect to an aesthetic property of one kind (or within one art form) will be an ideal viewer with respect to aesthetic properties of every kind (or within all art forms).

[30] The idea of an evaluative response is unclear, covering both evaluative judgements—judgements of an item's value—and such psychological reactions as pleasure and displeasure. Goldman leaves this ambiguity unresolved: Hume resolved it by identifying the two ideas.

properties). A broadly evaluative aesthetic property, such as beauty, is [relatively] unspecific as to what property or properties it relates a positive or negative response to: its ascription to an item leaves unspecified what it is about the object that makes it such as to elicit from a suitable spectator or audience the positive or negative response integral to the specification of the evaluative aesthetic property—a pleasurable response in the case of beauty. A [more] narrowly evaluative aesthetic property is more specific about what property or properties it relates a positive or negative response to: its ascription to an item indicates more specifically—partially but not completely—what the characteristics of the object are in virtue of which it has the power to elicit the implied positive or negative response. So:

'Graceful' always refers to formal properties, and only of certain kinds. Thick, straight, and sharply angular lines rarely make for a graceful drawing, and squat objects with jutting edges cannot be graceful. A graceful sculpture ordinarily has smooth and flowing curves and lacks sharply protruding parts...A daring or innovative work must contain features not possessed by its predecessors in the tradition to which it is related...[31]

I am going to consider the kind of analysis Goldman proposes only in application to narrowly evaluative aesthetic properties (while remaining non-committal about which aesthetic properties or what proportion of aesthetic properties are narrowly evaluative).

The crucial issue for this kind of analysis is whether ideal viewers (critics) as specified in terms of the characteristics indicated by 'V' will agree in their aesthetic judgements, which they will do only if their responses will coincide, i.e. be of the same kind. If they will not, if there will be no consensus, then, Goldman maintains, this account of aesthetic properties becomes incoherent, licensing both that an object does, and that it does not, have a certain aesthetic property.[32] Now although Goldman does not indicate it, this requires reading the Humean structure in a weak sense: an object is such as to elicit a response of kind R in ideal viewers of kind V if it is such as to elicit that response from *some* of those viewers. On this reading, if an object is such as to elicit from some ideal viewers a response of a kind integral to one kind of aesthetic property but from other ideal viewers a response of a kind integral to an aesthetic property of an incompatible

[31] Goldman, *Aesthetic Value*, 25.   [32] Ibid. 28–9.

kind, then the object both does and does not possess each of the aesthetic properties. If it is understood in a strong sense, crediting an object with the dispositional property only if it is such as to elicit the response from *all* the qualified viewers, the Humean structure is not rendered incoherent by lack of consensus. Rather, the absence of uniformity of response will imply that the object does not possess the aesthetic property in question. Non-realists maintain the possibility of disagreements amongst ideal critics which are not to be explained by ignorance, bias, or insensitivity, so that (reading the Humean structure in the weak sense) there are no facts of the matter about the disputed ascriptions of aesthetic properties to works of art. Such disagreements would reflect faultless differences in 'taste'.[33] In Goldman's view, ideal critics might well differ faultlessly in taste: it is not necessary that their responses to the same underlying properties of an object should coincide:

A painting with gently curving lines may be graceful to one critic and insipid to another.[34]

[T]he same [non-evaluative] property in a work that one critic [who approves of it] calls unity another [who disapproves of it] will call monotony. What is complex to one is disorganised or muddled or baffling to another, and what is intense to one is strident or raucous to another.[35]

Now it is not entirely clear whether Goldman intends to make the exceptionally strong claim that with respect to *any* object and *any* aesthetic property ideal critics might faultlessly disagree, or merely that, for each aesthetic property, it is possible for there to be cases in which there is no consensus among ideal critics as to whether a certain object possesses that property. This weaker claim might well be true. But to establish in the case of a particular narrowly evaluative aesthetic property that it is possible for there to be a set of non-evaluative properties suitable to be the basis of that property which is such that there can be faultless differences of taste among ideal critics, it would be necessary to show that the constraints imposed on the base properties by the nature of the aesthetic property and the criteria for qualifying as an ideal critic do not guarantee a consensus in aesthetic judgements. And to establish the weaker claim it would be necessary to show that this is true for each narrowly evaluative aesthetic

---

[33] Goldman, *Aesthetic Value*, 36–7.   [34] Ibid. 138.   [35] Ibid. 141.

property. Goldman's non-realist position is not compelling because it is unclear what characteristics it is right to require of an ideal critic (with respect to funniness, for example), and so it is unclear whether these characteristics allow for divergences in aesthetic judgements of ideal critics across all narrowly evaluative aesthetic properties and sets of non-evaluative base properties.

Now the (supposed) possibility of faultless disagreements among ideal critics about the narrowly evaluative aesthetic properties of works leads Goldman to modify the relational account of aesthetic properties—the Humean structure—by relativizing judgements that ascribe aesthetic properties to tastes, each person's aesthetic judgements being relativized to those ideal critics who generally share their taste, so that there might be no genuine disagreement in judgement, but only a difference in attitude or response, between two persons whose aesthetic judgements are apparently opposed. Accordingly: 'when I say that an object has a certain aesthetic property, I am saying that ideal critics who generally share my taste will react in a certain way to its more basic properties'.[36] This seems to be a bad move—for two reasons. First, there is nothing in Goldman's account to rule out the possibility that two ideal critics who generally share my taste might nevertheless faultlessly disagree in their aesthetic judgements about a certain work—in which case he is faced with the same problem that the relativizing move was designed to overcome. Secondly, it is not plausible to represent the content of a person's aesthetic judgement as being self-referential (or in any other way different from that of other persons'), which, on Goldman's relativization of the relational account, would imply that, unless those ideal critics who generally share my taste are the same as those who share your taste, your denying my attribution of an aesthetic property to an object would not constitute disagreement about its aesthetic properties. And no revisionary account of aesthetic judgements that ascribe narrowly evaluative aesthetic properties, which Goldman's clearly is, is needed to accommodate the possibility of faultless differences in taste. For there are two obvious non-revisionary strategies. The first is to read the Humean structure in the strong sense I indicated. The second is to understand a judgement that ascribes a narrowly evaluative aesthetic property to a work as making no reference to ideal viewers but rather as claiming that

[36] Ibid. 37.

the work uniquely *merits* a certain response, so that the response is *the right* response. In either case, if there can be faultless differences in taste, both of two opposed faultless aesthetic judgements will be false—in which case someone who is aware of the possibility of an opposed faultless response might be wise not to express her own response in the corresponding aesthetic judgement. In fact, the second of the two strategies would appear to be the more plausible. As his relativizing move indicates, Goldman understands his account of what it is for an object to possess an aesthetic property to give, not just the truth-conditions, but the content of a judgement that ascribes a narrowly evaluative aesthetic property. But whereas it might be plausible to build a reference to ideal critics into the truth-conditions of such a judgement—this would be one way of indicating what the truth of the judgement would consist in—it is not plausible to build it into the content. Accordingly, a response-dependent account of judgements that ascribe narrowly evaluative aesthetic properties should represent the content of such a judgement as being that the item to which the property is ascribed is such that the evaluative response integral to the property is the appropriate response to the item, the judgement being true if and only if any competing response is indicative of a defect in a person who responds to the item in that manner or an inadequacy in the person's engagement with the item.

2

Aesthetic Essence

1. Does the aesthetic have an essence? If so, can it be captured in non-aesthetic terms or is the aesthetic an irreducible concept?

Whatever the scope of 'the aesthetic' may properly be thought to be—I return to this issue in §2—three preliminary points are important. In the first place, 'the aesthetic' ranges over items in different categories: there are aesthetic judgements, aesthetic pleasures, aesthetic values, aesthetic attitudes, aesthetic interest, aesthetic sensitivity, aesthetic properties, aesthetic character, aesthetic appreciation, aesthetic responses, and so on.[1] Second, aestheticians have been inclined to privilege one of these categories of the aesthetic, assigning to it a basic status and explicating the others in terms of it. Thirdly, the various categories of the aesthetic are inter-definable, no matter which, if any, is taken as basic, how exactly they are related to one another (not everyone understanding them as being connected in the same manner), and despite disagreements about what should properly be thought of as falling within a particular category. Such disagreements arise from different requirements for membership of the category. For example, whereas some require an aesthetic judgement about an item to be one acquired through first-hand acquaintance with the item,[2] others allow a belief founded on the opinion of another to be an aesthetic judgement. Again, some of those who agree that pleasure in the perception of a single colour, sound, taste, or smell is an aesthetic pleasure operate with a notion of judgement, as Kant did, which is such that the mere announcement of such a pleasure in the linguistic form of a judgement—'It's pleasurable'—counts

---

[1] I do not engage directly with the somewhat nebulous idea of aesthetic experience, the intended scope of which is unclear to me, preferring instead to work with what I take to be rather more precise notions, such as the idea of the perception of an aesthetic property or the idea of aesthetic pleasure or of an experience involving an aesthetic response.

[2] See, for example, Frank Sibley, *Approach to Aesthetics* (Oxford: Clarendon Press, 2001), 34–5.

as the expression of an aesthetic judgement. Others hold that the linguistic expression of an aesthetic pleasure or response is an aesthetic judgement—is a judgement at all—only if it claims intersubjective validity, as no mere expression of pleasure, even one formulated in judgemental form, properly does: it would be an aesthetic judgement only if it claimed an item's capacity or suitability to give pleasure, or that it merits a pleasurable response. I will skirt disagreements of this kind.

Now the idea of aesthetic judgement might well be understood to include general, universal, and comparative (or superlative) judgements: 'Some/most/all of the [46!] prints in Hokusai's *Thirty-six Views of Mount Fuji* are wonderful'; 'Hokusai's *Thirty-six Views of Mount Fuji* is a finer set than Hiroshige's *Thirty-six Views of Mount Fuji*'. To illustrate the inter-definability of the various aesthetic categories, it will simplify matters if the idea of aesthetic judgement is restricted to singular judgements and is understood to include only judgements that are solely about the aesthetic value or character[3] of a single item: on the one hand, those that are purely evaluative, restricted to expressing an assessment of the aesthetic value of an item, grading it as aesthetically good, mediocre, or bad, for example ('verdicts', as Frank Sibley called them); on the other hand, those that attribute to an item a property that is a ground of aesthetic value (positive or negative), a property in virtue of which the item may be aesthetically praised or faulted, the set of such properties constituting the item's aesthetic character.[4] If any ground of an item's aesthetic value, as realized in the item, is itself called an aesthetic value (positive or negative) of the item,[5] then with the idea of aesthetic value assigned the basic role, and exploiting the ambiguity of the notion,[6] the ideas of aesthetic judgement, pleasure,

---

[3] I take the notion of aesthetic character from Frank Sibley: see his *Approach to Aesthetics*, 123.

[4] This will impose a restriction on the idea of an aesthetic judgement if an aesthetic judgement is understood, as it might well be, to be a judgement that attributes an aesthetic property to an item, an aesthetic property of an item being conceived of as any property of the item, relevant to an assessment of the item's aesthetic value, which is dependent on the lower-order properties of the item, and which the subject can experience the item as possessing. But on this more liberal conception of an aesthetic judgement (and an aesthetic property), the categories of the aesthetic remain, *mutatis mutandis*, inter-definable.

[5] I am not assuming that someone who perceives a ground of aesthetic value recognizes it as the value it is or even as a value at all.

[6] The notion of aesthetic value covers both the notion of an item's overall aesthetic value and the idea of any property that is a ground of it.

property, and attitude might be defined in some such economical fashion as this:

An aesthetic judgement is a judgement that ascribes (positive or negative) aesthetic value to an item.

An aesthetic pleasure is a pleasure taken in the apparent perception or imaginative realization of aesthetic value.[7]

An aesthetic property of an item is any property of it that has aesthetic value.

An aesthetic attitude is an attitude of a kind conducive to a reliable perceptual- or imagination-based judgement of aesthetic value.

If, however, the basic status is assigned to the idea of aesthetic judgement, the other categories might be defined in terms of it just as easily:

An aesthetic value is a value of a kind ascribed by an aesthetic judgement.

An aesthetic pleasure is a pleasure taken in the apparent perception or imaginative realization of a value rightly or wrongly ascribed to the object of pleasure by a positive aesthetic judgement.

An aesthetic attitude is an attitude towards an item of a kind that is conducive to an aesthetic judgement about the item being well-founded.

An aesthetic property is a property ascribed to an item by an aesthetic judgement.

And so on round the circle of aesthetic categories.

It follows that if any category can be defined in non-aesthetic terms, all can. Nevertheless, one category might still be basic if the others can be defined (in non-aesthetic terms) only in virtue of their connections with it, whereas it can be elucidated independently of its connections with them (as with a word used paronymously).

2. Any attempt to articulate the essence of the aesthetic runs up against the problematic scope of the aesthetic. For there are different conceptions of its scope, no one of which has a proper claim to be the right one.

---

[7] 'Apparent' is needed to accommodate the common phenomenon of misplaced aesthetic pleasure—delight in an object, usually a work of art, that is based on an aesthetic character the object does not possess, that is, which lacks the aesthetic values that seem to be found in it. 'Imaginative realization' is to be understood in a wide sense to cover every way other than perception in which aesthetic value might be experienced.

Consider purely sensory (or sensuous) pleasure. The crucial feature of
purely sensory pleasure, understood as pleasure in the perception of a single
undifferentiated colour expanse, as such, or in the perception of a sound
of a constant pitch, loudness, and timbre or a taste or smell in which
a single sensory quality, sweetness, or acidity, for example, is detected,
is that there is no variety in the object as it is perceived, just a single,
structureless, homogeneous quality. Accordingly, a pleasurable series of
such perceptions—successive perceptions either of coexistent items or of
items that occur one after another—each of which yields pleasure, the
pleasure of each being independent of the relation of its object to that
of any other, affords only sensory pleasure, since no pleasure is taken in
anything other than a homogeneous quality. Likewise, a single perception
of a complex object yields only sensory pleasure if different elements of it
delight one but not in virtue of any relations among them. Some think of
purely sensory pleasure as being a species of aesthetic pleasure. But, for
others, aesthetic pleasure, by contrast, involves variety in its intentional
object, pleasure being taken in the manner in which the various aspects
are related to one another or in a property generated by the character
of the aspects and the relations among them (so that the experience of
a 'well-balanced' wine qualifies, not as purely sensory, but as aesthetic).
Accordingly, it is not just that the intentional object of aesthetic pleasure
must be complex: the pleasure must be due to the way in which the
elements relate to one another. This conception distinguishes aesthetic
from purely sensory pleasure by the requirement that aesthetic pleasure is
pleasure resulting from structure (in one sense of that word).[8]

   This divergence in understanding of the scope of the aesthetic is not the
only one. As yet there has been no need to distinguish art from non-art
or to draw a distinction between one art and another, between different
works within the same art, or between different aspects of a work. But
for some, not all forms of artistic appreciation are aesthetic. In the first
place, there are those who, seeking to stay close to the original meaning
of the term, allow into the aesthetic only those arts that address a specific
sensory mode (or a number of such modes), the conduit and appeal of
these arts being specifically visual or specifically auditory, for example,

---

[8] Another attempt to distinguish aesthetic from purely sensory pleasure insists that pleasure is aesthetic
only if it involves the exercise of conceptual powers. I leave aside the question whether this criterion
succeeds in effecting the desired distinction.

open only to those who possess the necessary sense and use it to take in what the art offers (or who are able to imagine the work, as someone now deaf can imagine a piece of music by means of the score), thus placing the appreciation of literature—or at least literature the specific appeal of which does not reside essentially in the sounds or visual appearance of its constituent words—outside the aesthetic.[9] According to the simplest form of this conception, for those arts that fall within the domain of the aesthetic there is no distinction between a work's artistic and its aesthetic value, but for those that fall outside that domain, although a work possesses an artistic value it lacks an aesthetic value. Second, whereas the term 'aesthetic' is often used in a wide sense to cover not only the aesthetic appreciation of nature and non-artistic artefacts but every kind of artistic appreciation, some prefer to operate with a narrower sense of the term, effecting a distinction between two kinds of properties of works of art—aesthetic and artistic properties. For those who use the term in the wide sense, artistic appreciation just is aesthetic appreciation of works of art. For those who use it in the narrower sense, although the aesthetic appreciation of a work of art is part of its artistic appreciation, it does not exhaust it, since the distinction between the aesthetic properties of a work of art and its artistic properties carries with it a distinction between its aesthetic and its artistic value. Not everyone who recognizes the distinction between the two kinds of property, each kind being relevant to the artistic evaluation of a work that possesses such a property, draws it in just the same way. But perhaps it would be agreed that artistic properties, unlike aesthetic properties, are such that they cannot be directly perceived or detected by attending exclusively to the work itself, even by someone who has the cognitive stock required to understand the work, since they are properties the work possesses only in virtue of the relations in which it stands to other things.[10] It would, of course, be possible to combine these two conceptions, both excluding from the aesthetic any art that does not address a specific sensory mode (or a number of such modes) and imposing the distinction between aesthetic and artistic properties of a work of art. This would yield the result that

---

[9] One important distinguishing feature of fiction is that the engagement of the imagination, which is an essential feature of its aesthetic appeal, does not consist in the (imaginative) perception of the imagined characteristics or scenes in the constituents or material of the work itself.

[10] Jerrold Levinson provides the clearest rationale of the distinction in his 'Artworks and the Future', conveniently reprinted in his *Music, Art, and Metaphysics* (Ithaca, NY and London: Cornell University Press, 1990): see pp. 182–3.

the idea of a work's artistic value diverges everywhere from that of its aesthetic value.

There are two reasonable responses to this proliferation of conceptions. A proposed account of the essence of the aesthetic might be intended to capture one particular conception of the scope of the aesthetic, or it might, in virtue of the generality of its formulation, be sufficiently elastic to be moulded to fit a number of conceptions.

3. Two promising candidates for the status of the basic category of the aesthetic are the ideas of aesthetic pleasure and aesthetic value. Whether either is basic, or whether any category is basic, two impressive recent accounts propose definitions of aesthetic pleasure that do not presuppose a prior understanding of the aesthetic. One of them also advances a definition of aesthetic value based on the fundamental component of the idea of aesthetic pleasure.

The distinctive feature of Kendall Walton's account[11] is the crucial role assigned to the notion of *pleasurable admiration*. This figures in the following way in his initial definition of aesthetic pleasure: aesthetic pleasure is 'pleasure which has, as a component, pleasure taken in one's admiration or positive evaluation of something; to be pleased aesthetically is to note something's value with pleasure'. Pleasure taken in the object is part of one's aesthetic pleasure if it is combined with pleasure taken in one's admiration for the object. Correlatively, an item's aesthetic value is its capacity to elicit 'reasonable' or 'apt' pleasurable admiration—the pleasurable admiration must be appropriate or merited. In fact, Walton confesses to the temptation to define an item's aesthetic value, not just in terms of its capacity to elicit (appropriate) pleasurable admiration for some value, but in terms of its capacity to elicit pleasurable admiration for its capacity to elicit pleasurable admiration for that value. To appreciate a work of art is to reap the benefits of the work's value, and this involves taking pleasure in admiring it (judging it to be good).

The initial definition of aesthetic pleasure is modified in two ways. First, in order to rule out 'pleasure of a self-congratulatory sort in admiring something' from constituting aesthetic pleasure, Walton adds that 'Aesthetic pleasure is not just pleasure in *my* admiration of something, but in *its* getting

[11] Kendall L. Walton, 'How Marvelous! Toward a Theory of Aesthetic Value', *The Journal of Aesthetics and Art Criticism*, 51/3 (Summer 1993).

me to admire it'. Second, Walton broadens the range of attitudes that are such that, if pleasure is taken in them, the pleasure is aesthetic pleasure: the attitude need not be admiration, but, for instance, awe or wonder (attitudes that are especially pertinent in the case of aesthetic pleasure in nature), or even revulsion or annoyance.

Building on the idea that a work of art has a character and a content, which can include a variety of different kinds of property, formal (such as balance and unity), aesthetic (gracefulness, garishness), expressive (melancholy, cheerfulness), representational (a woman, a landscape), semantic (the meaning of words), and symbolic (of death or the disintegration of life), all such properties not being first-order properties but second-order properties that an item possesses only in virtue of its possessing other properties on which the second-order properties are dependent, Jerrold Levinson[12] proposes a very different account of aesthetic pleasure:

Pleasure in an object is aesthetic when it derives from apprehension of and reflection on the object's individual character and content, both for itself and in relation to the structural base on which it rests. That is to say, to appreciate something aesthetically is to attend to its forms, qualities and meanings for their own sakes, [and to their interrelations,][13] but also to attend to the way in which all such things emerge from the particular set of low-level perceptual features which define the object on a non-aesthetic plane.

And he maintains that in order for pleasure in a work's 'cognitive content, moral import or political message'—aspects of a work that have traditionally been reckoned not to be aesthetic—to be aesthetic it must involve 'appreciation of the *manner* in which—the work being viewed in its proper historical context—these are embodied in and communicated by the work's' 'particular perceptual substructure', its specific elements and their structure, the work's 'concrete construction'.

Although this account appears to be geared more to pleasure in art than pleasure in nature, Levinson rightly requires that aesthetic pleasure in art should be related intelligibly to aesthetic pleasure in nature, which is, he asserts, 'typically a multi-level affair, involving reflection not only

[12] 'Pleasure, Aesthetic', in David Cooper (ed.), *A Companion to Aesthetics* (Oxford: Blackwell, 1992), reprinted as 'What is Aesthetic Pleasure?' in Levinson's *The Pleasures of Aesthetics*.
[13] Added in the reprint.

on appearances *per se*, but on the constitution of such appearances and the interaction between higher-order [and lower-order][14] perceptions'.

4. Neither of these conceptions of aesthetic pleasure appears to be satisfactory, each being inadequate both to pleasure in art and pleasure in nature. But something can be learnt from each.

Walton's theory imposes no restrictions on what something is admired for: whatever something is admired for—whatever value it has that it is admired for having—if the admiration is pleasurable then it is an instance of aesthetic pleasure. But this opens the theory to counter-examples, for it is clear that the theory does not provide a *sufficient* condition of a pleasure's being appropriately thought of as aesthetic. Consider, for example, my pleasurable admiration of John's fortitude in finishing the race despite his bad cold, or any other pleasurable admiration taken in someone's heroic, sterling, or admirable performance in the face of danger or difficulty. By deeming these aesthetic, Walton's account is unattractively idiosyncratic. And this inadequacy of Walton's account of aesthetic pleasure is starkly revealed if we leave aside the notion of admiration and consider just the notion of *positive evaluation*—judging something to be good—that is often substituted for it. For 'noting something's value with pleasure' means nothing other than taking pleasure in something's possessing a valuable quality of some kind—pleasure in the reliability of one's car, the thickness of the walls of one's house, the speed of one's computer, the excellence of one's spectacles, the good fit of one's new shoes, the purity of the water, the power of the vacuum cleaner, the high level of one's IQ, the strength of the cable, the accuracy of the thermometer, and so on. But none of these is an aesthetic pleasure, each of them being disqualified by the fact that it is a *propositional* pleasure—pleasure in *the fact that* one's shoes fit so well, for example.

It seems clear that for pleasurable admiration of something's value to constitute aesthetic pleasure, the value must be *aesthetic* value and the pleasure non-propositional.

Now if admiration is merely judging something to be good, then, as Walton remarks, admiration is not necessarily pleasurable, for there is such a thing as grudging respect or admiration. But to experience admiration is not just to judge something good: it is to experience an emotion. So

[14] Added in the reprint.

whereas it is obvious that pleasure is not integral to judging something to be good, a pleasurable element might be integral to the experience of admiration. Indeed, the emotion of admiration might well be construed as something like pleasurable contemplation of something's value. But suppose that pleasure is not integral to admiration, as it is not to judging something to be in some manner good. It would then, it seems, be possible for someone to take pleasure in an object, to admire it—to judge it to be good—and yet not to take pleasure *in admiring it*. Would this preclude the person's pleasure in the object from being aesthetic pleasure? If not—and this seems to be the right answer—then pleasurable admiration is not a necessary condition of pleasure's being aesthetic. There is another problem for Walton's account if admiration is not necessarily pleasurable. An item's aesthetic value is said to be its capacity to elicit 'reasonable' or 'apt' pleasurable admiration. It follows that non-pleasurable admiration of a work of art is not a matter of judging the aesthetic value of the work favourably. But why does the addition of pleasure to admiration turn it into a judgement of *aesthetic* value? Furthermore, if it is possible to derive pleasure from listening to a piece of music or reading a poem or watching a film for the sake of it without judging it to be good ('I enjoyed it but it's kitsch, sentimental . . .'), then *admiration itself* (judging something to be good) seems to be unnecessary for a pleasure to count as aesthetic.

Now 'pleasure taken in one's admiration of something' must be understood to mean that the pleasure qualifies the experience of admiration, rather than taking the admiration as its object. This is recognized implicitly by Walton in his rejection of pleasure of a self-congratulatory sort—delightedly patting oneself on the back for one's sophisticated and subtle taste in recognizing something's merit—as being aesthetic pleasure. But Walton's qualification of his initial definition of aesthetic pleasure—'Aesthetic pleasure is not just pleasure in *my* admiration of something, but in *its* getting me to admire it'—appears to conceive of pleasurable admiration, not as admiring with pleasure, but as pleasure in an item's capacity to generate admiration, and fails to bring out the most salient feature of the example. A distinguishing mark of pleasure of a self-congratulatory sort, other than its being directed at one's own admiration, is that it is a *propositional* pleasure—pleasure in the fact that one's aesthetic sensitivity is of a superior kind. It is *this* distinguishing mark that counts decisively against the pleasure's being aesthetic.

Two final points: First, it is clear that the doubling of pleasurable admiration that Walton is tempted by—defining an item's aesthetic value, not just in terms of its capacity to elicit (appropriate) pleasurable admiration for some value, but in terms of its capacity to elicit pleasurable admiration *for its capacity to elicit pleasurable admiration for that value*—if imposed as a condition of a pleasure's being aesthetic, would increase the implausibility of the account. Second, Walton's final account represents aesthetic pleasure as requiring that a component of a person's pleasure must be pleasure, not necessarily in the person's admiration of an item, but perhaps in some other attitude, such as awe or wonder. Accordingly, 'The aesthetic value of sunsets, alpine meadows, waterfalls, and flowers may consist (in part) in our taking pleasure in the awe or wonder we feel towards them'. But although forms of awe and wonder are feelings that at least some of us often experience towards natural objects or phenomena, it appears not to be a necessary condition of someone's deriving aesthetic pleasure from such an item that the person should experience some such feeling towards it, rather than merely finding it inherently rewarding to look at. This seems clear if awe is understood as reverential fear or wonder, i.e. fear of or wonder at something held in deep respect, and wonder is an emotion excited by what is unexpected, unfamiliar or inexplicable, especially surprise mingled with admiration or curiosity. For surprise, curiosity, fear, the unexpected, or unfamiliar are often lacking when people take delight in the appearance of natural items; respect is appropriate only for forms of life and even so is hardly shown towards, for example, flowers whose lives are shortened by being picked for their beauty and displayed only briefly, perhaps in a buttonhole; and much in the natural world that is experienced as being beautiful or sublime is not thought of by many of those who find it so as being inexplicable.

The crucial defect of Levinson's account is that it elides the distinction between aesthetic *pleasure* and aesthetic *appreciation* (between which he often slips). First, it is over-demanding in requiring, in the case of pleasure in a work of art, that the subject should reflect on the relation between the work's 'character and content' and the vehicle of the work, the relation 'between what a work expresses or signifies, and the means it uses to do so', i.e. the way in which these are realized in the work. This is perhaps a requirement on the full appreciation of a work as art, since full appreciation of a work of art involves understanding, as it were, *how it works*—how its aesthetic properties are realized in and determined by its non-aesthetic properties—but it is not a necessary condition of pleasure taken in the work being aesthetic pleasure. Pleasure in the mere *apprehension* of a work's character and content, for its own sake, is deemed not to be aesthetic by Levinson's account: for apprehension of that character and content to be aesthetic it must be accompanied by reflection on the manner in which that character and content is determined by its structural base: a person's attention must be engaged, not solely by that character and content, but also by how the second-order properties emerge from the first-order properties. But how else would it be reasonable to characterize pleasure in the mere apprehension of a work's character and content, i.e. apprehension of the work's character and content in the relevant way, by listening, looking, reading or whatever, but without *reflection* on the relation of this character and content to the structural base, perhaps without the kind of attention to the structural base that is necessary for such reflection to take place—the kind of pleasure that many people derive from reading a gripping novel, watching a comedy, spending the average amount of time in front of a picture in an art gallery, or listening to a melody with a certain emotional quality—if not as aesthetic? Apart from exceptional cases, there appears to be no good reason to disqualify this kind of pleasure from being aesthetic.

It is equally clear, if not more so, in the case of aesthetic pleasure in nature that the account demands too much: for being favourably impressed by a mighty waterfall, being delighted by a glittering iceberg, the flickering reflections of clouds in a river, the gracefulness of a gazelle, or the beauty of a rainbow or an alpine meadow to count as aesthetic pleasures, no reflection of the kind required by the account—which involves attention to the 'perceptual and conceptual underpinnings' of nature's 'manifest effects'—is necessary. Levinson claims that:

Even to enjoy aesthetically something as simple as the luminosity of the sun's colour at sunset is to enjoy such luminosity as the upshot of a particular shade and brightness of yellow, and as somehow appropriate to the heavenly body which is the source of all life.

But this seems to be too strong even as a requirement on the aesthetic *appreciation* of a natural phenomenon as the phenomenon it actually is, let alone on the *pleasure* being aesthetic.

Levinson's explanation of how pleasure in aspects of a work that have traditionally been characterized as 'non-aesthetic' can be aesthetic pleasure might be thought to add plausibility to his position. But even if the claim is true, it does not follow that pleasure in *any* aspect of a work is aesthetic only if it involves reflection on the manner of embodiment of character and content, or attention to how higher-order properties emerge from first-order ones. Of course, to perceive or apprehend any higher-order properties of an item you need to *perceive* lower-order ones, and in particular those lower-order properties upon which the higher-order ones are dependent: whenever you perceive or apprehend higher-order properties you perceive or apprehend them, not in the abstract, but as they are realized in the item. But to derive pleasure—aesthetic pleasure, surely—from the graceful shape of a vase or the mournful quality of a melody, no reflection on the relation between the item's gracefulness or melancholy and its structural basis is required. Furthermore, it is one thing to claim, rightly, that 'the relationship of substructure and superstructure in the total impression that an object affords is *necessarily of concern* [my emphasis] when an object is approached aesthetically', or that various higher-order properties are not in themselves aesthetic virtues and constitute aesthetic merits only as they are realized in particular works, and another to claim that any pleasure taken in a work of art is aesthetic only if it involves reflection on the relation of substructure to superstructure. Here it is important to recognize that the relation of substructure to superstructure may be an essential determinant of one's pleasure in a work, and one's pleasure may be pleasure in the superstructure as embodied in the substructure, in the absence of any reflection on that relation. And this, it would seem, is all that is necessary for one's pleasure to be aesthetic. In order to accommodate under the banner of the aesthetic pleasure in aspects of a work traditionally conceived of as being non-aesthetic, it is unnecessary to insist that this pleasure must involve reflection on or appreciation (rather than mere awareness) of the manner in which they are realized in the work: it suffices that the pleasure should be pleasure in them *as so realized*.

5. We can bring away from our consideration of these accounts two significant features of aesthetic pleasure, whether this is aesthetic pleasure in a work of art or aesthetic pleasure in a natural item or an artefact that is not a work of art. From the consideration of Walton we take

the important fact that aesthetic pleasure is a non-propositional pleasure: for the account of aesthetic pleasure as pleasure taken in the perception of aesthetic value to be adequate, pleasure *in* the perception of aesthetic value must not be understood as simply pleasure *from* that perception. From the consideration of Levinson we take a near neighbour of his conception, weakening his account in order to jettison the over-strong requirement imposed by his eliding the distinction between aesthetic pleasure and aesthetic appreciation: aesthetic pleasure, as distinguished from purely sensory pleasure, is pleasure taken in relations among the elements of the object and/or in higher-order properties of the object—by which I shall understand properties dependent on the nature of its elements and the relations among them—as they are realized in the object. But this must be qualified in order to accommodate misplaced pleasure—pleasure misplaced through the misrepresentation of an item's aesthetic character, through the experience of the item as possessing aesthetic value that it lacks.[15] A plausible definition of aesthetic pleasure in non-aesthetic terms, which takes these features on board, which straddles both art and non-art, and which is flexible enough, if it is suitably tailored, to accommodate different conceptions of the scope of the aesthetic, is as follows. First, a minimal conception of aesthetic pleasure: aesthetic pleasure is non-propositional pleasure taken in the character of an item as experienced in perception and/or imagination. Second, a conception that discriminates against purely sensory pleasure: the minimal conception bolstered by the condition that the pleasure must be taken in the apparent relations among the elements of the item—in a pattern, for example—and/or in the item's apparent higher-order properties as they are realized in the item.[16] Third, a conception that allows into the aesthetic only those arts that address a specific sensory mode (or a number of such modes): the enhanced conception reinforced by the condition that if the item is a work of art, it must be of a kind that addresses a particular sensory mode (or set of modes). Fourthly, a conception that takes on board the distinction between aesthetic and artistic properties of works of art: the enhanced conception

---

[15] I leave aside the possibility of perverted aesthetic pleasure—pleasure taken in the perception of a property that from the aesthetic point of view is inherently a demerit (which I distinguish from pleasure taken in a work of art's badness—amusement at its remarkable crassness or vulgarity, for example).

[16] Pleasure in higher-order properties as they are realized in the item can now be understood to include, but not entail, attention to and pleasure in how the higher-order properties are generated by lower-order properties.

strengthened by the condition that if the higher-order properties are properties of a work of art, then they must be directly detectable as realized in the work itself.[17] If something along these lines is acceptable, then, having achieved an account of aesthetic pleasure in non-aesthetic terms, it might seem that this can be used as the basic category and the other categories of the aesthetic defined in non-aesthetic terms by means of it, the set of definitions of the various categories encapsulating the essence of the aesthetic. Accordingly, operating with the minimal conception strengthened by the condition that discriminates against purely sensory pleasure, restricting the categories to those previously considered, and disambiguating the notion of aesthetic value:

> An aesthetic value—a positive aesthetic value—of an item is a relation among its elements, or a higher-order property as realized in the item, which is fit to yield non-propositional pleasure in the perception or imaginative realization of it.
>
> An item's overall aesthetic value is its fitness to yield non-propositional pleasure in the perception or imaginative realization of it in virtue of the ensemble of the relations among its elements, its higher-order properties as realized in it, and the interrelations of these.[18]
>
> An aesthetic judgement (one that is not a verdict) is a judgement that ascribes to an item a relation among its elements or a higher-order property and which is true if and only if the item possesses that relation or property and this is such that, as realized in the item, it is fit to yield non-propositional pleasure or displeasure in the perception or imaginative realization of it.

---

[17] I am unconvinced that many of what are taken to be artistic properties—being influential, for example, or originality (as it is often understood)—are in themselves relevant to an assessment of a work's artistic value (its value as a work of art). By far the best examination of the concept of originality in art is Frank Sibley's 'Originality and Value', conveniently reprinted in his *Approach to Aesthetics*.

[18] This is a simplification, for more than one reason. In the first place, it needs to be adjusted to accommodate the fact that overall aesthetic value is a matter of degree and involves the weighing of merits and demerits. But this rectification is easily made. Second, the notion of an item's overall aesthetic value—where this means its overall aesthetic value considered as the kind of thing it is (work of art, non-artistic artefact, or natural object, more specifically, cubist painting, church, or stone pine, etc.)—not only imposes requirements on the cognitive stock of the perceiver but is afflicted by a number of uncertainties. For example, the notion of the aesthetic value of a natural object, so I have argued, suffers from an indefiniteness that does not attach to the idea of the aesthetic value of a work of art. See my 'The Aesthetics of Nature', *Proceedings of the Aristotelian Society*, 50/2 (2000). The starting point for reflections on the aesthetic significance of the categories to which objects belong is Kendall Walton's seminal 'Categories of Art', *The Philosophical Review*, 79/3 (1970).

An aesthetic property of an item is any relation among the elements or any higher-order property of it that, as realized in the item, is fit to yield non-propositional pleasure or displeasure in the perception or imaginative realization of it.

An aesthetic attitude is an attitude of a kind conducive to the reliable perception or judgement of an item's fitness to yield non-propositional pleasure or displeasure in the relations among its elements or its higher-order properties as they are realized in it.

A word of explanation. There is a contentious issue I have not as yet acknowledged, and definitions of the category of aesthetic judgement in terms of pleasure will vary with the side adopted. While it is clear that an assessment of the aesthetic value of an item (a verdict) is an evaluation, there is an ongoing dispute between those who, following Sibley, regard the attribution of a property that is, from the aesthetic point of view, in itself a merit or demerit, as being purely descriptive and which does not require that the person making the judgement should regard the possession of the property as a value or disvalue,[19] and those who maintain that the attribution to an item of a ground of aesthetic value (positive or negative) should properly be understood as an expression of a favourable or unfavourable attitude towards an aspect of the item, one that indicates, perhaps, that the person making the judgement considers the experience of the aspect as being fit to yield pleasure or as being fit to yield displeasure. I intend to skirt this disagreement, although my formulation, in terms of a judgement that ascribes a property that is fit to yield pleasure, rather than a judgement of a property's fitness to yield pleasure, expresses my belief that it is not of the essence of the attribution of a ground of aesthetic value that it carries with it an evaluative attitude.

However, although this set of definitions does perhaps capture a certain narrow conception of the aesthetic, the concept of pleasure is not a sound foundation on which to build a broader and more usual conception of the aesthetic. For unless the idea of an experience in which we take

---

[19] I simplify Sibley's position by expressing it in terms not of the nature of words but of the attribution of properties, and by representing it as applying to all, rather than to the majority of, attributions. See Sibley's incisive discussion in his 'Particularity, Art and Evaluation', conveniently reprinted in his *Approach to Aesthetics*. Sibley's position is well defended in Jerrold Levinson's 'Aesthetic Properties, Evaluative Force, and Differences of Sensibility', in Emily Brady and Jerrold Levinson (eds.), *Aesthetic Concepts* (Oxford: Clarendon Press, 2001).

pleasure is understood in an unnaturally wide sense, so that it is equivalent to an experience that we find inherently rewarding to undergo, it is not possible to elucidate the notion of artistic value—the value of a work of art as art—in terms of pleasure.[20] Moreover, this is not due to the distinction between a work's artistic and its aesthetic value drawn by those who distinguish artistic from aesthetic properties of works: this notion of a work's aesthetic value is itself resistant to explanation in terms of pleasure. The point is, rather, that the experience of a work of art can be intrinsically rewarding to undergo, worth undergoing for its own sake—rewarding to undergo independently of any beneficial consequences that might be anticipated to accrue to one as a result of having had the experience—for reasons other than the pleasure the experience might afford; and the right idea to use to elucidate the notion of artistic value is not that of pleasure but the more fundamental idea of the rewards intrinsic to experiencing a work of art with understanding.[21] The modifications in the above accounts of aesthetic categories necessary to accommodate this conclusion are easily made:

> An aesthetic value—a positive aesthetic value—of an item is a relation among its elements, or a higher-order property of it, which, as realized in the item, is fit to make the perception or imaginative realization of it intrinsically rewarding.
>
> An item's overall aesthetic value is its fitness to make the perception or imaginative realization of it intrinsically rewarding in virtue of the ensemble of the relations among its elements, its higher-order properties as realized in it, and the interrelations of these.[22]
>
> An aesthetic judgement (one that is not a verdict) is a judgement that ascribes to an item a relation among its elements or a higher-order property and which is true if and only if the item possesses that relation or property and this is such that, as realized in the item, it is fit to make the perception or imaginative realization of it intrinsically rewarding or unrewarding.

[20] The best discussion of this issue is Jerrold Levinson's 'Pleasure and the Value of Works of Art', conveniently reprinted in his *The Pleasures of Aesthetics*.

[21] See my *Values of Art* (London: Allen Lane/The Penguin Press, 1995), pt. I. For a general conception of an aesthetic response in terms of an experience that is found to be intrinsically rewarding (or not inherently worthwhile, even worth not having), see my *The Aesthetic Appreciation of Nature* (Oxford: Clarendon Press, 2002), 14–15.

[22] See n.17.

An aesthetic property of an item is any relation among the elements or any higher-order property of it that, as realized in the item, is fit to make the perception or imaginative realization of it intrinsically rewarding.

An aesthetic attitude is an attitude of a kind conducive to the reliable perception or judgement of an item's fitness to make the experience of the relations among its elements or its higher-order properties as they are realized in it intrinsically rewarding.

It counts in favour of the approach I have suggested if these accounts of categories of the aesthetic are, as I believe, independently plausible.

3

The Acquaintance Principle

In *Art and its Objects* Richard Wollheim refers to what he takes to be 'a well-entrenched principle in aesthetics, which may be called the Acquaintance principle, and which insists that judgements of aesthetic value, unlike judgements of moral knowledge, must be based on first-hand experience of their objects and are not, except within very narrow limits, transmissible from one person to another'.[1] Wollheim says nothing about what the 'very narrow limits' of transmission might be, what it is about judgements of aesthetic value that allows transmission—transmission of what might be aesthetic knowledge—within these limits, and what restricts transmission to these limits. Note that on Wollheim's understanding of the principle it is about judgements of aesthetic *value* (which might be understood either as judgements of absolute or comparative overall aesthetic value or, perhaps, as judgements of inherent aesthetic merit- or defect-constituting properties), although the principle has not always been so restricted.

In fact there are two related but rather different aesthetic principles, the principle of Acquaintance and the principle of Autonomy, which tend to be conflated, but, so I maintain, with good reason. The principle of Acquaintance, whether applied to judgements of aesthetic value or more widely to other kinds of aesthetic judgement, maintains that such

---

[1] Richard Wollheim, *Art and its Objects*, 2nd edn (Cambridge: Cambridge University Press, 1980), 233. Wollheim's pronouncement rather confusingly contrasts aesthetic (value) judgements, not with moral judgements, but with judgements of moral knowledge. My principal concern is the claim that (well-founded) aesthetic judgements must be based on first-hand, not second- or third-hand, experience, rather than the view that aesthetic knowledge must be so based (although that view, which in what follows I am not always at pains to distinguish from it, also falls within my compass). I shall understand first-hand experience to include, where appropriate, perception, not of the object itself, but of an adequate reproduction, one that provides a good idea of the object's appearance. Difficulties in elucidating the idea of an adequate alternative to perception or awareness of the object itself are well expressed in Paisley Livingston's 'On an Apparent Truism in Aesthetics', *The British Journal of Aesthetics*, 43/3 (2003).

judgements must be based on acquaintance with the item in question, so that, lacking this acquaintance, it is not possible for one to make a (warranted) judgement about an item's aesthetic value or any of its aesthetic properties. The principle of Autonomy, as explicated by Robert Hopkins,[2] maintains (roughly) that it is never justifiable to change one's mind about an item's aesthetic value or its possession of a certain aesthetic property—one's mind having been made up through acquaintance with the item—solely on the basis of the disagreement of others, no matter how many or how well-qualified they may be. These are different principles, but it is clear that the principle of Acquaintance is fundamental, the principle of Autonomy being implied by it, resting upon it, and serving merely as a means of eliciting the intuition of, or gaining support for, the principle of Acquaintance. It rests upon it, because what other ground could there be for denying that the strength of the verdict of others could ever warrant a change of mind (especially if one's mind had been made up very quickly on a cursory inspection)? The rationale of the principle of Autonomy surely must be that the basis of a judgement about any of an item's aesthetic properties must be one's own experience of the item, in that it is the character of this experience—perhaps as the item is revisited in memory—that must determine one's judgement: one's judgement must arise from this experience as an expression of its character.

How well-entrenched the principle of Acquaintance is in aesthetics is a moot point. There appears to be a paucity of arguments in support of it. Although it is often said that this principle has its roots in Kant, he certainly cannot be appealed to in support of it (or the principle of Autonomy). This is so for two reasons. The first is that Kant distinguishes a very small number of kinds of aesthetic judgement and it is only in the case of his principal interest, a so-called judgement of taste, a judgement of free or dependent beauty, which concerns (at least) an object's perceptual structure (although its predicate 'is beautiful' does not serve to characterize the nature of that structure), that he *argues* that the judgement must be based on the subject's experience of the object judged. He does not acknowledge, and so expresses no view of, the immense variety of other judgements that ascribe aesthetic properties. The second is that, in any case, the considerations he produces

² Robert Hopkins, 'Kant, Quasi-realism, and the Autonomy of Aesthetic Judgement', *European Journal of Philosophy*, 9/2 (2001), 166–89.

in support of the principle of Autonomy (or Acquaintance) as governing judgements of beauty are manifestly insufficient to establish it even in this single case. These considerations are put forward in support of his claim that a judgement of taste cannot be determined by 'bases of proof' and consist of these two assertions: (i) there are no a priori principles that could provide the basis for a proof of a judgement of taste, and (ii) there is no empirical basis of proof that could compel someone to make a judgement of taste. In support of these two assertions Kant makes essentially the same point, namely that one cannot, in virtue of the contrary opinion of however many others, be talked into feeling the pleasure that is the canonical basis of a judgement of taste—which manifestly fails to establish the principle of Acquaintance (or Autonomy) for such judgements: the canonical basis of a certain kind of judgement is not thereby a necessary condition of a person's making a judgement of that kind, the essential basis on which the judgement must rest for it properly to be deemed such a judgement. It is true that Kant *defined* an aesthetic judgement as one whose basis can be nothing other than the subject's hedonic response to the item judged. But his tendency just to fall back on his conception of a judgement of taste as one the determining ground of which must be pleasure, which reduces the issue to a definitional one, achieves nothing. For if we take Kant's prime example of an aesthetic judgement—a judgement of free beauty—although his definition precludes characterizing my belief, based on your reliable testimony, that the flower you are looking at is beautiful as being an aesthetic judgement, this does not imply that you have not transmitted to me the knowledge that it is beautiful. It is true that people are in general less reliable in their judgements of aesthetic value than in their judgements of colour, for example. But it would be a mistake to conclude from this that nobody could ever be in a position in which they have adequate justification to credit another with exceptionally good aesthetic judgement and so to accept that person's verdict on an item they themselves have not perceived. In fact, there is no insurmountable barrier to knowledge of something's being beautiful being transmitted from one person to another, and the Acquaintance principle, understood as a thesis about judgements of overall aesthetic value, has no plausibility.

As I have emphasized, Wollheim's formulation of the Acquaintance principle renders it as governing judgements of aesthetic value. Others take the principle to apply also to judgements of aesthetic *properties*, understood in a wide Sibley-style sense. Michael Tanner, who accepts the Acquaintance principle for judgements of aesthetic properties, has suggested that part of the explanation of why the principle holds is that the ascription of aesthetic properties 'does not follow from the description of the phenomenal properties on which they supervene in such a way that from the phenomenal description the aesthetic properties can be inferred'.[3] It is clear that, if the principle does hold and if this fact does constitute part of the explanation of its holding, this fact could not be the complete explanation. For in itself it implies nothing about the impossibility of aesthetic judgements being transmitted from one person to another. Tanner proceeds to make another claim:

judgements of aesthetic, and in some cases moral, value must be based on first-hand experience of their objects not simply because one is in no position to assert the presence of the requisite properties without the experience, but also because one is not capable of understanding the meaning of the terms which designate the properties without the experience.[4]

But the assertion that one cannot understand the meaning of evaluative terms that designate the properties ascribed to objects without first-hand experience of those objects, which Tanner puts forward as having universal validity in aesthetics, is based on loose reasoning. For it does not follow from the fact which he emphasizes—that it is possible to encounter works of art which provide one with one's concept of greatness and which serve as touchstones for judging works of art—that every term that designates a value-laden aesthetic property is such that its meaning can be understood only through acquaintance with whatever particular work it happens to be applied to.

---

[3] Michael Tanner, 'Ethics and Aesthetics are—?', in José Luis Bermúdez and Sebastian Gardner (eds), *Art and Morality* (London: Routledge, 2003), 29. This is a familiar line of thought that derives from Frank Sibley. For example, Sibley suggests that the reason a person needs to experience a work of art in order to judge that it possesses a merit-constituting property is that there is no conceptual connection between its possessing a determinate merit-responsible property and its possessing the merit-constituting property for which the determinate merit-responsible property is responsible. See Frank Sibley, 'Particularity, Art and Evaluation, reprinted in his *Approach to Aesthetics*, ed. John Benson, Betty Redfern, and Jeremy Roxbee Cox (Oxford: Clarendon Press, 2001). An item's aesthetic properties could not in general be derived from a description of its phenomenal properties, for its aesthetic properties are a function of various features other than its phenomenal properties, such as its artistic category. I leave aside the question of the truth or falsity of the view that the possession of an aesthetic property cannot legitimately be inferred from a description of all of the item's relevant non-aesthetic properties because of the manifest insufficiency of the view to establish the Acquaintance Principle.

[4] Tanner, 'Ethics and Aesthetics are—?', 33.

For Roger Scruton, the Acquaintance principle holds for (so-called) aesthetic *descriptions* precisely because one must embrace a non-realist conception of them: the acceptance condition of an aesthetic description is not a belief (that the item described has the property ascribed to it); rather, one can assert or assent sincerely to such a characterization only if one has had a certain (typically affective) experience of the item so characterized.[5] But it is unnecessary to engage here with the general issue of aesthetic realism/non-realism. For although Scruton's form of non-realism certainly does imply the Acquaintance principle, it is an extreme conception, one that has unacceptable consequences, and more plausible forms will not commit themselves to the Acquaintance principle. The distinctive feature of Scruton's form of anti-realism about the attribution of aesthetic properties is that it prioritizes in a particular manner the cognitive state of a person who, on the basis of his or her acquaintance with an item, makes such an attribution, explicating the meaning of the attribution as an expression of the experience undergone by the person. Hence it is forced to posit a semantic distinction between attributions based on acquaintance and attributions not so based.[6] For an attribution by one who is unacquainted with an item cannot be an expression of the experience undergone by the person in acquaintance with the item, since there is no such experience. Accordingly, this version of anti-realism maintains that a sentence used to express an aesthetic judgement about an object is ambiguous, meaning one thing in the mouth of someone acquainted with the object and something else in the mouth of one who is unacquainted with the object; and, furthermore, it commits itself to the claim that without first-hand experience of the object one cannot understand perfectly the meaning of the sentence as uttered by one acquainted with it. It follows that if an aesthetic attribution, no matter who makes it, means just the same—if the sentence 'O is beautiful (or amusing, dynamic, sentimental, graceful, harmonious, expressive of happiness, or whatever)' has a unitary meaning, whether in the mouth of someone acquainted with O or of someone unacquainted with O—this form of anti-realism collapses immediately.

[5] Roger Scruton, *Art and Imagination* (London: Methuen & Co Ltd, 1974), esp. ch. 4.

[6] This commitment has never, I believe, been explicitly acknowledged by Scruton himself. In his 'Quasi-realism, Acquaintance, and the Normative Claims of Aesthetic Judgement' (*The British Journal of Aesthetics* (44/3 (July 2004)) Cain Samuel Todd, who adheres to Scruton's form of non-realism, recognizes the commitment and embraces it.

This appears to be exactly the fact of the matter. If someone tells me that *Sons of the Desert* is an amusing film or *The Makioka Sisters* a great novel, and, to put it crudely, I take his word for it, then if I tell another, wisely or foolishly, that the film is amusing or the novel great, I mean exactly what my informer meant. I contradict someone who says 'Greuze's paintings are generally sentimental' when I say, on another's testimony, 'Greuze's paintings are in general not sentimental'. Unfamiliar with the work, I can ask someone acquainted with Schoenberg's First String Quartet (in D minor) whether its opening is dynamic, in just the same sense as he thinks it is or is not. I can wonder whether a rue-leaved saxifrage, which I am unacquainted with, is as beautiful as a fritillary, which I am acquainted with, without falling into incoherence. Without first-hand experience of O I can understand perfectly the meaning of 'O is expressive of happiness' as said by one acquainted with O, for, being acquainted with P, it cannot be denied that I understand the meaning of 'P is expressive of happiness' in the mouth of one acquainted with P, and the difference in meaning between 'O is expressive of happiness' and 'P is expressive of happiness', each spoken on the basis of acquaintance, is solely a matter of the difference in meaning/reference between 'O' and 'P'. And so on throughout the variety of ways in which expressions occur in our aesthetic talk and thought, in generalizations, questions, doubts, comparisons, etc. So it is unsurprising that upholders of this form of anti-realism provide no scrap of evidence for the existence of a duality of meaning or for the associated denial that someone unacquainted with an object can understand perfectly an aesthetic attribution to it, and that no account of the alleged meaning of such an attribution by one unacquainted with the object in question is forthcoming. In the light of the linguistic facts it is, I believe, a constraint on any adequate theory that it should recognize the univocal nature of aesthetic attributions: if a theory credits each kind of aesthetic attribution with two meanings, one for those acquainted with the object of attribution, the other for those who are not, it has gone wrong. But this does not imply a realistic theory of aesthetic attributions (of whatever kind): there are forms of non-realism other than this extreme one—ones that do not imply the acquaintance principle.[7]

---

[7] [2007] Roger Scruton has recently indicated that a different form of non-realism—one that I have outlined elsewhere—now seems preferable to him (private communication).

So leaving aside this implausible version of non-realism, is there some other kind of reason for thinking that it is necessary to be acquainted with something in order to be able sincerely to assert (justifiably) or (with due warrant) assent to an aesthetic description of that thing?[8]

Philip Pettit, in the process of countering Scruton's anti-realism, has advanced a claim about aesthetic characterizations—characterizations of a work of art as 'graceful or awkward, tightly or loosely organised, dreamy or erotic, inviting or distancing', for example—that is tantamount to the Acquaintance principle taken in the strongest sense, as not admitting transmission even within 'very narrow limits'. He takes aesthetic characterizations to be 'essentially perceptual', by which he means that 'the putatively cognitive state one is in when, perceiving a work of art, one sincerely assents to a given aesthetic characterization, is not a state to which one can have non-perceptual access'. Accordingly, even though someone, who has good reason to trust the testimony of one who has perceived a particular work, might properly say, relying solely on that testimony, that she knows that a certain aesthetic characterization is true of that work, her cognitive state is not the same as that of the one whose testimony is the source of her knowledge. So 'Aesthetic characterisations are essentially perceptual in the sense that perception is the only title to the sort of knowledge—let us say, to the full knowledge—of the truths which they express.'[9]

Pettit's explanation of the essentially perceptual nature of aesthetic characterizations is that, if 'p' is a sentence offering such a characterization of W, then what is expressed by 'p' as this is asserted by one who perceives

---

[8] The Acquaintance Principle maintains that aesthetic knowledge must be acquired through first-hand experience of the object of knowledge and cannot be transmitted from person to person. This implies that aesthetic knowledge of an object cannot be acquired either from an accurate description of the non-aesthetic features of the object or from reliable testimony of its aesthetic character. I give scant consideration to the possibility of deriving knowledge from a non-aesthetic description. If this were to be a real possibility, it would certainly disprove the Acquaintance Principle, but its impossibility would not establish it. Furthermore, if the way knowledge were to be derived from a non-aesthetic description were through its enabling a person to imagine the object (as one might imagine music from a score), a defender of the Acquaintance Principle might simply deem imagining to be a form of first-hand experience. I focus on the possibility of acquiring aesthetic knowledge through reliable testimony because here there is a style of argument that, if correct, would rule out the possibility of knowledge of an item's aesthetic properties being transmitted to someone who lacks the requisite first-hand experience, and the manoeuvre of including imagining under the head of first-hand experience is not available.

[9] Philip Pettit, 'The Possibility of Aesthetic Realism', in Eva Schaper (ed.), *Pleasure, Preference and Value: Studies in Philosophical Aesthetics* (Cambridge: Cambridge University Press, 1983), 24–5.

W cannot be fully understood by one who does (and has) not. Suppose that 'p' characterizes W as being ø. Then Pettit's idea is that what is expressed by 'p' is given by this associated conditional: 'W is ø iff W is such that it looks (sounds, etc.) ø under standard presentation and under suitable positioning that is allowed by the appropriate constraints'. By standard presentation is meant presentation in appropriate conditions of observation (which vary across different art forms and even within the same art) to a competent person (competence again varying from work to work). By suitable positioning that is allowed by the appropriate constraints is meant, in short, correct positioning, positioning in the right reference class, that is, perceiving W against the background of, or by reference to, the class of relevant contrasts (which, simplifying, is a certain class of discernible variations on W).[10] An understanding of what standard *presentation* involves is unproblematic for someone who stands only in a testimonial relation to W. Pettit's claim is that only someone who perceives W can identify the right *positioning*—can understand what that positioning is—and so only such a person can fully grasp what is expressed by 'p'.[11] Accordingly, aesthetic characterizations are essentially perceptual.

However, if a correct specification of the right positioning suffices for the identification of it, Pettit's claim would seem to be unwarranted, since one who has not perceived W might be informed of the right positioning by one who has. For Pettit's claim to go through, identification must preclude specification (or specification understandable by one who has not perceived W). But if identification of the right reference class precludes specification, it becomes unclear what identification consists in. Pettit maintains that the right reference class is available only through imagination and that only someone who is perceiving W and putting it imaginatively through various positionings can understand what that positioning is under which W looks (sounds, etc.) ø—understanding being

[10] For my present purpose it is not necessary to engage with Pettit's notion of positioning. His basic idea is that perception of a work of art, if it is to be such as to reveal the work's true aesthetic properties, must be informed by relevant background knowledge.

[11] The associated conditional could be understood in two ways: either 'standard presentation' and 'suitable positioning that is not incorrect' are short for what constitutes them or they are not. If not, it would be possible for one unaware of the right reference class to have a full understanding of the associated conditional and so of 'p'. For on this reading the associated conditional does not require one who understands it to know what the right reference class is. But Pettit intends it to be understood in such a manner that, just as understanding standard presentation requires knowing what it involves, so understanding appropriate positioning requires identification of the right reference class.

achieved only in so far as the person succeeds in making W look (sound etc.) ø.[12] Now this is certainly too strong: no putting of a work through various positionings is necessary to perceive the applicability of an aesthetic characterization to a work previously unfamiliar to one—it might well be obvious immediately—and you do not need to be perceiving a work you are familiar with in order to have a full understanding of an aesthetic characterization of it that you experienced it under when you did perceive it. But this can be left aside. There is a more important point: to adopt, or be able to adopt, the right positioning does not imply the ability to spell out what the appropriate reference class is. Now if adoption of the right positioning never guaranteed this ability, precisely because it is never possible to spell out the appropriate reference class, it might be thought that this would be sufficient to establish Pettit's claim. But it would not, for an understanding of the appropriate reference class might be acquired, not by a direct indication of the class, but by a reference to it as being the same as the one that is the appropriate reference class for another work that one is familiar with. What Pettit's argument needs is that knowledge of the right reference class is restricted to those who have interacted with W in the right manner. But given that the knowledge need not be specifiable by one who has it—and cannot be if Pettit's claim is to hold—it would seem that what possession of the knowledge comes to is simply the ability to perceive W as looking (sounding, etc.) ø, which ability might well be possessed by someone unfamiliar with W. Furthermore, Pettit's reliance on the associated conditional, understood in the manner he intends, is questionable. Even if I have no idea under what (correct) positioning an unfamiliar work presents a certain aesthetic appearance, I understand perfectly the claim that the work is graceful or awkward, tightly or loosely organized, dreamy or erotic, inviting or distancing, for example. And I might have forgotten what the positioning was that enabled me to perceive a certain work under a particular aesthetic characterization, and yet fully understand my characterization of it.

The stratagem of distinguishing two different understandings of the notion of an aesthetic judgement—as a judgement that is a direct expression of the character of one's own experience of an item, and as a judgement of an item's aesthetic character arrived at in any way (on the basis of another's

---

[12] Pettit, 'The Possibility of Aesthetic Realism', 33.

testimony, for example)—would be an ineffective means of coming to terms with the Acquaintance principle. The idea would be that in the first sense an aesthetic judgement of a work of art must be based on first-hand experience of the work, but in the second sense it need not: opposition to the Acquaintance principle derives from not distinguishing the two senses. A closely related idea is that an unqualified ascription of an aesthetic property or value to a work will be regarded as misleading or improper if it is not based on first-hand experience: such an assertion is expected to be a reflection of the speaker's experience of the work, not of another's, no matter how reliable the other may be. The avowal of an aesthetic characterization is in this respect like an avowal of liking a taste: it would not be right to say of something you haven't tasted that you like its taste, even if you are reliably assured that you will or would like it. But—leaving aside the question of their plausibility—what each of these positions fails to address is the issue in question: whether one can be justified in forming a firm judgement on another's testimony about the aesthetic character of a work of art—a judgement that has the same content as one based on first-hand experience. It is just this possibility that the Acquaintance principle denies, and neither the distinguishing of different notions of aesthetic judgement nor the indication of a conversational implicature precludes a belief about an aesthetic property, based on testimony, from being justified and having the same content as one based on acquaintance.

In fact, there *is* a crucial difference between the cognitive states of someone unfamiliar with a certain work, who wholeheartedly accepts the view of a reliable informer as to an aesthetic characterization of the work, and the reliable informer as he perceives the work—and, usually, for some time, perhaps an indefinitely long time, afterwards; but this difference is not a difference in their understandings of the characterization of the work. Suppose the work is characterized as being graceful. The reliable informer, as he perceives the work, will not just perceive the work as being graceful but will perceive the gracefulness *as it is realized in the work*. And when he quits the work he will retain some memory, perhaps a detailed memory, of the realization of the aesthetic property, a memory that, unless it is reinforced, is liable to become ever more sketchy as time passes. In contrast, the one who has no first-hand experience of the work will, given the infinitely many strikingly different ways in which gracefulness can be realized in a work of art, have little or no idea of the work's appearance simply in virtue of knowing at second-hand that the work is graceful.[13] As the reliable informant's unreinforced memory of the work gets ever more dim, his cognitive state will diverge less and less from the virtually blank state of the one who has no first-hand experience of the work; and a time might well come when the reliable informer no longer has any idea of the work's appearance, and yet remembers that the work is graceful. If this happens, the crucial difference between the cognitive states of the two people has vanished. Now appreciation of a work is not a matter of knowing what its aesthetic properties are, but of perceiving them as realized in the work. So you do not appreciate a work even if you know at second-hand as full a characterization of its aesthetic properties as might be given by one who is perceiving the work. And attitudes and reactions linked to appreciation—liking or disliking, admiration, contempt, revulsion, and so on—are denied to you: you cannot like a work's gracefulness if you are unacquainted with the work. In terms of transmission, we might put the point by saying that an item's gracefulness, in contrast to its being graceful—likewise, an item's beauty, unlike its being beautiful—cannot be transmitted from person to person through testimony. If anything can be identified as the prime provider of false sustenance for the strong version of the Acquaintance principle, as applied to aesthetic characterizations or judgements of aesthetic properties, it is, perhaps, this fact about the lack of transmissibility of appreciation and associated attitudes and reactions. Although aesthetic judgements do not carry appreciation with them, judgements of aesthetic properties are as transmissible from one person to another as are other kinds of judgement.

Postscript [2007]

It will be clear that I take the crucial claim which adherents of the Acquaintance principle, understood in its strongest sense, must embrace to be that it is impossible for someone who has not experienced a certain

---

[13] Here there is a marked difference between aesthetic properties and many other properties that need to be perceived in order to be detected: the indefiniteness of the knowledge of something's appearance given by the possession of an aesthetic quality is vastly greater than that given by colour, shape, and other perceptible properties.

item—or (perhaps) an item of a relevantly similar kind (usually, one that is identical in appearance)—to understand exactly which property is being predicated of the item by an aesthetic attribution made by one acquainted with it and whose attribution accurately reflects their experience: a necessary condition of grasping the specific aesthetic property attributed to an item is acquaintance with the item. What other possible explanation of the Acquaintance principle could there be? For if what is expressed by a sentence offering an aesthetic characterization of a work of art, as it is asserted by a perceiver of the work, can be fully understood by someone unacquainted with the work, then that person could have the perceiver's judgement transmitted to her: she could then believe it, know that the perceiver is an exceptionally good judge of the aesthetic features of works of the kind in question, perhaps a better judge than she herself is, and so be justified in relying on the perceiver's opinion, and, accordingly, properly claim to know that the work is as so characterized.[14] To resist this conclusion by having recourse to an extreme scepticism about the possibility of aesthetic knowledge would be a desperate and unwarranted strategy, which would in any case achieve only a pyrrhic victory: the acquisition of aesthetic knowledge through testimony would be ruled out simply through aesthetic knowledge being deemed impossible. But how could this crucial claim be true? If the reasoning Pettit advances in support of it is untenable, from what else could the claim receive support? As far as I can see the claim could be true only if the attribution of aesthetic properties is implicitly indexical. Now this has indeed been claimed. For example, it has been maintained that if an object possesses an aesthetic property, G, say, its G is different from that possessed by any other object (except those objects perceptually indiscriminable or almost

---

[14] I leave aside the insistence that certainty based on testimony which there is good reason to believe reliable is nevertheless always insufficient for aesthetic knowledge. The outstanding investigation of the possible degree of support that testimony might provide for one particular kind of aesthetic judgement—a judgement of beauty, understood in a somewhat Kantian manner as indicating a response of pleasure to a beautiful object—is Robert Hopkins' 'Beauty and Testimony', in Antony O'Hear (ed.), *Philosophy, the Good, the True and the Beautiful* (Cambridge: Cambridge University Press, 2000), 209–36. I do not regard the concept of knowledge as sufficiently sharp and robust enough to underpin the claim that no amount of testimony can ever provide sufficient grounds for an aesthetic judgement (of whatever kind) formed on the basis of testimony to be deemed knowledge. But in any case I would be happy to retreat, if that is what it would be, to the position that one can understand an attribution of an aesthetic property to an object one is unacquainted with by a person or number of persons whom one has exceptionally strong reason to regard as reliable in their judgements of that kind of property and so to believe, justifiably, in the attribution of that property to the object.

indiscriminable from it). For aesthetic terms incorporate a (hidden) indexical or demonstrative component, so that to talk of the G of W is to talk of a different aesthetic property from that of the G of an easily discriminable X: '(almost) every graceful painting confronts us with a unique quality of grace'.[15] Hence a person will understand the judgement that W possesses G (is graceful) differently after acquaintance with W than before such acquaintance: acquaintance with W will always introduce a difference into the understanding of the aesthetic judgement. But not only does this view, the appeal of which has always eluded me, lack a solid foundation, it is confused. Its foundation is the claim that—I simplify—every item that possesses aesthetic property G possesses a different G from that possessed by any perceptually discriminable item. I have never seen a convincing argument for this proposition and my suspicion is that it depends for its plausibility on being conflated with the manifest truth that the realization of G in W is not the same as the realization of G in X. But in any case the view is founded on a false inference. For even if it were to be true that each perceptually discriminable item that possesses a certain generic aesthetic property possesses its own unique quality of that property, this does not touch the *attribution* of the generic property to an item and so the understanding of that attribution: these remain at the generic level. The most that could follow from perceptually discriminable items necessarily possessing their own unique quality of some generic aesthetic property G is that acquaintance is essential for knowing, not that an item possesses G, but exactly which quality of G it possesses—and that is not the acquaintance principle. It is, of course, sometimes true that although two works equally possess G, the G of W is not the same as the G of X. But when this is so it is not just because W is, if it is, (easily) discriminable from X, but because there are different species or varieties of G, one of which is possessed by W and another by X. When John W. Bender asks 'Is the poignancy of a Debussy prelude *the same property* as the poignancy of a

---

[15] Iuliana Corina Vaida, 'The Quest for Objectivity: Secondary Qualities and Aesthetic Qualities', *Journal of Aesthetics and Art Criticism*, 56/3 (Summer 1998), 283–97. Her tactic of representing an attribution of an aesthetic property as a combination of a judgement of alikeness and an indexical component (*this* G) is immediately vulnerable to the thought that, since there is no essential connection between the two elements that yokes them inseparably together, the self-subsistent generic judgement constitutes an attribution of an aesthetic property unacknowledged by and inconsistent with the insistence that aesthetic language always has a dual function in singular judgements, subsumption *and* indexical.

Brahms sonata? Or are these attributions implicitly indexical . . .?', [16] the answer is that these *attributions* are not implicitly indexical, so that the same generic property is being attributed to the Debussy prelude and the Brahms sonata. But, of course, if there are different kinds (species) of poignancy, each attribution allows of further specification of the kind in question, which, if the specifications differ, will mean that the revised attributions attribute different properties.

[16] John W. Bender, 'Aesthetic Realism 2', in Jerrold Levinson (ed.), *The Oxford Handbook of Aesthetics* (Oxford: Oxford University Press, 2003), 85.

4

The Intersubjective Validity of Aesthetic Judgements

1. By an aesthetic judgement I shall mean a judgement of an object (event or process) for which the canonical basis of such a judgement is a person's aesthetic sensitivity as exercised in an experience of the object.[1] This is not to say that for someone's judgement of an object to be an aesthetic judgement it must be based on the person's aesthetic sensitivity as exercised in an experience of that object: it allows for the possibility that the person's judgement derives, at one or more removes, from another's judgement, whether reliable or not, that is so based.[2]

Aesthetic sensitivity is dependent upon other sensitivities, sensitivities which are not themselves specifically aesthetic, such as sensitivity to difference in colour, shape, taste, sound, or the meaning of words. How is the idea of aesthetic sensitivity itself to be understood? I propose to understand it as sensitivity to the aesthetic character of an object. I follow Frank Sibley in meaning by the aesthetic character of a work 'the quality or assemblage of qualities in virtue of which it may be aesthetically praised or condemned—its grace, serenity, dynamism, gaiety, balance, unity, vividness, psychological perceptiveness, profundity, banality, sentimentality, etc.'[3] Accordingly, a person's aesthetic sensitivity is exercised in detecting (or seeming to detect) aspects of an object, dependent on characteristics of the object for which aesthetic sensitivity is not required, that are relevant to an assessment of its aesthetic value. Aesthetic sensitivity is sensitivity, refined,

---

[1] For simplicity's sake I have framed this to fit singular judgements, which I will focus on. But with slight modifications it will cover comparative, general, and universal aesthetic judgements.

[2] In this way it diverges from Frank Sibley's favoured conception. See his *Approach to Aesthetics* (Clarendon Press: Oxford, 2001), 34–5.

[3] Sibley, *Approach to Aesthetics*, 123.

crude, or malformed, to whatever higher-order characteristics of an object might be cited in explanation of a judgement of aesthetic value, to inherent aesthetically meritorious or deleterious characteristics of an object, or to whether a feature or aspect of an object enhances or detracts from the object's aesthetic value, and it is expressed in the aesthetic value accorded the object.[4]

2. There are significantly different kinds of aesthetic judgement, which can be classified in a number of ways. A fundamental distinction is between evaluative and non-evaluative judgements, the former expressing an aesthetic evaluation of the object by the subject, the latter not doing so but instead offering some kind of characterization of the object of the judgement. However, for my present purpose I need, at first, a more refined classification. I propose to distinguish three kinds of aesthetic judgement, which I shall do by reference to the character of the predicates of sentences used to express them. The three sorts of predicate, and accordingly the three kinds of judgement, are: purely evaluative, purely descriptive, and evaluation-added.[5] A purely evaluative predicate signifies a high, medium, or low degree of aesthetic value but without indicating any properties of an item, in particular those properties in virtue of which the item is attributed the value. So the aesthetic judgement that a certain work of art is superb, great, good, mediocre, weak, or poor, is purely evaluative. A purely descriptive predicate signifies a property but without indicating any value, even in those cases where the property it stands for is in fact a value of the item, given the kind of thing it is. Accordingly, the judgement that a musical phrase sounds melancholy or a poem is sombre is purely descriptive. An evaluation-added predicate signifies a property and also a value in the sense that the (sincere) application of the predicate indicates that the person who applies it values or disvalues the property. So the judgement that a painting is garish (where 'garish' means 'obtrusively bright') is an evaluation-added judgement, representing the painting as being not just brightly coloured, but obtrusively so. Perhaps it will be thought that in order to exhaust the possibilities it is necessary to add a further kind of aesthetic judgement,

---

[4] 'Aesthetic sensitivity' is to be understood in a wide sense, so as to embrace artistic sensitivity, where this includes sensitivity to an object's artistic values.

[5] It will be clear that I am here following Frank Sibley, although I have adjusted his terminology slightly. See his 'Particularity, Art and Evaluation' conveniently reprinted in his *Approach to Aesthetics*, 91–3.

one that is evaluative but which contains or implies a restrictive element, limiting the judgement to a particular aspect of the judged object, explicitly (as with the judgement that the colouring of a painting is wonderful) or implicitly (as with the judgement that a painting is balanced, which is concerned with the interrelation of its parts, or the judgement that a movement is graceful, which is concerned with the smoothness of the transition from one position to another). But with a suitable understanding of the conception of object this is unnecessary: the relevant objects in the preceding examples are the colouring of the painting, the interrelation of the painting's parts, the smoothness of the transition from position to position. But although aesthetic judgements are susceptible of this threefold division, there is no need to deal separately with evaluation-added judgements. For the evaluative element of an evaluation-added judgement has as its specific object the property attributed to an item, as, for example, the brightness of the colouring is the specific object of the evaluative element of the judgement that a painting is garish. Hence an evaluation-added judgement can be assimilated, in one respect to a purely evaluative judgement, and, in another respect, to a purely descriptive judgement. It is in fact a combination of two judgements, one purely descriptive, the other purely evaluative: its purely descriptive element consists in attributing the signified property to an object and its purely evaluative element consists in the signified aesthetic value (of the property attributed).[6] So an adequate treatment of the topic of the intersubjectivity of aesthetic judgements, which must be based on an account of the nature of such judgements, can restrict itself to two issues, aesthetic evaluation and aesthetic description.[7]

The more refined classification of aesthetic judgements appears to effect a division of them into, on the one hand, those that claim to represent the world as being a certain way, attributing a property to their object, and, on the other hand, those that ascribe an aesthetic value to their target, whilst it allows for judgements that straddle the division, such judgements being partly representational and partly evaluative. If this were so, then for each

---

[6] This follows immediately from the concept of an evaluation-added judgement. Sceptics about the separability of the descriptive element of an aesthetic judgement that is not purely descriptive should engage with Jerrold Levinson's 'Aesthetic Properties, Evaluative Force, and Differences of Sensibility', in Emily Brady and Jerrold Levinson (eds.), *Aesthetic Concepts* (Oxford: Clarendon Press, 2001).

[7] This point is not affected by the fact that there is a kind of evaluative aesthetic judgement that I have not yet explicitly acknowledged (see §11).

category of aesthetic judgement the first question would be into which side it fits or whether it has a foot in each camp. And then, for judgements that fall on one side, their intersubjective validity would be a matter of 'descriptive' or 'representational' accuracy; for judgements that fall on the other side, this validity would be a matter of what is valuable from the aesthetic point of view; and the intersubjective validity of all other aesthetic judgements would consist in a double success, both representing the object as it is in a certain respect and according this character of the object its appropriate value from the aesthetic point of view. But the matter is not as simple as this.

3. It is customary for both purely descriptive and evaluation-added aesthetic judgements to be thought of as ascribing or withholding 'aesthetic properties', a term of art that is understood variously and has no agreed extension. I shall follow this custom, but for me it is just a matter of terminology, merely reflecting the surface grammar of the sentence in which such a judgement is directly expressed. Note that the property signified by the predicate of an evaluation-added judgement need not itself be an aesthetic property (as with the bright colouring of 'garish'). Purely descriptive aesthetic judgements are, rightly or wrongly, liable to both realistic and non-realistic constructions. The realism/non-realism distinction can be drawn in different ways. One conception of realism deems a property to be realistic if the possession of it by an object is independent of our attitudes towards or evaluations of the object. On this conception, it follows at once that all purely descriptive aesthetic judgements are to be understood realistically, and the only question is which, if any, aesthetic judgements are purely descriptive. Another conception requires that the possession of a property by an object should be independent of our affective responses to it, responses of pleasure or emotion, for example. And these two conceptions can be combined—they are often not distinguished—requiring that the possession of a property by an object should be independent, not just of our attitudes towards or evaluations of the object, but also of our affective responses to it. By a realistic view of such judgements I shall mean one that construes their canonical basis as being purely representational. A non-realistic view denies that these so-called aesthetic properties are properties represented to us in our perception of items that apparently possess them. Rather, we *react* to what *is* represented in our perception and 'project' this onto the object represented, certain reactions and projections being

the right or appropriate ones. In other words, a non-realistic conception of purely descriptive aesthetic judgements construes their canonical basis as including some kind of non-representational response (a response that need not be affective) to what is represented in the experience of the object judged. It is not to my immediate purpose to determine which, if any, purely descriptive aesthetic judgements should be construed realistically, and which, if any, should be understood in a non-realistic manner. The point is that, despite appearances, it is only for (at most) those purely descriptive aesthetic judgements which are properly construed realistically that the question of their entitlement to intersubjective validity is simply a matter of whether the world is such as the judgement represents it to be.

4. The most interesting question about any purely descriptive or evaluation-added aesthetic judgement concerns its content or point. This is often not easy to determine since it is rarely manifest in the judgement's linguistic expression. Typically, aesthetic properties are ascribed either by the use of an expression that has nothing other than an aesthetic use ('elegant', perhaps), or by the use of an expression as a metaphor—an expression whose present literal use is confined to signifying a property in another domain, or, if it has a number of literal senses, to a number of properties in other domains—or by the use of an expression ('balanced', perhaps) that is by now tailor-made for the purpose, possessing a literal sense in which it signifies the aesthetic property, although in the past it lacked this sense, applying literally (as it still does) to some other property (or set of properties), or by the use of an expression that has a unitary sense suitable for aesthetic and non-aesthetic purposes ('monotonous', for example). More complex characterizations, especially of works of art, may combine a number of these uses or, as Wittgenstein emphasized, may consist in the drawing of an explicit comparison with something else, as in Proust's description:

The violin had risen to a series of high notes on which it rested as though awaiting something, holding on to them in a prolonged expectancy, in the exaltation of already seeing the object of its expectation approaching, and with a desperate effort to last out until its arrival, to welcome it before expiring, to keep the way open for a moment longer, with all its remaining strength, so that the stranger might pass, as one holds a door open that would otherwise automatically close.[8]

[8] Marcel Proust, *Remembrance of Things Past*, i, trans. C. K. Scott Moncrieff and Terence Kilmartin (London: Penguin Books, 1981), 375.

If an aesthetic property is ascribed to an item by an expression that stands for a property that cannot be possessed literally by that kind of item, either the expression (or a synonym) is essential to the characterization or it is not. If it is not, either some other expression that stands for a property that the item cannot possess literally is essential to the characterization or it is not. If some such expression (or a synonym) is essential, then the content of an aesthetic judgement that ascribes the aesthetic property includes the concept of the property signified by the expression in its home domain. This can hold in two kinds of case: where the sentence is a metaphor or where the sentence looks like a metaphor but is only an ellipsis. There is no general problem about this possibility, one concept often being included in the definition or analysis of another. Rather, for an aesthetic judgement of this kind, the crucial issue is how exactly this is so, that is, how the sense of the aesthetic attribution is related to the sense of the non-aesthetic attribution so as to render the concept of the foreign property integral to the identity of the aesthetic property. For the nature of the claim to intersubjective validity made by an aesthetic judgement the content of which includes the concept of some property that the object judged cannot literally possess turns on the precise nature of the conceptual connection. Consider, for example, a judgement about the emotional quality of a piece of music, or the emotion it is expressive of, a judgement that is generally (but not universally) recognized to be of this kind. How is the predication of sadness or joyfulness of a melody integrally related to the predication of sadness or joyfulness of a person, the implications of the two being so different? Many suggestions have been made as to what this connection is, elucidating it in terms of the arousal or expression or projection of emotion, the relational property of resemblance to emotion or to emotion's expression, or (in a variety of ways) the imagination of emotion. Some of these suggestions in effect construe 'The melody is sad (or expressive of sadness)' as a metaphor, others as an ellipsis, and whereas some understand the aesthetic judgement realistically, others interpret it non-realistically. Theories that explicate the musical expression of emotion in terms of the relational property of resemblance are liable to construe the sentence as an ellipsis and the judgement as realistic; imagination-based theories are liable to construe the sentence as a metaphor and the judgement as non-realistic. I am not here concerned to adjudicate this disagreement about the emotional qualities of music: my present interest is the different characters of the claims to intersubjective validity entailed by these interpretations, whichever of them is correct. The nature of the claim is in general straightforward for interpretations of the sentence as an ellipsis, but is not so easy to determine for metaphorical interpretations.

5. Nelson Goodman, unlike most theorists of artistic expression, does not restrict a work's expressive qualities, i.e. those qualities that it expresses, to psychological qualities. In fact, on his understanding of the matter, a work of art can express qualities of more or less any kind. It might be thought that the idea of metaphorical exemplification, the heart of Goodman's conception of expression, covers at least the great majority of cases in which the concept of a property from an alien domain is embedded in the content of a purely descriptive aesthetic judgement. For it involves both the characterization of an object as possessing a property metaphorically and reference to that property. However, I shall argue that Goodman's conception is unfit to achieve this end. It suffers from a neglected defect which entails that it has little application to works of art of any kind. Goodman's account of artistic expression has, of course, often been criticized. Anthony Savile and Richard Wollheim have emphasized that it is not invariably true that if a work expresses a certain quality it possesses that quality metaphorically: a picture can express boredom, or desperation, or anxiety, for example, without being a boring (or bored) picture, a despairing (or desperate) picture, an anxious picture.[9] The conclusion is that Goodman's account fails to provide a necessary condition for the relation of artistic expression. But it must be remembered that Goodman is fully aware of the varying use of 'expresses' and is concerned only to isolate 'a characteristic and peculiar relation of expression, as distinguished from representation and from reference of other kinds in the arts'.[10] Accordingly, the fact that his conception is unacceptable as an account of some commonly recognized idea of artistic expression is of little concern—as long as the relation his conception identifies has widespread application in the arts. In my view, Goodman himself is prone to exaggerate the applicability of his conception. Consider these examples: a certain Katherine Sturgis drawing

---

[9] Anthony Savile, 'Nelson Goodman's *Languages of Art*: A Study', *The British Journal of Aesthetics*, 11/1 (Winter 1971), 13; Richard Wollheim, 'The Sheep and the Ceremony', reprinted in his *The Mind and its Depths* (London: Harvard University Press, 1993), 6.

[10] Nelson Goodman, *Languages of Art* (London: Oxford University Press, 1969), 45.

expresses flashing action, a Pollaiuolo engraving expresses poised power, a 'Daumier lithograph may express weight, a passage from Vivaldi express visual or kinaesthetic patterns of skaters, and Joyce's *Ulysses* express an infinite cycling of time', pictures by Vermeer, de Heem, van der Heyden and van Everdingen express the domestic quality of seventeenth-century Holland, a painting might express abject poverty.[11] Not many of these can easily be made to conform with his own account of expression as metaphorical exemplification. But be that as it may, the problem I shall highlight is not any alleged failure of fit between Goodman's notion of artistic expression and some more familiar one. It is a problem internal to Goodman's notion of metaphorical exemplification, a defect that renders it of little use in thinking about the aesthetic properties of works of art and in particular about those cases in which the concept of a property from an alien domain is embedded in the content of a purely descriptive aesthetic judgement.[12]

For Goodman, what is expressed is metaphorically exemplified. His conception of artistic expression is, loosely, that a work expresses (only) those metaphorical properties of it that, as a symbol of its kind (the kind of art it is an instance of),[13] it refers to; more precisely, that a work expresses a certain property only if some label that is coextensive with (i.e. has the same literal denotation as) a label of the property is referred to by and metaphorically denotes the work. It seems to be a straightforward inference to the conclusion that characterizations of a work in terms of a property it is said to express are such that the concept of that property is essential to the characterization or, in other words, that every judgement that attributes an expressive characteristic to a work of art is such that the concept of a property from an alien domain is embedded in the content of that judgement. But the formulations I have presented are open to misinterpretation and in order to assess the usefulness of Goodman's conception it is vital to grasp its true character.

[11] Nelson Goodman, *Ways of Worldmaking* (Brighton: The Harvester Press, 1978), 28–9, 33; Nelson Goodman and Catherine Z. Elgin, *Reconceptions in Philosophy and Other Arts and Sciences* (London: Routledge, 1988), 20–1.
[12] I am grateful to Rob Hopkins for improvising so quickly the best defence of Goodman's conception of artistic expression against my criticism, which I sprang upon him one afternoon: the fact that this defence, so it seemed to me (but not, perhaps, to him!), was not able to resist the thrust of my attack, confirmed my faith in its strength.
[13] This is to be taken as read in what follows.

In the first place, it is rarely recognized that Goodman regards apt metaphorical descriptions of a work of art as being in theory replaceable by complex literal descriptions and in effect descriptions of properties the work possesses literally:

[Musical] Works differing widely in detail may all have the same property of sadness; and the common structural property, the literal correlate of sadness, is not easily specified...Theoretically, these metaphors [descriptions of 'a work or passage as muscular, electric, spatial, curvilinear, brittle, or floating'] can be supplanted by complex literal descriptions; but even as metaphors, they are in effect descriptions of structural features.[14]

Now (literal) exemplification is possession of a property plus reference to it and expression is fundamentally a matter of metaphorical exemplification. But what is referred to in the case of metaphorical exemplification? Is it the property signified by the literal use of the metaphor or the structural (or other) property the metaphor in effect describes? If the former, then the content of a judgement of an object that it expresses a property includes the concept of that alien domain property; if the latter, it does not. Immediately after the passage quoted above, where Goodman is concerned to show that expression has an importance even for a formalist, he sums up his view of expression like this:

Briefly, the feelings a work expresses are properties it has, not because the work literally has feelings, but because the feeling-terms applied are metaphorical descriptions of structural (or other) properties the work has and exemplifies.[15]

This seems unequivocal and if it is taken at face value—it certainly is in conformity with Goodman's emphasis on an expressive work's exhibiting, showing forth, manifesting, what it expresses—it implies that for a work to express sadness (or anything else) it must possess the literal correlate of sadness (or whatever), a certain structural property, and exemplify *that structural property*. Accordingly, the aesthetic judgement that a work is expressive of a certain quality, where expression is understood à la Goodman, attributes a structural (or other) property to the item, which, it claims, is referred to by the item: in describing a work as expressing

---

[14] Nelson Goodman, *Problems and Projects*, 127. See also his *Languages of Art* (Indianapolis and New York: Bobbs-Merrill, 1972), 93.

[15] Goodman, *Problems and Projects*, 127.

melancholy, I am in effect indicating a structural property (for which I have no literal label) which, I claim, the work exemplifies, i.e. both possesses (literally) and refers to. Hence no judgement of Goodmanian artistic expression is one in which the concept of a property from an alien domain is embedded in the content of a purely descriptive aesthetic judgement, and the truth conditions of any such judgement are unproblematic: it is correct just if the work possesses the property (in effect attributed to it) and refers to that property.[16]

But it is clear that this is not how Goodman's idea of metaphorical exemplification should be understood. Consider the summary account at the end of chapter 2 of *Languages of Art*:

if *a* expresses *b* then: (1) *a* possesses or is denoted by *b*; (2) this possession or denotation is metaphorical; and (3) *a* refers to *b*.[17]

This is formulated in such a way as to accommodate those, unlike Goodman, with a preference for properties, rather than labels, and reading it in terms of properties delivers the result that the property referred to in a case of metaphorical exemplification is the property that is possessed metaphorically, that is, the property signified by the literal use of the metaphor. Now this entails that the concept of the home domain property is included in the content of a judgement of an item that it expresses that property. But this understanding of Goodman's conception of artistic expression raises a problem about the existence and establishment of the required referential relationship, which, Goodman asserts, is a matter of singling out that property for attention.[18] It is easy to see how an object that possesses a property literally, as with the structural property that is the literal correlate of musical sadness, might also refer to the property, and so exemplify the property. It is exceptionally well-placed to refer to the property and if it does so this will be, as Goodman indicates, in virtue of the fact that it exhibits it, typifies it, shows it forth, makes it manifest, serves as a sample of it and thereby heightens it in our consciousness or focuses attention upon it.[19] But metaphorical exemplification is not a case of (literal) exemplification. A work does not exemplify a property that it possesses

---

[16] Of course, whether a particular work possesses the structural property supposedly attributed to it may not be easy to settle decisively without a non-metaphorical identification of the property.

[17] Goodman, *Languages of Art*, 95.   [18] *Languages of Art*, 88.

[19] *Languages of Art*, 86, and in many places in *Ways of Worldmaking*.

only metaphorically: it is not a sample of that property.[20] What is referred to in the case of metaphorical exemplification is not the structural (or other) property the metaphor in effect describes but the property signified by the literal use of the metaphor. So the route of reference that might be taken in the case of the structural property is closed for metaphorical exemplification: a work that does not possess a certain property literally cannot, in any obvious sense, exhibit that property, typify it, show it forth. Of course, there are other ways in which an item can refer to a property it does not literally possess. But it is unclear that any other route of reference is widely available and frequently used in art so as to link a work that can be characterized by a metaphor to the property the predicate signifies literally. It is certainly not the function of a poem *qua* poem, a painting *qua* painting, a piece of music *qua* music, to refer to the property literally signified by whatever predicate might appropriately be applied metaphorically to it as an instance of the kind of artwork it is. It is not integral to a work of art's being the kind of work it is that if a predicate can appropriately be applied to it metaphorically *qua* being of that kind, the work thereby refers to the property signified by the literal use of the predicate. It is strange that Goodman provides no evidence that, or indication how, works of art that can appropriately be described by a term used metaphorically ever (as works of their kind) refer to the property that the term signifies when used literally. If, as I believe, very few musical passages that can appropriately be described by the use of a metaphor—'muscular', 'electric', 'spatial', 'curvilinear', 'brittle', 'floating'—can also correctly be said to refer in some manner to the property possessed metaphorically, and likewise for works of other art forms, the scope of Goodman's conception of artistic expression is exceedingly narrow.

Perhaps it will be thought that this appearance of, on the one hand, a notion of possibly wide scope—one for which the concept of the home domain property is not included in the content of a judgement of an item that it expresses that property—and, on the other hand, a notion of exceedingly narrow scope—a notion for which the concept of the home domain property is so included—arises only because Goodman's conception of expression has been rendered in terms of properties. If we

---

[20] Contrast Goodman's wayward assertion that a symbol can serve as a sample of properties it metaphorically possesses (*Ways of Worldmaking*, 68).

decide not to indulge the 'prissy prejudice'[21] for talking of expression of properties, rather than of predicates (or other labels), will not the apparent oscillation between the two views disappear and the wide scope that Goodman believes his conception commands be seen indeed to attach to it? No: it makes no difference whether we think in terms of properties or predicates. Goodman's view of metaphor is, in a nutshell, that 'In metaphors, symbols moonlight',[22] that a metaphor is 'a way we make our terms do multiple moonlighting service'.[23] His basic idea is that used metaphorically a predicate does a different job from the one it does when used literally. In each case it is used to classify items, but the classifications it effects are different, its metaphorical extension being different from and typically not included in its literal extension. A predicate used as a metaphor resembles an ambiguous predicate in having more than one extension, and differs from a merely ambiguous predicate solely in the fact that the earlier of its extensions (assuming just two) influences what the later extension is. If as time passes the two uses achieve equality and independence, what began as a metaphorical use becomes a new literal use and the predicate is now merely ambiguous.[24] Consider now Goodman's summary account given above. The crucial final part, read in terms of predicates, requires the expressive object to refer to the predicate that metaphorically denotes the object. But that predicate has two different extensions according as it is used literally or metaphorically. So—just as would be necessary with merely ambiguous predicates—if Goodman's preference for talking of predicates rather than properties is to do its job properly it is vital to indicate whether the expressive object refers to the predicate in its literal or its metaphorical use, or, if one prefers, to the literal or metaphorical use of the predicate. As it stands the final part of Goodman's summary account is ambiguous; disambiguated in favour of the literal use it yields a notion of exceedingly small scope.[25] It is, I believe, Goodman's preference for predicates and failure to disambiguate the referent that conceals the limitation of his conception.

---

[21] *Languages of Art*, 87.

[22] Nelson Goodman, 'Metaphor as Moonlighting', *Critical Inquiry*, 6/1 (Autumn 1979), 130.

[23] *Ways of Worldmaking*, 104.   [24] *Languages of Art*, 71.

[25] It would be mere evasion to insist that if a predicate figuratively denotes an item, the item is then well-suited to exhibit, typify, show forth, make manifest, and thereby focus attention upon and so exemplify the predicate in its figurative application, which entails reference to the predicate. (Compare Goodman, *Reconceptions in Philosophy and Other Arts and Sciences*, 71.) This is clear if we allow ourselves to speak of the properties signified by the predicate in its two uses.

I have deliberately left aside the consideration that in fact virtually no work of (non-literary) art ever refers to a predicate (or any other kind of label), in order to focus on what I take to be a more significant weakness in Goodman's conception of artistic expression. Note also that, although I do not share these views, I have not chosen to dispute Goodman's idea that metaphors are used to effect a classification of items in some new fashion and that a sentence taken metaphorically will be true if, in accordance with the new mode of classification, it classifies an item correctly, that is, if the item falls within the extension of the predicate understood metaphorically. Would it not be possible to protect Goodman's conception of artistic expression as metaphorical exemplification against the line of criticism I have pursued by adopting a different theory of metaphor from Goodman's own theory? Not if the alternative theory of metaphor is the most plausible theory, for this would mean the effective abandonment of Goodman's conception, all the work being done by 'metaphorical possession' itself (see §8).

6. There is no special problem about the intersubjective validity of a purely descriptive aesthetic judgement which ascribes a property by the use of an expression that has a unitary sense suitable for aesthetic and non-aesthetic purposes. The judgement is correct only if the item, when judged from the aesthetic point of view, satisfies the criteria required by the expression in its non-aesthetic use, i.e. possesses the property signified by the expression. Taking 'monotonous' in its purely descriptive meaning, a poem is monotonous if and only if *qua* poem it lacks variety. If a purely descriptive aesthetic property is ascribed by the drawing of an explicit comparison, the intersubjective validity of the judgement turns on the aptness of the comparison. If a purely descriptive aesthetic property is ascribed by the use of an expression that is now tailor-made for the purpose or that has nothing other than an aesthetic use, the crucial issue is how the expression is to be understood, which remains to be explored.

7. The subtlest defence of the intersubjective status of descriptive aesthetic judgements, of the idea that aesthetic characterizations, or—to use the language of properties that he was so wary of—attributions of aesthetic properties, can be true or false in the straightforward sense in which colour judgements, for example, can be, is Frank Sibley's examination of the similarities and differences between characteristic features of aesthetic terms

and colour words.[26] Sibley does not rest his defence on an account of the nature of aesthetic properties: apart from their dependent or emergent character and their lack of entailment by the properties responsible for them, he leaves their nature unspecified. Jerrold Levinson has proposed the most sophisticated account of the nature of aesthetic properties consonant with Sibley's work, one that, at least in its main line of thought, might be used to provide a perspicuous explanation of the intersubjective standing of judgements that attribute aesthetic properties. The conception of aesthetic properties he has articulated represents them as being, roughly, 'higher-order phenomenal impressions', more precisely, higher-order perceptual 'ways of appearing'—properties that reveal their natures in their perceptual appearances and are dependent in a holistic manner on lower-order ways of appearing (such as colours, which are visual ways of appearing, or timbres, aural ways of appearing).[27]

As it stands, this conception lacks a certain amount of definition and needs to be sharpened in two related respects. This stems from the fact that there are indefinitely many terms—'lifeless', 'serene', 'powerful', 'tragic', 'moving', 'balanced', 'unified', 'sentimental', 'monotonous', 'naive', 'blatant', 'nostalgic', 'wistful', 'majestic', 'sprightly', 'frenzied', and so on—that are used to ascribe aesthetic properties to, on the one hand, works of art that belong to art forms that address different sense modalities, or, on the other, works belonging to an art form that does address a particular sense modality (or more than one) and works belonging to an art form that addresses none at all. It is clear that if the perception of an aesthetic property which is a higher-order way of appearing is confined to one sense modality, vision or audition, for example, this conception allows that it can be correctly described in a manner that restricts it to that modality: if its way of appearing is confined to vision or to audition, it can be said to be a look or a sound.[28] However, to consider just one example, both a painting and a

---

[26] Frank Sibley, 'Objectivity and Aesthetics', conveniently reprinted in his *Approach to Aesthetics*, 71–87.

[27] See Jerrold Levinson, 'Being Realistic about Aesthetic Properties', *The Journal of Aesthetics and Art Criticism*, 52 (1994), 351–4; 'Aesthetic Properties, Evaluative Force, and Differences of Sensibility', in Emily Brady and Jerrold Levinson (eds.), *Aesthetic Concepts: Essays after Sibley* (Oxford: Clarendon Press, 2001), 61–80; and especially 'Aesthetic Properties', *Proceedings of the Aristotelian Society*, Supplementary Volume 78 (2005), 211–27, upon which I will focus. His view is (see later) that many aesthetic properties, some of them simply, some only in part, are such higher-order ways of appearing.

[28] 'Aesthetic Properties', 219.

piece of music might equally well be described as dynamic, that is, power-fully energetic, but on the basis of very different perceptual experiences, the first visual, how the painting looks, the second, auditory, how the music sounds. If it is right to think of the function of the term 'dynamic', used to attribute an aesthetic property, as indicating a higher-order way of appearing, then it would seem that at least two such ways of appearing go by that name, the aesthetic property of dynamism being a different property for each sense-modality, in the one case a look, in the other a sound. If, on the other hand, the aesthetic property of dynamism is neither a look nor a sound but a property common to items in both perceptual domains, a property that can be realized both by a look and by a sound, it would seem that what unites them under the same term, 'dynamic', is not their sharing a common higher-order perceptual way of appearing but some other feature—whatever property it is that is signified by the use of such a term as 'dynamism'. But now the point can be taken further. For consider 'nostalgic' (or 'unified' or 'monotonous' or 'high-spirited' or 'lifeless'—there are many more such terms): a poem, short story, or novel might just as well be described as nostalgic (or unified or monotonous or high-spirited or lifeless) as might a piece of music. The nostalgia (and so on) of a short story or novel, even of a poem, the appreciation of which, more than any other literary form, includes the sounds of the words and the feel of the words in the mouth, would not seem to be a perceptual 'way of appearing' or 'phenomenal [or perceptual] impression' at all. If this is so, and it is right to think of the nostalgia of a piece of music as a higher-order way of appearing, then the function of the term 'nostalgic', used to attribute an aesthetic property, is diverse, on some occasions (when applied to music, for example) indicating a higher-order perceptual way of appearing, on others (when applied to poetry, say) not doing so. But if the nostalgia of a piece of music is also not a higher-order perceptual way of appearing, the function performed by the term 'nostalgic' when used to attribute an aesthetic property might be unitary, a nostalgic poem and a nostalgic piece of music sharing a common aesthetic property which is not a way of appearing at all.

Leaving these two issues unresolved, Levinson's view is that some kinds of aesthetic property are simply higher-order perceptual ways of appearing, whereas certain aesthetic properties seem not to be simply higher-order perceptual ways of appearing but properties the concepts of which include the idea of distinctive kinds of feelings, so that they are, to put it loosely, a matter of how perceiving a higher-order perceptual way of appearing makes people feel. (If there are such aesthetic properties, they might be designated by the rebarbative expression 'higher-order perceptual ways-of-appearing-perceived-with-feelings'.) But before I consider the examples he gives of properties that supposedly fall into these classes, it is necessary to come to terms with a highly significant issue.

8. The main obstacle faced by any relatively comprehensive attempt to answer the question 'How many kinds of aesthetic property conform to these characterizations?' arises from the previously mentioned fact that the content or point of a purely descriptive aesthetic judgement is rarely manifest in the judgement's linguistic expression. This difficulty is exacerbated by the fact that aesthetic judgements with the same linguistic expression can be intended differently. For example, the purely descriptive aesthetic judgement that a sound is silky, which manifestly likens it to silk (in some unspecified respect), and so, taken at face value, attributes the relational property of resembling silk to the sound, might well be intended only to direct attention to a certain aspect of the sound, an aspect that resembles a feature of silk (its softness, its smoothness, its lustre)—a feature that might vary from judgement to judgement—in which case the reference to silk is inessential to the identification of the property. Moreover, descriptions used to ascribe aesthetic properties are often ambiguous as between purely descriptive and evaluation-added. For example, since the term 'monotonous' can mean either 'lacking in variety' or 'tedious through sameness', the judgement that a poem is monotonous might claim just that it lacks variety or, in addition, that its sameness is tedious. This is not to say that there are no simple cases, such as those where the attribution of an aesthetic property does not proceed through a metaphor. But many descriptive aesthetic judgements are expressed by the use of predicates used metaphorically (indefinitely many predicates being available to be used metaphorically to express such judgements); the concept signified by the metaphor might or might not be essential to the characterization of the object; and a metaphor always stands in need of interpretation: without an interpretation the appropriateness of the metaphor cannot be assessed. To decide whether the aesthetic property of dynamism is a higher-order way of appearing and a different property when

attributed by sight and by hearing, in the first case a look, in the second a sound, or instead a property common to them, a property that can be realized both by a look and by a sound,[29] it is necessary to elucidate the content or point of the aesthetic judgement that a work is dynamic. What do two works have in common, if anything, in virtue of which each can be said to be dynamic? Is the concept of dynamism integral to the concept of the aesthetic property signified by the term 'dynamic' used in the ascription of the property? In advance of an answer to these questions, the character of the aesthetic property, what kind of property it is, must be veiled.

The question 'How should the ascription of an aesthetic property by the use of a metaphor be understood?' arises both where the use of the metaphor is essential—the predicate is such that the concept of the property its literal use signifies is included in the concept of the aesthetic property attributed—and where it is non-essential. Now so far it has not been necessary to express an allegiance to any particular theory of metaphor, which is why, although I have sometimes chosen to use the notion of content loosely, I have referred a number of times to the content or point of an aesthetic judgement. For this pair of alternatives accommodates both sides of what I take to be the basic division in theories of metaphor: on the one hand, theories along Goodmanian lines, which attribute a special content to predicates that are to be understood metaphorically, and on the other, those that favour the approach of Donald Davidson, for whom a sentence used as a metaphor has no cognitive content in addition to the literal, says nothing other than its literal meaning, but does have a point, intimating unspecified likenesses, similarities, common features, parallels, or analogies of some kind that one needs to pick up on in order to understand the metaphor.[30] But now, given that my conception of metaphor is in this fundamental respect Davidsonian, how should we understand a purely descriptive aesthetic judgement that is expressed by the use of a metaphor?

First, we need a certain refinement of the approach. For whatever exactly the point might be of an utterance or inscription of a sentence which has a

---

[29] Levinson (private communication) is inclined to think that a dynamic painting and a dynamic musical passage have an aesthetic property of dynamism in common, both presenting a dynamic appearance, the one visually and the other aurally or sonically. As will become clear, I believe that this plays fast and loose with the idea of a perceptual way of appearing, relying on an unexplained notion of a dynamic appearance.

[30] Donald Davidson, 'What Metaphors Mean', *Critical Inquiry*, 5/1 (Autumn 1978), 31–47.

predicate that is to be understood metaphorically—provoking or inviting a view of its subject or getting us to notice or appreciate something about the subject or attend to a likeness between it and other things—if the sentence has been used to express a judgement (which is our sole concern), the possible or intended effects of the inscription or utterance are one thing, the judgement the sentence has been used to express is another, although, of course, there will be a close relation between the two. In addition we must acknowledge the fact that since the ordinary, literal meaning of a predicate is compatible with a sentence for which it is the predicate being intended as a metaphor in a variety of different ways, the particular point or function of a sentence used metaphorically on a certain occasion—what it is then being used to do, or what the judgement it expresses is—cannot be uniquely determined by what it means. Furthermore, the judgement that corresponds to that token sentence can be made without being expressed. I think it is best, or at least simplest, to think of a purely descriptive aesthetic judgement which is expressed in a sentence with a metaphorical predicate, in terms of what it commits one to, which will typically be that there is a resemblance between some feature of the item described and the property signified by the predicate used literally, a resemblance one can indicate: in making or embracing the judgement you commit yourself to there being some respect in which the two are alike. This is not in general true of metaphors. One kind of exception is where the basis of the metaphor is fancy, rather than fact. Isaiah Berlin's judgement that whereas Dante is a hedgehog, Pushkin is a fox, did not commit him to holding that Dante was in a certain respect like a hedgehog rather than a fox, whereas Pushkin was in that respect like a fox rather than a hedgehog. For his judgement was based on Archilochus' remark that 'The fox knows many things, but the hedgehog knows one thing', so that in fact the commitment was not to there being a parallel to an actual difference but to a supposed difference. It is not uncommon for metaphors to be rooted in something other than fact. However, my sole concern here is metaphor as it figures in purely descriptive aesthetic judgements, which in general lack this character (and the character of other kinds of exception), and the typical commitment is to an actual resemblance. But it should be remembered that the commitment concomitant with a sentence with a metaphorical predicate can vary from token to token; the commitment can be minimal, amounting to no more than that the predicate is well-suited to indicate some aspect of the item characterized; and the commitment is likely to be to some extent indefinite, not something specific and clearly circumscribed in one's mind, but liable to development through further study and reflection.

Accordingly, in order to get clear about a purely descriptive aesthetic judgement that is expressed by the use of a metaphor, it is necessary to grasp what the particular point of the metaphor used to ascribe the aesthetic property is, which is to say what particular commitment is undertaken by embracing it. If the judgement is to be intersubjectively valid the metaphor must be a good one, which means that the entailed commitment is justified, in the typical case the object described having a character appropriately like the property signified by the predicate understood literally.

In developing his conception of metaphor, Davidson focuses exclusively upon the effects of or reactions to a metaphor, what it makes us notice or see, and eventually aligns metaphor with Wittgenstein's notion of 'seeing as', or seeing an aspect, under which Wittgenstein gathered a motley collection of instances of seeing something in a manner which in one way or another involves reference to something else, and also various related phenomena.[31] Wittgenstein held that in some cases imagination is required to perceive an aspect, as when seeing a triangular figure as half a parallelogram or a bare triangular figure as depicting an object that has fallen over, but not in other cases, as when seeing the principal aspects of the so-called double cross.[32] Davidson's view is that metaphor 'makes us see one thing as another by making some literal statement that inspires or prompts the insight'.[33] This alignment, which is often overlooked, is used by Davidson, who does not distinguish different forms of seeing-as, but refers only to the perception of Wittgenstein's so-called 'duck-rabbit figure' derived from Jastrow, merely to illustrate what he takes to be the generally non-propositional character of the insight prompted by a metaphor, what a metaphor makes us notice.[34] It suggests, however, a different possibility for the commitment undertaken by one who makes

[31] Wittgenstein's notion of seeing-as is considerably wider than that of seeing one thing as another. For example, it includes seeing a resemblance between one thing and another and seeing a row of dots as grouped in a certain manner.

[32] Ludwig Wittgenstein, Last Writings on the Philosophy of Psychology, i (Oxford: Basil Blackwell, 1982), §§698, p. 703; Philosophical Investigations (Oxford: Basil Blackwell, 1958), p. 207.

[33] Donald Davidson, 'What Metaphors Mean', 47.

[34] Of course, he allows that it may be propositional, 'and when it is, it usually may be stated in fairly plain words' (Davidson, 'What Metaphors Mean', 47).

a purely descriptive aesthetic judgement which is expressed in a sentence with a metaphorical predicate, and this possibility is especially appropriate for certain[35] aesthetic uses of metaphorical predicates that signify properties the concept of which is included in the concept of the aesthetic property attributed. If the judgement is, as it might be, an expression of a person's seeing or hearing or imaginatively experiencing an item as possessing the property signified by the predicate used literally, in one or other of the various forms of experience that fall under the head of 'perceiving-as', the commitment might be that it is right, or at least appropriate, or perhaps just worthwhile, to see or hear or use the imagination to experience the item as possessing that property. The strongest commitment—that the item should be experienced in the specified manner—is likely for works of art; the weakest is likely for inanimate natural phenomena. So—to take the artistic case—there are many forms of imaginative engagement with works of art, as Kendall Walton, above all others, has emphasized and articulated, and wherever one of these is mandatory it is because its operation is necessary to understand and appreciate the work properly. An interpretation of the commitment, of whatever strength, along these imagination-based lines yields an elucidation of the claim to intersubjective validity made by the judgement. For works of art the implicit claim will be that to experience the work with understanding it is necessary to engage in the relevant form of imaginative perception and perceive the work as possessing the property signified by the predicate used literally.[36]

9. We can now return to consider Levinson's conception of aesthetic properties as wholly, or only in part, higher-order perceptual ways of appearing and his assignment of the various kinds of aesthetic property that

---

[35] Certain, but not all. For one other possibility, see my 'The Characterisation of Aesthetic Qualities by Essential Metaphors and Quasi-Metaphors', *The British Journal of Aesthetics*, 46/2 (April 2006), 133–44 (reprinted as Essay 7).

[36] I am broadly in sympathy with Brandon Cooke's account of the significance of the imaginative experience of a work of art ('Imagining Art', *The British Journal of Aesthetics*, 47/1 (January 2007), 29–45), especially in its leading anti-realism theme, despite its unnecessary and, I believe, wrong-headed, rejection of Davidson's view of metaphor. Cooke prefers Roger White's conception of metaphor, which represents a metaphorical sentence as being a conflation of two other implied, grammatically analogous sentences. This seems to me to muddle what a sentence means with what might be in the mind of someone who utters the sentence. Nevertheless, although Cooke does not express his view in this precise manner, he recognizes that many descriptions of works of art in metaphorical terms attribute to the work aesthetic properties, the nature of which can be captured only in terms of the property the metaphor literally signifies.

he distinguishes to one or the other category.[37] Since my principal interest is not so much to determine whether Levinson is right to slot them into the categories he does but to clarify the claims to intersubjective validity they entail if interpreted correctly, I shall not consider every one of his examples. For aesthetic properties that fully fit the conception of them as higher-order perceptual ways of appearing, the intersubjective validity of judgements that attribute them will be unproblematic, comparable to that of judgements that attribute other perceptual ways of appearing, non-aesthetic ways of appearing, but displaying certain differences from those non-aesthetic and lower-order perceptual ways of appearing in virtue of their higher-order nature.[38] For those aesthetic properties that fit the conception only in part, the nature of the claim to intersubjective validity carried by judgements that attribute them remains to be determined.

I begin with such stylistic categories of painting as impressionist, fauvist, cubist, and futurist: if these are properly counted as aesthetic properties then, as Levinson claims, they seem to be higher-order perceptual ways of appearing, the look of each manifesting the nature of its stylistic category, demanding of the observer only a particular recognitional ability. Then there are so-called formal aesthetic properties, such as balance, unity, dynamism, and fluidity. Levinson regards these also as being higher-order perceptual ways of appearing, but they seem to me a mixed bag, none of which is a higher-order perceptual way of appearing, even in part. Whereas 'balance', used to ascribe an aesthetic property, is no longer a metaphor, and 'unified' never was, 'dynamic' and 'fluid' still are. The aesthetic property of being balanced is hard to determine, because of the variability of the language. As normally understood, it does not seem to be a purely descriptive property, for to describe a composition as being balanced is, standardly, to commend it. A characterization of a composition as being balanced, however exactly this is to be understood, implies that the composition is not unbalanced. This would normally be taken to mean that the composition lacks a certain kind of aesthetic defect, a balanced composition being one in which the parts fit harmoniously together,

---

[37] I am grateful to Derek Matravers, for both talking with me about and later sending me comments on my critique of Levinson's view of aesthetic properties.

[38] Frank Sibley explores some of these differences in his 'Objectivity and Aesthetics', conveniently reprinted in his *Approach to Aesthetics*.

working together to integrate the work by virtue of the relations among the parts, no feature being over-emphasized or misplaced, so as to produce an aesthetically pleasing effect. But perhaps, at least sometimes, 'balanced', used as an aesthetic term, is what Sibley called a descriptive merit-term and so signifies an aesthetic merit-quality.[39] Unity as an aesthetic property is just the property of unity—being composed of parts that constitute a whole—understood from the aesthetic point of view: the parts form an aesthetic whole. It is simply a rather more general property than balance, and being found across all the arts, including drama, fiction, and poetry, it, like balance, is not a higher-order perceptual appearance.

Levinson suggests that the most important kind of aesthetic property is the class of expressive properties and he is inclined to believe that the expressive qualities of music—tenderness, solicitousness, hesitancy, mournfulness, lugubriousness, cheerfulness, confidence, and good-heartedness, for example—are (wholly) higher-order audible ways of appearing. But, first, on his own account of these expressive qualities, a listener is encouraged by a piece of music that possesses such a quality to perceptually imagine that he is hearing the outward expression of the quality by an indefinite persona in a *sui generis* manner.[40] Leaving aside the acceptability of such an account,[41] which in the sense I have given to the term (although not Levinson's) advances a non-realist view of aesthetic judgements about expressive qualities, it seems that this conception of them can be reconciled with their being audible ways of appearing only if something can still count as a perceptual way of appearing if its perception involves imagining what one perceives (the music) to be something that one knows it is not. This would seem to be an extension of the conception of properties that reveal their natures in their perceptual appearances, being a very different case from that of such stylistic categories as impressionist, cubist, and so on, which demand of an observer only a particular recognitional ability, not the capacity to imagine of some perceived object that it is something else, and in doing so, perhaps, to transform one kind of perception into another. I regard it as unhelpful to

---

[39] Frank Sibley, 'Particularity, Art, and Evaluation', 91–2.

[40] See, for example, his 'Hope in *The Hebrides*', in his *Music, Art, and Metaphysics* (Ithaca, NY, and London: Cornell University Press, 1990), 338, and 'Musical Expressiveness', in his *The Pleasures of Aesthetics* (Ithaca, NY, and London: Cornell University Press, 1996), 107.

[41] In fact, the account is essentially the same as that suggestion of R. K. Elliott which I expounded and rejected in my *Music and the Emotions* (London: Routledge & Kegan Paul, 1985), ch. 7, §§6–17, and which, rightly or wrongly, I have seen no reason to change my mind about.

bracket such different cases together, but I assume that, although Levinson does not intimate this, he is willing to embrace this expansion of the concept. It might be objected to his account of the expressive qualities of music that it does not generalize across the arts. This, however, is beside the point unless there is a univocal concept of artistic expression equally applicable across the arts, which is something Levinson rejects. In fact, it is not necessary in principle to deny univocity in order to acknowledge manifest differences in expression across the arts. For the question whether a concept is univocal—whether it is invariant across its range of application—is not the same as the question whether any instantiation of the concept comes to the same thing: although a concept might be unambiguous, what it is for the concept to be instantiated—what constitutes its instantiation—might vary from domain to domain. As Crispin Wright has emphasized,[42] the concept of identity is invariant across different ranges of individuals, but what constitutes identity is subject to considerable variation as the kinds of objects vary: identity of material objects, of numbers, of shapes, of directions of lines, of persons, is in each case just identity, the very same notion, but what constitutes the identity of one kind of thing is not the same as what constitutes the identity of another kind of thing. The variety of artistic expression could therefore be accommodated by maintaining that what varies across the arts is not the concept but what constitutes its instantiation. But leaving this aside, the characterization of works of art by the terms 'tender', 'mournful, 'confident', and so on, is not restricted to music (they could all be applied to passages in poetry, for example); there is no good reason to believe that their meaning changes when used across different arts; and if the applicability of such a characterization to a work is sufficient to indicate an aesthetic property, it would seem that these terms stand for the same aesthetic properties across the arts.[43]

Now consider the aesthetic property of dynamism, which seems on a par with the expressive properties mentioned above. If 'dynamic' is a non-essential metaphor in the ascription of an aesthetic property, then there is a principled way of settling whether a dynamic painting and a dynamic musical passage share an aesthetic property, even if the outcome

---

[42] Crispin Wright, 'Truth in Ethics', in Brad Hooker (ed.), *Truth in Ethics* (Oxford: Blackwell, 1996), 6–7.

[43] I am here ignoring the distinction that is sometimes drawn between music's being tender, mournful, or confident and its being expressive of tenderness, mournfulness, or confidence.

is not easy to determine. For the crucial issue is whether the point of the 'dynamic' metaphor, used to characterize a painting or a piece of music, is the same or different in the two cases. As similarity in linguistic expression is no guarantee of sameness of metaphor, aesthetic attributions of dynamism might diverge in the commitments they carry. But they might well be the same, the entailed commitment in each case being simply that the work is in some way like something that is energetically powerful (even if the respect in which this is so differs). However, on the assumption that 'dynamic' is a non-essential metaphor in the ascription of an aesthetic property, the point of the characterization would be, not to attribute the relational property of resembling a powerfully energetic thing or activity—for that would render the concept of dynamism an ingredient of the concept of the aesthetic property—but to draw attention to an aspect of the object that bears that resemblance; and these aspects will differ in the two cases, so that there will not be a single appearance of dynamism shared by the works. This will carry over to the terms used to ascribe expressive properties, if they also are non-essential metaphors, no one of them being used to designate a certain higher-order perceptual way of appearing.

But this conclusion is not dependent on 'dynamic' and expressive terms being understood as non-essential or eliminable metaphors. In fact, 'dynamic', in its use to ascribe an aesthetic property, would appear to be, at least often, an ineliminable or essential metaphor, some term with that meaning being required to specify the character of the aesthetic property, the concept of dynamism being an essential ingredient of the concept of the aesthetic property. (Perhaps—this is certainly not the only possibility—a painting, such as Fragonard's *Les Beigneuses* (Louvre), might be said to be dynamic to indicate that it looks as if it has been painted with great élan, whereas a piece of music, such as the opening of Elgar's Second Symphony (E flat major), might be said to be dynamic to indicate, not that it sounds as if great energy was necessary to compose it (or to produce the sounds that constitute a performance of it), but that it creates the impression of something exploding into powerful forward movement). This essential character is, I believe, a common feature of the expressive terms that Levinson indicates, as I am sure he recognizes. But if it is, and given the wide range of application of the terms, covering both arts that address a particular sense modality, or a combination of sense modalities, and arts that address no particular sense modality, no one of them designates a higher-order perceptual way of appearing, their application to works of different arts being unified by something other than sameness of perceptual appearance, no matter how much this idea might reasonably be stretched.[44]

10. One aspect of Levinson's thought about aesthetic properties still demands attention: the idea that certain aesthetic properties are higher-order perceptual ways-of-appearing-perceived-with-feelings. By a 'feeling-added' judgement I shall mean a judgement with a feeling-added predicate, one that signifies a property and also a feeling in the sense that the (sincere) application of the predicate indicates that the person who applies it experiences the feeling towards the (instantiation of the) property. Unlike an evaluation-added judgement, a feeling-added judgement is an aesthetic judgement only if the property towards which the feeling is felt requires aesthetic sensitivity to detect it. Levinson's idea that certain aesthetic properties are higher-order perceptual ways-of-appearing-perceived-with-feelings would be mistaken if it were construed as representing judgements that attribute such properties as being feeling-added judgements. Consider human facial beauty, which Levinson represents as essentially involving a distinctive kind of pleasurable feeling tinged with desire being produced by a higher-order visual appearance of a human face and directed at that appearance (or, perhaps, at the person with the face).[45] Even with the relativization to a specific ethnic or cultural sensibility that Levinson suggests might need to be built into the conception, interpreted as a thesis of feeling-added judgements it would be false. For not only are there at least two distinct kinds of human facial beauty, male and female, but those who do not experience physical desire for the sex in question are not thereby denied the capacity to perceive the facial beauty of members of that sex. In fact, their attributions might well match those of persons who do experience physical attraction to members of that sex. Although Levinson writes in a manner that to a certain extent invites this interpretation, I am sure this is wrong. But what might therefore appear to be an unnecessary deviation is intended to bring out two things. The first is that the appearance of human facial beauty, even if it is at least in part a higher-order way of appearing, is

---

[44] Much the same result would follow if the use of the term 'dynamic', or some expressive term, to ascribe an aesthetic property should be understood not as a metaphor but as an ellipsis.

[45] I have ignored some uncertainty in the text in order to capture Levinson's true view (private communication).

in one sense independent of the feeling distinctive of it, in that the feeling is not supposed to transform what would otherwise be the appearance of facial beauty into a different appearance. The second is the importance of an elucidation of the connection between the property of human facial beauty and the distinctive feeling to which it is claimed to be essentially tied, something about which Levinson is vague. For whether there are aesthetic properties that fit the conception of them as being higher-order perceptual ways-of-appearing-perceived-with-feelings and the nature of the claim to intersubjective validity made by attributions of them depends on how exactly the concepts of such properties include the idea of distinctive kinds of feelings, that is, the nature of the relation between the way of appearing and the feeling. There is, first of all, the question of relativization. What exactly does this come to? Are attributions of facial beauty *tout court* to be understood as containing an implicit restriction to a face of a particular ethnic kind, Anglo-Saxon, Melanesian, or whatever? Then there is the relevant range of those who experience the distinctive feeling. Is this supposed to be restricted to those of the same race or culture as the face in question? Finally, there is the nature of the attachment of the distinctive feeling to the way of appearing. I assume that this is to be explicated in dispositional terms: the perception of the way of appearing is disposed to induce the feeling in a person who satisfies certain conditions in appropriate circumstances. If this is so and I am one of those who does not satisfy the conditions, this would not deny me the ability to detect the higher-order way of appearing, but would give me reason not to care about it in the way those liable to the distinctive feeling do; and if non-satisfaction of the conditions is not inherently a defect in a person, I would be justified in differing about the aesthetic merits of an item that possesses the aesthetic property, rightly taking this to be understood relatively, not absolutely.

Levinson regards it as an open question whether garishness, gracefulness, and the like are simply higher-order perceptual ways of appearing or ways-of-appearing-perceived-with-feelings, since the feeling that the way of appearing is disposed to elicit might be a mere concomitant of the aesthetic property, not an essential ingredient of it. In other words, although the way of appearing is disposed to elicit the feeling, the concept of the disposition to elicit the feeling might not be included in the concept of the aesthetic property, this concept just being the concept of the way of appearing. This may be so. But actually it does not matter what the answer to the open question is. Perhaps 'garish' and 'graceful' are ambiguous. In fact, 'graceful' now has, perhaps, a predominantly aesthetic use and in its most common use the aesthetic property of being graceful is, I believe, not descriptive. Some might well think of it as being an evaluation-added property or as in some way 'feeling-added'. But the aesthetic property of gracefulness, as I understand it, is a near-relative of an affective quality (see next section), indicating not only the suitability of a certain kind of response, but to some extent the character of that to which the response is made. For something to be graceful (aesthetically) is for it to be attractive or pleasing in virtue of the generally smooth, non-abrupt transition from one element of the item to another, from one position to another of a line or series of lines or a movement, from one part to another of a shape or form, a transition of this kind requiring minimal effort to take in perceptually. Be that as it may, the substantial issue concerns what the nature of the claim to intersubjectivity amounts to if these (actual or possible) aesthetic properties are interpreted on a higher-order perceptual way-of-appearing-perceived-with-feeling model.[46]

11. A certain sort of aesthetic judgement has a content that is not only unproblematic but is indicative of the content of evaluative aesthetic judgements of all kinds, whether these are directed at art, other kinds of artefact, or nature. Unlike an evaluation-added predicate, the predicate of such a judgement does not signify a property and also a value in the sense that the (sincere) application of the predicate indicates that the person who applies it values or disvalues the property. For the predicate does not in the same sense signify a property at all. Judgements of this kind, which attribute what are sometimes called 'affective' qualities, characterize their object only in a certain, indirect manner, in terms of a psychological reaction or attitude, often an emotional response. The reason why their content is

---

[46] I take musical tension, understood in accordance with Kendall Walton's pioneering theory (which Levinson cites), not to be a higher-order perceptual way-of-appearing-perceived-with-feeling, for the reason that it is not, even in part, a higher-order perceptual way of appearing. On Walton's account, the canonical basis of a judgement that a passage of music is tense is (roughly) an experience of tension induced by the music which causes the listener to feel as though in the presence of something tense, and musical tension is (roughly) the property of being apt to make listeners feel as though in the presence of something tense through making them tense. See Kendall Walton, 'Projectivism, Empathy, and Musical Tension', *Philosophical Topics*, 26 (1999), 407–40.

unproblematic is that these judgements have precisely the same content as their counterpart-judgements about non-aesthetic matters. For although it is implicit in such a judgement as 'X is interesting, boring, moving, horrifying, lovable, exciting, touching, repulsive, amusing, exhilarating . . .' that its subject is being judged interesting (or whatever) *as the kind of thing it is*, or *from a certain point of view*, the sentence in which the judgement is expressed does not change its meaning according as its subject is a different kind of thing, a play, a lecture, a piece of music, an unexpected development, or the point of view is moral, astronomical, archaeological, botanic, or whatever. There is often also an implied restriction to a particular class of people or kind of person. A judgement that something is interesting will normally be understood to indicate that the object judged interesting is such as to merit, command, retain, and reward the interest, not necessarily of everyone, but of those who are interested in, or are capable of developing an interest in, some particular area or phenomenon. But this does not rule out the possibility that there is no implied restriction, since it is the subject's view that everyone ought to be interested in this sort of thing. Judgements that attribute an affective quality indicate an emotion or some other psychological state and the claim implicit in them is that this emotion or state is an appropriate response to the item, considered as the kind of thing it is or from the implied point of view.[47] If an emotion is indicated, it may be somewhat indefinite, as with the judgement that a work is moving, although it would be wrong to think that 'moving' signifies merely that the work is fit to move to some emotion or other, no restriction being imposed on the kind of emotion. For there is an implicit restriction to 'sympathetic' emotions, the implied claim being that it is right for one who enters imaginatively into the experience offered by the work to be moved to experience one of the 'softer' emotions (not, e.g. excitement, fear, horror, anger). But whatever the psychological reaction or attitude indicated, affective judgements that attribute an aesthetic property to an item claim that the response they indicate is an appropriate response to the

---

[47] Compare Sibley's comment (Sibley, 'Tastes, Smells, and Aesthetics', in his *Approach to Aesthetics*, 233) that 'as with many adjectives, like "exciting", "moving", or "thrilling", so "sickening", "disgusting", "offensive" etc. may be used to indicate that a taste or smell is such that one should be sickened, disgusted, offended by it'. Of course, judgements that ascribe emotional affective qualities to things (including works of art) are not always aesthetic or evaluative judgements: their function might be to ascribe a mere disposition to evoke the emotion they mention in some class of persons, usually unspecified (and, if specified, not identified in aesthetic terms).

item from the aesthetic point of view—the response is suitable, apt, fitting, even right or merited, perhaps.

Accordingly, the intersubjective validity of an aesthetic judgement that attributes an affective property to an item turns on whether the item, considered from the aesthetic point of view, merits or is worthy of the indicated response or is such that it is right, appropriate, or fitting to respond to it in that manner; and since the kinds of consideration that would justify or undermine an affective reaction to an object, in particular to a work of art, are apparent, it follows that everything turns on the resources available to criticism in the particular case, which might well not be easy to resolve or which might even have no clear resolution.

12. For a kind of activity that has an aim, performances of the activity are, as such, evaluated against the aim: those who engage in the activity perform it well or poorly inasmuch as their performance is effective in attaining or making progress towards the aim; and both the merits and demerits and the limits and precision of assessment of performances of the activity are determined by the character of that aim. The making of art is an activity—one which, characteristically, creates a product that exists after the activity ceases—but does it have an aim against which performances of the activity and their products, the creations of the activity, can be assessed? If so, what constraints does this aim impose upon the comparative evaluation of artists and works of art? Some, impressed by the fact that works of art always have been created for a variety of purposes and to perform many different functions, have denied that art has an aim; but in one sense it certainly does, for whatever other aims an artist may have the aim of the artist *as artist* is to create, in a medium of some sort, whether stone, paint, tones, words, human bodies, or whatever, a work which is valuable as art. In this sense a work of art which is valuable as art—a work that issues from the artist's activity *qua* artist and in general outlives it—is the aim of art. But this sense in which art possesses an aim is illuminating only if we have an answer to the question 'What is a work's artistic value, its value as art?' If a specification of the aim of art is what is needed to understand why certain characteristics count as merits or demerits of works of art and why the evaluation of artists and their works is limited in just the manner it has often correctly been recognized to be, an account of a work's artistic value must be forthcoming. Given the level at which this is

pitched—one that spans everything that is art—it is certain that the aim of art must be highly abstract.

It is clear that works of art should be conceived of under the general notion of achievement: a successful work of art is a certain kind of achievement, one the value of which is determined in a particular manner.[48] Elsewhere I have outlined the overarching element of this conception like this:

> a work of art is intended to be understood *as* a work of art; the experience a work of art offers is one in which the work is understood; the meaning of a work of art—how it should be interpreted—is tied to the conception of the work under which the artist created it, the style in which it is executed, the works of art to which it alludes and the view of the world and life out of which it arose; and the appreciation of a work of art is the appreciation of the artistry of the artist, which requires an appreciation of the artistic achievement the work represents, so that experience of the work must be informed by an understanding of the aesthetically relevant facts about the work's history.[49]

However, this omits what is a crucial component of any viable conception of artistic value, the aim of art, the particular kind of achievement aimed at by the artist and against which his or her product is to be evaluated as art. But the nature of this aim becomes clear, I believe, from reflection on two considerations concerning the way in which works of art matter to us when we value them as art.

The first is that when we value a work of art *as* a work of art we value it on account of what it provides us with in the experience of it, rather than for something not present in the experience but which it achieves by means of our interaction with the work. This is reflected in the fact that unless we find a musical work intrinsically rewarding to perform or listen to, we do not value it as music; only if we find a novel intrinsically rewarding to read, or a painting intrinsically rewarding to look at, do we value it as literature or as painting; and so on. Furthermore, the more rewarding we find it to engage with the work, the more we value it as art, and the ways in which we find it rewarding indicate those qualities for

---

[48] In his *An Ontology of Art* (Basingstoke and London: Macmillan Press, 1989), Gregory Currie provides an excellent defence of the view that to appreciate a work of art is to appreciate the artistic achievement it represents.

[49] Malcolm Budd, *Values of Art* (London: Allen Lane, The Penguin Press, 1995), 11.

which we value it. The value we attach to a work is a non-instrumental value, fully transparent to us in the experience we undergo in experiencing it with understanding. The second consideration, in its unqualified form, is that when we value a work of art as a work of art we do not regard it as being intersubstitutable with another work of art: we regard the experience of the work as being irreplaceable by the experience of any other work. But, as I have signalled, this requires a qualification. For someone can value a work of art as a work of art because she finds the experience of part, but not all, of the work intrinsically rewarding: her attitude might not be one of unqualified admiration. She might experience the work as having a part or aspect that is both unrewarding in itself and contributes not at all to what is rewarding about the experience of the complete work, not even as a foil or relief, and these rewards might be sufficient to outweigh the lack of reward from the uninteresting or defective part. If so, she values the work as a work of art, but only in part: it is for her a partial success as a work of art. Accordingly, she might well regard the work as intersubstitutable with another work that differs from the first only in the unvalued part: this other work has an equally unrewarding, but different, unvalued part. So the third consideration must be amended. It can be reformulated like this: for someone who values a work of art as a work of art without qualifications—for her admiration of it to be unqualified—the experience of the work must be irreplaceable by a different experience, one offered by a different work of art. That is, if the experience of the work were not to be available to her, then, no matter what alternative experiences were to be available, something that is of value to her would be lost.[50]

Putting these two thoughts together, then, in the first place, the aim of art—the aim of art as art—is, not to change the world, but to enrich it through the creation of an object which is intrinsically valuable to appreciate, one the appreciative experience of which is uniquely valuable. Secondly, the fact that someone who values equally two works nevertheless does not regard them as intersubstitutable implies a distinction between

---

[50] To value a work unqualifiedly is not to regard it as supremely valuable or unimprovable or such that no alteration in it would yield an equally good work. In the sense at issue, I might value a print unqualifiedly even though I regard a different state of the same print as equally fine or even better, and although I regard neither as art of the highest order. (I regard states of the same print as being, in effect, different works of art. But if this should be objected to, it is easy to substitute a different example.)

a work's *specific* artistic value (to use Sibley's terminology)[51] and a work's artistic value in the sense of how good a work of art it is. In this second sense artistic value is a matter of degree, some works being better than some others to a greater or lesser extent. Thirdly, experience of a work of art does not just put us in a position to make a judgement of a work's artistic value, one that will be undermined if the work is not correctly understood in undergoing the experience. The connection is more intimate than that, for, unlike most things, a work of art is made to be experienced, or, more precisely, is made by the artist from the point of view of what experience it is intended to yield or afford; and a work is to be evaluated as art by reference to the nature of the experience integral to understanding it, an experience in which the work is perceived aright, its meaning manifest.[52] To talk of the experience integral to understanding a work should not be understood simplistically: to experience a work with understanding may require many different experiences, in no particular order, as in the appreciation of a building or statue, which require to be looked at from different points of view and in various lighting conditions. Of course, except for relatively simple works, the experience a work offers, if this means one in which it is fully understood, every aspect of it being experienced with perfect understanding, is an ideal to which we can approach but never reach in a single experience. But this does not rule out good approximations, even of the most complex works, upon which sound judgements may rest. And if, often, no actual experience—no reading through of Proust, no looking around while walking in and about Sienna cathedral, no listening to a performance of Bach's *The Art of Fugue*—delivers everything that a work has to offer, what is rewarding about the work being too manifold to be fully appreciated in one experience (under constant conditions), this does not imply that there is something other than what is deliverable in an informed experience of the work that determines its value as art. There is not: any aspect of a work's artistic meaning is such that it can be experienced in a proper engagement with the work by one who has the requisite grasp of the work's place in the history of art and understands

---

[51] Sibley, *Approach to Aesthetics*, 122–3.

[52] Compare Richard Wollheim's remark that the artist is essentially a spectator of his work, and Wollheim's account of the meaning of a painting as resting upon the experience induced in an adequately sensitive and informed spectator who engages with the work in a particular manner. Richard Wollheim, *Painting as an Art* (London: Thames and Hudson, 1987), 22, 39.

the way in which it should be perceived. And it is what a work offers to experience, what it offers to one in the very experience of it, that defines its value as art: inasmuch as what it offers is in itself worth experiencing, it is valuable. Accordingly, construing 'rewarding' as an affective term with an entailed merit-claim[53] and a wide scope covering all positive psychological reactions and attitudes, the natural way to think of artistic value is that a work of art possesses artistic value in so far as what it offers to experience is intrinsically rewarding. Artistic value is a non-instrumental value intrinsic to a work; it is inherent in the work in the sense that it is determined by the intrinsic value of an informed experience of it, an experience in which it is understood; and a work is valuable as art to the degree that the experience it offers is valuable, not in virtue of anything absent from the experience itself but which might be brought about by undergoing an experience of this kind, but in itself. In short: fine art is the achievement of intrinsic value in a medium.

If what is integral to the idea of the artist, namely the aim of producing something distinctive which is valuable in itself, something that in the very engagement with it is such as to reward one who understands it, is inserted into the outline account of art that I presented earlier, it yields a conception of a work of art which immediately invites assessment of the magnitude of its particular achievement, which is a matter of the extent and degree to which what it offers to experience is intrinsically rewarding, that is, how inherently valuable it is to experience it with understanding—with all that understanding involves—or, in other words, how intrinsically valuable the experience it offers is.

13. There is more than one objection that this account of artistic value is liable to attract. I will engage here with just two.

One likely charge against this conception represents it as locating a work's artistic value, not in the work itself, but in the experience of it; alternatively as reversing the dependence of one value on another, assigning priority to the experience of a work over the character of the work itself; and in either case failing to recognize or do justice to the value that is intrinsic to or inherent in a work of art itself. For, the objection maintains, a work of art is a good work of art because or in virtue of the constellation

---

[53] See §11.

of qualities it instantiates, and the experience that a good work of art offers is valuable because or in virtue of the fact that the work is a valuable work, rather than vice versa. But this is a misunderstanding of the conception of artistic value I have proposed. The objection opposes two propositions: (i) the experience offered by a good work of art is a valuable experience because the work is a good work, and (ii) a work is a good work because the experience it offers is a valuable experience.[54] But rather than favouring one of these claims, which is the ground of the objection, my view that what it is for a work to possess artistic value is for it to be of such a nature that the experience it offers is intrinsically valuable, embraces them both. And it can do so because of the aim it attributes to the artist, which is to endow the work with properties that make it intrinsically rewarding to appreciate. If a work of art is a good work, that is so in virtue of its nature or character, the constellation of properties that constitute it: it is these properties that need to be cited in support of an assessment of the work's value. And the reason why a work of this nature or character is a valuable work of art is that the experience offered by this work—the appropriate experience *of* this constellation of properties—is intrinsically rewarding: the intrinsic value of the experience is a measure of the artistic worth of the constellation of properties that compose the work. What makes this possible is that the question, 'What makes an object a good object of its kind?', can be understood in at least two different ways: about a certain object it might ask for those qualities of the object that make it a good thing of that kind; about the kind in question, it might ask for the reason why certain qualities are desirable or meritorious features of an object as being something of that kind. That is to say, the word 'because', as it appears in the propositions (i) and (ii) above, refers to two different relations. Accordingly, not only are the propositions not in opposition, but both are true. A work's artistic value and the intrinsic value of the experience it offers cannot be pulled apart: each is an index of the other.

A different objection alleges that there are properties of works of art that are neither included in what is appreciated in the experience of perceiving a work with understanding nor determined by it but which are relevant to an assessment of its artistic value. Many instances of this objection operate with a simplistic, over-narrow conception of the experience offered by a

---

[54] I am grateful to John Hyman for this formulation of the objection (private communication).

work of art, conceiving of it as merely a registering of what is before the
mind of anyone who engages with the work, neglecting what is built into
the idea of an informed experience of the work, which includes whatever
properties of the work a properly informed person can rightly experience
it as possessing, perception or imaginative experience being transformed by
whatever concepts are introduced into them, and in particular those under
which their objects are appropriately brought. Other instances operate with
a wider conception of the experience, but fail to recognize the full range of
kinds of property that can fall within it. Perhaps the prime example of such
a lapse is the claim that originality or the lack thereof is a property of a work
which is relevant to an assessment of its artistic value but which cannot be
appreciated in an experience of perceiving the work with understanding.[55]
For this overlooks the fact that appreciation of the artist's artistry in the
creation of his or her work is an integral part of the experience offered
by a work of art, and it is only if originality is understood in such a
fashion that originality is no part of the artist's artistry, that, on the account
I have advocated, originality is not a factor to be taken into account in
an assessment of the magnitude of the artist's achievement. If this is how
originality is to be understood (and it certainly can be understood in a
variety of ways), it is indeed irrelevant to the assessment of artistic value;
but on a more plausible understanding of the notion, an artist's originality is
a matter of how and to what extent he or she is creative in the construction
of his or her work, in which case it does not fall outside those properties
of the work that are integral to the experience of perceiving a work with
understanding. An essential part of my conception of artistic value is, as I
have explained, that 'the appreciation of a work of art is the appreciation
of the artistry of the artist, which requires an appreciation of the artistic
achievement the work represents, so that experience of the work must be
informed by an understanding of the aesthetically relevant facts about the
work's history' (p. 91). So the objection fails.[56]

14. The prime fact of artistic value is that artistic value is a matter of
degree, some works being better than others to a greater or lesser extent,

---

[55] See, for example, Matthew Kieran, *Revealing Art* (London: Routledge, 2005), ch. 1.

[56] Frank Sibley's 'Originality and Value', in his *Approach to Aesthetics*, 119–34, is the best examination
of artistic originality. See also Bruce Vermazen's 'The Aesthetic Value of Originality', in Peter A.
French, Theodore E. Uehling, Jr, and Howard K. Wettstein (eds.), *Midwest Studies in Philosophy*, 16
(Indiana: University of Notre Dame Press, 1991), 266–79.

some incontestably so. This follows at once from the differing intrinsic values of the experiences offered by various works.[57] On the aim that I have assigned to art *qua* art, the intersubjective validity of a judgement that attributes a high, medium, or low artistic value to a work is determined by how valuable it is to experience the work with understanding. It is clear in general what characteristics of a work—there are indefinitely many of them—can make it intrinsically rewarding to experience with understanding: it is a matter for criticism to make out the case for a particular work's fitness or unfitness, strengths or weaknesses. But the aim and variety of art imposes severe restrictions on well-founded claims to intersubjective validity of judgements about the relative worth of works of art. For it does not follow from artistic value's being a matter of degree that each work of art possesses artistic value to a precise degree, enabling the construction of an order of rank in which each work of art is either a precise amount above or below, or at exactly the same level as, any other work. In fact, if one work is better than another, it is never better by a definite amount: artistic value does not possess a precise metric. Moreover, artistic value does not impose even a unique ordering on works of art, for issues of comparative artistic value are sometimes, indeed often, indeterminate: it is not true that, for any pair of works, either one must be better than the other or they must be exactly as good as each other. Sometimes, but not always, the most that can be said about the comparative ranking of two works, whether of the same art form or different art forms, is that they are of roughly the same order of merit. For example, Poussin's *Landscape with the Gathering of the Ashes of Phocion* (Walker Art Gallery) is undoubtedly a better work than Holman Hunt's *The Awakening Conscience* (Tate Gallery), and Beethoven's Piano Sonata in A flat (op. 110) is a better work than Rachmaninov's Piano Sonata in B flat minor (op. 36). But if it is conceded that neither the Poussin nor the Beethoven can be said to be superior to the other, the insistence that they must be precisely equal in value imposes an unreal precision on the concept of artistic value; and this is not because the works of Poussin and Beethoven belong to different arts, for the Beethoven is better than the Holman Hunt and the Poussin better than the Rachmaninov.

---

[57] It is regrettable that artistic value is a species of a form of value for which there exists no adequate account. Nevertheless, it would be absurd to subscribe to the view that no experience is in itself less rewarding than any other, or that no experience offered by any work of art is in itself more rewarding than that of any other.

The incommensurability of artistic value is, of course, one reason why the question whether one work is finer than another is generally of no, or at most little, interest, whereas an articulation of the strengths and weaknesses of works will always lie at the heart of criticism. But why is artistic value incommensurable and why are so many issues of comparative evaluation indeterminate? The incommensurability of artistic value and the indeterminacy of many issues of the comparative rank of works of art is readily explained by the conception of the intrinsic value of things as being constituted by their 'unity in diversity', their 'organic unity', degree of intrinsic value being a matter of degree of organic unity, a function of, on the one hand, degree of diversity of material to be unified—for works of art: colour, represented scene, expressive character, sound, meaning, brush stroke, texture, function, decoration, form, theme, act, verse, chapter, movement, and so on—and, on the other hand, degree of unification effected, a conception best articulated by Robert Nozick, and one that has often been advanced as an account, not of intrinsic value *per se*, but, more specifically, of artistic value.[58] For there is no prospect of a precise measure of the degree of diversity or the degree of unification of different works—works which will generally have different components and unifying relationships—and so no prospect of a formal measure of degree of organic unity—one which, to be plausible, would need to deliver assignments of degree of organic unity that accord with our soundest estimates of artistic value.[59] And without a formal measure, based on an account of what constitutes diversity (as such), how degree of diversity is to be assessed, what constitutes a set of elements being (more or less) unified, and how degree of unity is to be assessed, whilst two works might properly be said to be of roughly comparable value, it would be wrong to insist that it must be that either one of the values is the greater or the two values are exactly the same.

[58] Robert Nozick, *Philosophical Explanations* (Oxford: Clarendon Press, 1981), 413 ff. In fact, Nozick qualifies this conception in order to allow the possibility that some realms of value have, in addition, their own special values. His view is that degree of organic value is the basic dimension of intrinsic value (perhaps the only one).

[59] This is especially clear if, as Nozick insists (rightly, if degree of organic unity is to provide a plausible representation of artistic value), the magnitude and importance of the themes of a novel, and the diversity that these themes unify, are to be part of the total diversity unified by the work (Nozick, *Philosophical Explanations*, 416 fn.).

But the practice of criticism does not support the conception of artistic value as residing in degree of organic unity. The degree of organic unity instantiated by a work (however this might be described) is rarely, if ever, referred to as the (complete) reason why one work is better than another, and many of the reasons that are given seem, on the face of it, to have nothing to do with degree of organic unity and allow of the possibility that a work with a higher degree of organic unity might be inferior to one with a lower degree. In fact, the practice of criticism appears to provide no support for any unitary account of what the intrinsic value of good works of art consists in, attributing to them a variety of meritorious features that seem to have nothing that is common and peculiar to them other than their contribution to making the experience offered by the works that instantiate them intrinsically valuable. And this is as it should be. The truth is that the incommensurability of artistic value and the indeterminacy of many issues of the comparative rank of works of art arises from the fact that there are many different kinds of quality that can make a work intrinsically rewarding to experience and so endow the work with artistic value, or that can detract from a work's being intrinsically rewarding to experience and so adversely affect its artistic value. For, in the first place, there is no common unit that would allow the contribution (positive or negative) of different kinds of quality to a work's artistic value to be measured, there being no definite amount by which one outweighs the other, their comparative value—how much more or less intrinsically rewarding one is than the other—resisting measurement. Furthermore, there is no intersubjectively valid order of rank of the comparative values possessed by these different kinds of quality, from the highest positive to the lowest negative quality (or qualities); and most of these qualities can be possessed by works to varying degrees, for which there is no precise metric. Moreover, works themselves vary in size and density and so in the number of such qualities they possess, and there is no intersubjectively valid method of determining the relative rank of works with different numbers of such qualities, positive and/or negative—one work possessing many positive and some negative qualities, another only positive qualities but fewer than the first, for example. Finally, even if qualities that, considered in themselves, are artistic merits or demerits were susceptible of either measurement of or ordering in value, a quality that in one context constitutes an artistic merit can in other contexts detract from a work's artistic value by being combined in an incongruous manner with other qualities of the work, so that the contribution of a quality to a work's artistic value is not an individual matter but holistic. In many cases this set of facts precludes any well-founded comparative evaluation of two works; in many others it does not.[60]

Where there is no determinate answer to the question whether one work is better than another, there is room for blameless aesthetic preferences: if you prefer to give your time to one work rather than the other, you are not thereby making a misjudgement. David Hume, having reached the conclusion that 'the true standard of taste and beauty' is 'the joint verdict' of his 'true judges', acknowledged an unavoidable degree of diversity in judgements arising from blameless differences in people, such as age or temperament.[61] Such differences understandably affect people's responses to works of art, bringing about an inevitable divergence of sentiments that does not reflect adversely on those whose judgements about artistic value fail to agree:

it is almost impossible not to feel a predilection for that which suits our particular turn and disposition. Such preferences are innocent and unavoidable, and can never reasonably be the object of dispute, because there is no standard, by which they can be decided.[62]

However, Hume muddies the waters by his identification of a person's judgement about a work's artistic value with the sentiment it arouses in the person, which implies that a judgement of comparative artistic value is identical with the person's more pleasurable or strongest sentiment, that is, their preference. This is a mistake and it is vital to realize that in fact there is always room for blameless aesthetic preferences, not just in those cases where there is no uniquely correct judgement about the relative values of works. For preferences are just that—preferences—not judgements about comparative artistic values, and where the comparative rank of two works is a determinate matter, to prefer the less valuable to the greater is not as such to make any kind of mistaken judgement. Furthermore, such a

---

[60] For an excellent account of the reasons for the incomparability of the artistic values of works and the conditions under which comparative evaluations are in place, see Bruce Vermazen, 'Comparing Evaluations of Works of Art', *Journal of Aesthetics and Art Criticism*, 34 (1975), 7–14.

[61] David Hume, 'Of the Standard of Taste', in Eugene F. Miller (ed.), *David Hume: Essays Moral, Political, and Literary*, rev. edn. (Indianapolis: Liberty Classics, 1987), 226–49.

[62] Ibid. 244.

preference is not only compatible with a recognition of the superior value of the less preferred, but there are many different ways in which the preference can be justified. One's favourite works are not necessarily those one thinks the best, and to prefer one work to another is not thereby to judge it to be the better work. Of course, aesthetic preferences are often expressive of a person's aesthetic judgement, and certain preferences are indicative of one or another defect in character, and may even be harmful. But not always. And if, simply in virtue of blameless diversity in people, in age, character, or temperament, for example, there is divergence of artistic judgement about the relative merits of works, neither party's judgement is intersubjectively valid, and, if advanced without qualification, each is incorrect.

15. I began by defining the idea of aesthetic judgement in terms of the concept of aesthetic sensitivity, which in turn I defined in terms of the notion of aesthetic character, a notion that incorporates the idea of aesthetic value. I have left in abeyance two questions that these definitions were likely to provoke: (i) What is it to be an aesthetic value of an item? (ii) What is an item's overall aesthetic value? Now is the time to answer them.

Elsewhere I have proposed the following accounts of purely aesthetic value:

An aesthetic value—a positive aesthetic value—of an item is a relation among its elements, or a higher-order property of it, which, as realised in the item, is fit to make the perception or imaginative realisation of it intrinsically rewarding.

An item's overall aesthetic value is its fitness to make the perception or imaginative realisation of it intrinsically rewarding in virtue of the ensemble of the relations among its elements, its higher-order properties as realised in it, and the interrelations of these.[63]

With suitable modifications, these can be turned into accounts of specifically artistic value. The first of these can then be used to deliver a criterion—one that yields results in accordance with the practice of criticism—for a property's being, in terminology drawn from Sibley,[64] an inherent aesthetic

[63] 'Aesthetic Essence', in Adele Tomlin and Richard Shusterman (eds.), *The Value of Aesthetic Experience* (London: Routledge, 2007) (reprinted as Essay 2).
[64] See Frank Sibley, 'Particularity, Art and Evaluation' and 'General Criteria and Reasons in Aesthetics', conveniently reprinted in his *Approach to Aesthetics*, 94, 105.

merit- or defect-constituting property of a work of art, a criterion that Sibley did not himself provide; and the second will fit neatly together with the conception of artistic value I have advocated. However, these two sets of definitions will do more than this: they provide the necessary link between evaluative aesthetic judgements of works of art and evaluative aesthetic judgements of non-art objects.

Although a unified aesthetic must comprehend the aesthetics of everything, it will not provide a uniform account of the aesthetics of each kind of thing or activity open to aesthetic experience. For just as there are significant differences between one art and another which must be reflected in the aesthetics of their products, so there are between, on the one hand, the products of the arts and, on the other, phenomena of other sorts, in particular those that are not artefacts. And if aesthetic evaluation is understood as aesthetic evaluation of an object as the kind of thing it is, the nature of the kind of thing that is the object of aesthetic appreciation will determine how it should be evaluated aesthetically, and especially which aspects of the object must inform the aesthetic appreciation of it. Accordingly, and in particular, although the aesthetics of nature must stand in a readily intelligible relation to the aesthetics of art, which must be articulated, the two must not be assimilated. Of course, natural items can be used to compose works of art, either partly (as with Ikebana) or wholly (as is possible with landscape gardening). But this does not undermine the distinction between judging aesthetically a natural item as such, and judging aesthetically a work of art in which a natural item figures. It is a moot point how exactly or in what ways aesthetic judgements about nature—judgements that acknowledge that their objects are the products of nature, not humanity—differ from aesthetic judgements about works of art (which here should be understood to include judgements about a work's artistic value). I have written about this elsewhere[65] and will here confine myself to a brief comment on a single line of thought directed towards a contrast between the evaluation of art and the aesthetic evaluation of nature.

This line of thought maintains that evaluative aesthetic judgements are applicable only to works of art and other artefacts, and bases itself on

[65] Malcolm Budd, *The Aesthetic Appreciation of Nature* (Oxford: Clarendon Press, 2002).

the idea that there are no bad or good natural objects as there are bad and good poems or paintings or pieces of music. It concludes from this that there is no valid standard of good taste, and, hence, no objective way of estimating and grading aesthetic responses to natural things, so that the idiosyncratic preferences of individual spectators (for clouds rather than trees, flowers rather than birds, tulips rather than roses, or whatever) are immune to criticism.[66] Note, first, that this must be taken to mean that judgements of overall aesthetic value are not applicable to nature, since evaluation-added judgements or judgements that attribute evaluative aesthetic qualities to natural things (the graceful gazelle) and comparative judgements of this kind (a gazelle is more graceful in movement than a hippopotamus) are untouched by the consideration that there are no kinds of natural thing which can be divided into the good and the bad things of that kind. But, even so, the view is not secure. In the first place, a bad or good poem is one that is bad or good *as* a poem. So the claim that there are no bad natural objects and good natural objects as there are bad poems and good poems must mean that there are no trees, for example, that are good as trees or bad as trees. Now if this refers to species of tree, it might be acceptable, for different species are fit to flourish in different environments and conditions, none of which has a greater claim than any other to be the standard against which the fitness of trees should be judged. But if to be bad as a tree is to be a tree that does not perform well the natural functions of a tree of its kind, then there are good and bad trees—healthy and diseased oaks, elms or cherries, for example. Leaving this specific consideration aside, some natural things, regarded in themselves and appreciated under standard conditions, do have a greater aesthetic value than others. This might be in virtue of their having so much more to offer (a cedar of Lebanon versus a grain of sand), or because they are healthy instances in their prime of the natural kind to which they belong, rather than dead, withered, injured, badly damaged, deformed, diseased, or in some other way deficient examples. It must be admitted, however, that the fact that natural things are not artefacts designed to fulfil a certain purpose and to be judged from that point of view, that many natural things are not forms of life and so lack natural functions, and that the requirement of appreciating a natural item as the kind of natural item it

---

[66] See Pepita Haezrahi, *The Contemplative Activity* (London: George Allen and Unwin, 1954), 63–4.

is does not limit the conditions under which observation should take place or the relevant aspects of the item to be attended to, restricts severely the sense and force of comparative judgements about the aesthetic values of natural items.[67]

[67] I would like to thank Peter Lamarque for his very helpful comments on a late draft of this essay.

5

The Pure Judgement of Taste as an Aesthetic Reflective Judgement

1. The idea of a reflective judgement lies at the heart of Kant's critical aesthetics. Both of the pure aesthetic judgements that Kant identifies, the pure judgement of taste and the judgement of the sublime (in nature), which occupy the bulk of his attention, are conceived of as being reflective judgements (*FI*, §XII);[1] the judgement of dependent (adherent) beauty incorporates a reflective judgement (the pure judgement of taste); and the notion of reflection integral to the idea of a reflective judgement plays a crucial role in underpinning the claims to intersubjective validity of the pure judgement of taste and the judgement of the sublime.

Kant introduces the idea of a reflective judgement through a distinction between two ways in which the power of judgement—the ability to think the particular as contained under the universal—can be exercised, and, accordingly, between two kinds of judgement (*CJ*, Introduction, §IV, *FI*, §V). Judgement can be exercised in a *determinative* or a *reflective* manner, the upshot being in the first case a determinative and in the second a reflective judgement. A determinative judgement is one that *determines* a *given* universal (a principle, law, rule, or concept) by subsuming a given empirical representation under it; when judgement is exercised reflectively one *reflects on* a *given* particular, in accordance with a certain principle, in order to *find* a universal under which it can be brought. In other

---

[1] All references to Kant's works are, unless indicated otherwise, by section number and/or the pagination in the relevant volume of the standard Prussian Academy edition of Kant's works. Abbreviations: *Critique of Judgement* = *CJ*; *First Introduction to the Critique of Judgement* = *FI*; *Critique of Pure Reason* = *CPR*.

words, in a determinative judgement you possess a certain concept and bring some empirical item under it; in reflective judgement, you are aware of something and attempt to acquire a concept under which it can be brought.[2] To reflect is to hold given representations up to, and compare them with, either other representations or one's cognitive powers, with respect to a concept which is thereby—by means of this comparison—made possible. The idea of comparing a given representation *with other representations* with respect to a concept that is made possible by means of this comparison is straightforward: by comparing a given representation with others we can form a concept—an 'empirical' concept—by extracting from the various representations what they have in common. The idea of comparing a representation *with our cognitive powers* is more problematic and requires a more complex elucidation.[3] The principle in accordance with which reflection takes place is an a priori principle, a principle that the power of judgement necessarily presupposes, a principle that effects a direct relation of the power of judgement to the feeling of pleasure or displeasure. But this principle assumes two forms, one passive and the other active, as it were, the first for the pure judgement of taste, the second for the judgement of the sublime. The principle is that of nature's *subjective purposiveness*, its first form being nature's purposiveness concerning the subject, its purposiveness *for the (reflective) power of judgement*, which means its being such that it makes possible something desirable concerning the power of judgement, its second form consisting in its being suitable to make palpable, to arouse a feeling of, a purposiveness that exists a priori in the subject (*CJ*, Introduction, §VII; *FI*, §XII). This subjective purposiveness is *intrinsic* in the case of the pure judgement of taste, being based in the representation of the object judged beautiful itself; it is *relative* in the case of the judgement of the sublime, arising only from the (supersensible) *use* made of the representation of the object (*FI*, §XII), a use (in the case of judgements of the sublime *in nature*) of intuitions

---

[2] This formulation appears to be better suited to the attempt to find higher and higher empirical laws under which lower ones fall, one of Kant's concerns in the *Critique of Teleological Judgement*, than to so-called aesthetic reflective judgements, as will become clear.

[3] [2007] In his 'The Harmony of the Faculties Revisited', in his *Values of Beauty: Historical Essays on Aesthetics* (Cambridge: Cambridge University Press, 2005), 97, Paul Guyer, citing this first section of my essay, claims that I 'may suppose' that the categories can be applied to objects independently of any determinate concepts. Not only is there no trace of this view in this section, but, as will be seen, it is something I am at pains to deny in the essay.

of nature that enable us to feel 'a purposiveness within ourselves entirely independent of nature' (*CJ*, §23). In each case, the comparison involved in the reflection is with *our cognitive powers*, not with other representations.

Two questions immediately arise about Kant's conception of an aesthetic reflective judgement:[4] 'What does it mean to compare a representation with our cognitive powers (and how is this connected with a judgement's being aesthetic)?', and, 'What concept is, and in what sense is it, thereby made possible?' In this essay I shall consider only the pure judgement of taste.[5]

2. A number of lines of thought have been proposed about what, in judging an item's beauty, Kant has in mind by the comparison of a representation with our cognitive powers, a comparison which is involved in reflection on the (form of the) item, an idea that occurs in different formulations in various places in the main text and the two introductions. What is incontestable is that, for Kant, the two cognitive powers involved in the making of a perceptual judgement—in perceiving that something is the case and in particular in perceiving something to be an object of a certain kind—are the imagination and the understanding, the understanding supplying the concept of the kind of item the subject perceives an object to be.

A condition of the possibility of perceptual judgement is that the imagination should run through and take together (or combine) the manifold of sensible intuition, which is necessary for the manifold to be represented *as a manifold* contained *in a single representation*, and that the understanding should effect the synthetic unification of the manifold in the concept of an object, so that the manifold is represented not just as a manifold but *as a manifold combined in an object*, is thought as belonging to one object, and in that sense as forming *a unity*—'that unity that constitutes the concept of an object', 'that unity which must be encountered in

---

[4] 'Aesthetic judgements of reflection' is a better characterization than 'aesthetic reflective judgements'. For although such judgements are not determinative judgements in the sense of subsuming the object under what Kant calls an empirical objective concept or a determinate concept, they are genuine judgements, subsuming the object under a concept, judgements that (supposedly) *issue from* reflection. (Kant's view that sublimity cannot properly be predicated of a natural object does not imply that the judgement of the sublime is not a genuine judgement.)

[5] Kant confesses the presence of a certain amount of obscurity, an obscurity 'not always avoidable', in his derivation of the phenomenon of aesthetic judgement—he has in mind pure judgements of taste—from the a priori principle of nature's subjective purposiveness (*CJ*, Preface, 171).

a manifold of cognition in so far as it stands in relation to an object', an object being 'that in the concept of which the manifold of a given intuition is *united*'.[6] Since 'the regularity leading to the concept of an object is the indispensable condition (*conditio sine qua non*) for apprehending the object in a single representation and determining the manifold in the object's form' (*CJ*, 242), although a pure judgement of taste does not itself attribute a perceptible property to an object, and so is not itself a perceptual judgement, in the reflection involved in a pure judgement of taste the manifold *is* brought under the concept of an object, the requirements of the possibility of perceptual judgement *must* be satisfied, as Kant makes abundantly clear:

in calling a judgement about an object aesthetic, we indicate immediately that, while a given representation is being referred to an object, by judgement we mean here not the determination of the object, but the determination of the subject and of his feeling.

(*FI*, §VIII, 223)

This apprehension [of an object by means of the imagination in relation to the understanding] occurs by means of a procedure that judgement has to carry out to give rise to even the most ordinary experience. The only difference is that in the case of ordinary experience the imagination has to engage in the procedure in order to perceive an empirical objective concept, whereas in the present case (in aesthetic judging) it has to do so merely in order to perceive that the representation is adequate for harmonious (subjectively purposive) activity of the two cognitive powers in their freedom . . .

(*CJ*, §39)

Here Kant refers to a common procedure and a difference of aim and he is making use of his vital distinction between the *categories*, which are 'a priori concepts of the systematic unity of the manifold of intuition' (*CJ*, §36), and *empirical objective concepts*. The essence of his thought about a pure judgement

---

[6] *CPR*, A105, A109, B137. The concept of an object is 'the concept of something in which [representations] are necessarily connected' (*CPR*, A108), which means that they are not determined 'arbitrarily or at pleasure' (*CPR*, A104), but 'necessarily agree in relation to [the object]'. Given the variations in Kant's articulation of the activities of the mind essential for experience as he struggled to express them in the A and B versions of the 'Transcendental Deduction of the Pure Categories of the Understanding', and as re-expressed in *CJ*, no formulation could accurately represent Kant's thought. I have chosen one that, although it glosses over certain unclarities and variations in the details of Kant's view, accords reasonably well with Kant's terminology in *CJ* and does not omit anything crucial to his conception of the experience of the beautiful or his deduction of judgements of taste.

of taste is that the normal aim in the unity imposed on the manifold of intuition, namely, to issue in a determinative perceptual judgement, one that subsumes the object under an *empirical* concept, is replaced by a different aim, which is to be achieved by reflection on the (form of the) object. Accordingly, when Kant writes 'Only where the imagination is free when it arouses the understanding, and the understanding, without using concepts, puts the imagination into a play that is regular, does the representation communicate itself not as a thought but as the inner feeling of a purposive state of mind' (*CJ*, §40), by 'concepts' he means 'empirical objective concepts', and the regularity he refers to is that required for the manifold to be brought under the concept of an object. His fundamental idea is that in making a pure judgement of taste, rather than being concerned to identify what kind of thing a given object is, what is in common between this object and others in virtue of which they fall under a certain empirical concept, which in a sense involves an implicit comparison with other objects—in other words, rather than being concerned with the object *as a thing of a particular kind*—we are concerned with just the individual form of the given object, the form itself, not what kind of thing it is the form of, 'the apprehension as such of this form, in so far as that form manifests itself in the mind' (*CJ*, §30, 279) as favourable to classification by the understanding and as a form the mere apprehension of which is rewarding.

Given, then, that the reflection involved in assessing an item's beauty presupposes the conditions of the possibility of perceptual judgement, how is this reflection, a reflection that consists in holding a given representation up to, and comparing it with, the cognitive powers, to be understood? Clearly, if Kant's account is to be true to the phenomenology of the experience of finding something beautiful, the comparison must not be thought of as taking place intentionally or even as requiring the subject to engage in an activity that presupposes the possession of the concepts of the imagination and understanding. So it must be possible for this reflection to take place without the subject's being aware of her activity as involving a comparison with the cognitive powers. Now in the context of the frame of mind that is integral to judging an item's beauty—the lack of concern about what kind of object is being perceived, the exclusive focusing on the object's form—the subject's cognitive functions are entirely taken up with the mere representation of the item, the synthesis of apprehension by the imagination of the form of the object given in intuition and the synthetic unification of the manifold in the concept of an object, the essential preconditions of perceptual judgement, the ability to think a given particular as contained under a universal. In this sense there is an implicit 'comparison' with or reference to the relation in which the imagination and understanding must stand to each other whenever perceptual knowledge of an object is possible, whenever it is possible to 'use the power of judgement objectively' (*FI*, §VIII, 223). This is how Kant's idea of a given representation's being referred to *cognition in general*,[7] of how 'in a merely reflective judgement imagination and understanding are considered as they must relate in general in the power of judgement' (*FI*, §VII, 220), and allied ideas should be understood.

Now this implicit comparison might reveal that the form of this object is especially well suited to the joint operation of the two cognitive powers involved in the representation of it,[8] in the sense that, not only does neither hinder the work of the other, but each helps or enables that activity (*FI*, §VIII, 223)—in other words, they mutually assist each other in the representation of the object. If the implicit comparison does reveal this, it reveals it through the fact that contemplation of the item's form, independently of any particular empirical concept under which it might be brought, is found disinterestedly pleasurable, the pleasure engendered being an indication (in fact, the only possible indication) that the two cognitive powers that are at play in reflection on the item's form are working especially harmoniously together. The pleasure is an indication of this harmonious interplay in virtue of the fact that the pleasure just is the feeling of this 'free play' of the cognitive powers: the activity that the pleasure is being taken in is one of representing an object as having a form of such a nature as to induce the harmonious interplay of the cognitive powers—consciousness of the harmonious interplay *is* the pleasure. If this inherently pleasurable

---

[7] See, for example, *CJ*, §9.

[8] The requirement of its being *especially* well suited is needed to avoid the conclusion that everything is (equally) beautiful, a conclusion uncongenial to Kant but one that appears to follow from a number of his formulations that demand only the harmony required in general to unite an intuition with concepts so as to produce a cognition (*FI*, §VIII, 223–4, *CJ*, Introduction, §VIII, 192, for example). In addition, it appears to be demanded by the variability in proportion of the attunement of the cognitive powers required for cognition in general that Kant admits in a crucial passage (*CJ*, §21, 238–9) and that is required to avoid the repugnant conclusion.

operation of the cognitive powers takes place, the object is experienced as being *purposive* for the power of judgement and the object is said to possess *formal subjective purposiveness*, a purposiveness with respect to the subject's cognitive powers, the representation of this subjective purposiveness being identical with a feeling of pleasure (*FI*, §VIII, 228). This is what it is to experience an object as being beautiful. Accordingly, since a pure judgement of taste is not based on a concept of the object, in particular a concept of the object's purpose (or natural functions), Kant characterizes beauty as 'an object's form of *purposiveness* in so far as it is perceived in the object *without the representation of a purpose*' (*CJ*, §17, 236), the form of the object 'seem[ing] to be, as it were, pre-adapted to our power of judgement' (*CJ*, §23, 245).

3. One interpretation of Kant's thought insists that in making a pure judgement of taste, not only must the manifold be brought under the concept of an object, but the object judged must be conceptualized *as the kind of thing it is*,[9] for there is no such thing as the form of an object considered independently of how it is conceptualized: the form of an object is relative to what kind of thing it is represented as being.[10] But in the relevant sense the form of an object is *not* relative to how it is conceptualized. Consider the visual perception of a perceptually motionless object. It will often be the case that when the object is brought under a concept it was not formerly brought under there will be no change at all in the *perception itself*, and so no change in the object's perceived form, but only a change in the *interpretation* of the object (what kind of object it is). If I study a lump of metal and after a few seconds recognize it as being copper I do not thereby see it as having a different *form*; if at one time I see a tree but without the ability to identify its kind, and at a later time, when I have acquired the ability, see it as being an aspen, its form is not thereby represented to me differently; and the represented form of a whale does not change when it is seen as being a mammal, rather than a fish. This is not to say that there will never be a change in the perception itself when an object is brought under a concept it was not formerly seen under. For instance, the change will not merely be one of interpretation in the variety

---

[9] This must mean *some* kind of thing it is, each thing being of many kinds.

[10] Anthony Savile, *Kantian Aesthetics Pursued* (Edinburgh: Edinburgh University Press, 1993), 108–10, and *Aesthetic Reconstructions* (Oxford: Basil Blackwell, 1987), 115.

of 'seeing-as' cases explored by Wittgenstein. And an object, seen as an instance of a certain kind, may in a certain sense be perceived to have a structure and unity it will not be seen to possess if it is not seen as being this kind of object: if, for example, the object is a chair, it will be seen to consist of seat, back, legs and perhaps arms, each part performing a function integral to the object's purpose, the parts being unified through their essential contributions to the fulfilment of that purpose. But this notion of structural unification is not Kant's notion of form, which for spatial objects is a matter solely of shape (outer and inner shapes), the perceptible spatial structure of the formed matter that composes the object (CJ, §14, 225).[11] Hence this interpretation lacks its only foundation.

4. This brings out the inadequacy of a view that places too stringent demands on one who makes a pure judgement of taste. The temptation to embrace this view is admittedly encouraged by certain of Kant's formulations. For example: 'a merely *reflective* judgement about a given individual object *can be aesthetic*; if (before we attend to a comparison of the object with others) the power of judgement, having no concept ready for the given intuition, holds the imagination (as it merely apprehends the object) up to the understanding' (FI, 224).[12] Formulations such as this, which indicate the temporal priority of the harmonious activity of imagination and understanding to the conceptualization of the intuition in which an object is given, unlike those that refer only to a concept's not being presupposed by that harmonious activity, provide support for the view that interprets Kant as requiring not only that an object whose beauty is to be judged should not be judged with reference to the kind of thing it is, but that the object must not be perceived as falling under that (empirical) concept. Accordingly, if I am concerned to determine whether this rose is beautiful I must not conceptualize it as being a rose, or a flower, or an instance of any other empirical kind. But since (i) perceiving an object as being an instance of a certain kind does not entail that its form is represented differently from how it is represented when it is perceived but not as an

---

[11] The inclusion in an object's perceptual form of relations amongst colours, in addition to outer shape and inner contours, would not rescue the interpretation from the objection that the form of an object is not relative to what kind of thing it is represented as being. Neither would admission of Kant's speculation (CJ, §§14, 51) that colours admit of reflective awareness of their forms.

[12] The continuation of this passage not only seems to carry this implication but, like certain other formulations, also seems to imply that every object can rightly be judged to be beautiful.

instance of that kind, and (ii) perceiving an object as being a rose, say, does not disable one from abstracting from its being a rose and contemplating its form independently of the kind it exemplifies, the idea that to judge an item's beauty it must not be perceived as an instance of any kind of thing lacks a *raison d'être*. So the only viable interpretation of Kant's view is that in judging an item's beauty, although it may well be recognized as being something of a certain kind, its being an instance of that kind must not be allowed to figure in the process of reflection, which must focus solely on the object's form. In fact, it is easy to see that the reflection involved in a judgement of taste must allow the subject to abstract from what the object is seen to be. For to perceive the object's form it is necessary to perceive the formed matter that composes the object, which (for visual perception) will involve seeing the distribution of apparent colours (chromatic or achromatic) across its facing surface, seeing it *as being* red here and white there, say. It is therefore integral to judging an object's beauty that it is seen under empirical concepts, concepts of colour, for example.[13] Hence what is required is only that the appeal that might accrue to the object in virtue of its possessing these properties should be discounted in judging the object's beauty.

5. The mental state integral to finding an object beautiful is characterized by Kant in a variety of ways. For example: imagination and understanding are in free play (in so far as they harmonize with each other as required for cognition in general), because no determinate concept restricts them to a particular rule of cognition (*CJ*, §9); each is quickened to an activity that is required for cognition in general but is indeterminate (*CJ*, §9); what occurs is the facilitated play of imagination and understanding quickened by their reciprocal harmony (*CJ*, §9); the mental state is a mutual quickening of imagination and understanding (*CJ*, §21); the imagination is in free play, its product not determined by concepts, in harmony with the understanding's

---

[13] [2007] Paul Guyer agrees with this view but seems to believe that the concepts must be such specific concepts as *hummingbird, sunset, painting, symphony, facade of the building*. He appears to derive this conclusion from two propositions: (i) an aesthetic judgement does not have the form 'This is beautiful', but 'This F is beautiful', and (ii) the objects of such judgements can be individuated only by means of such concepts. This overlooks the following facts: we may not know what kind of object something that lies before us is; we can individuate the object by using just concepts of colour and shape ('That red, yellow and black round thing over there'); and an aesthetic judgement can be of the form 'I don't know what that is, but it certainly is beautiful'. See his 'The Harmony of the Faculties Revisited', 94–5.

lawfulness in general (*CJ*, §22, General Comment on the First Book of the Analytic); the imagination in its freedom and the understanding in its lawfulness reciprocally quicken each other (*CJ*, §35). One frequently iterated description of the imagination is that it is free (in so far as it satisfies the understanding's requirements for cognition). Kant asserts three things about this freedom. First, the imagination is free because it is not restricted by a particular rule of cognition, that is, it is not required to be adequate to some particular (empirical) concept.[14] Second, its freedom consists in its schematizing without a concept (*CJ*, §35, 287). Third, on the one hand, the imagination is *not* really free because—leaving aside its need to conform to the requirements of cognition—it is required to represent accurately the form of the given object. On the other, it *is* free in the sense that it is proceeding in a way in which it would be disposed to do if it really were free: although it is being required to produce a particular form, this form is one of the kinds of form it would be disposed to produce if it were free (*CJ*, General Comment on the First Book of the Analytic). The three characterizations are intimately linked. In Kant's epistemological theory a schema of an empirical concept is 'a representation of a general procedure for providing a concept with its image' (*CPR*, A140/B179–180), 'a way of putting the manifold together in space and time'[15]: it mediates between intuitions and concepts, enabling intuitions to be subsumed under concepts (and so judgements made about the objects intuited), or, as Kant puts it, enabling a concept to be exhibited. It signifies a rule of the synthesis of the imagination in accordance with the concept, no particular image being necessary for the application of the concept, the concept allowing of indefinitely many different images that can be brought under it as instances of the concept. For imagination to schematize *without a concept* would therefore be for its activity to be such that its product can be brought under some (unspecified) empirical concept, and so is such that a perceptual judgement about the object represented is possible. So this is really no advance on the first characterization: the imagination's freedom consists in its not being constrained by the requirement of being adequate

[14] If the implication is that the imagination would be required to produce an image of a different *form* if it were subject to an empirical concept, the critique of the idea that the form of an object is relative to what kind of thing it is represented as being shows that the implication is unwarranted.

[15] A formulation taken from Kant's *Reflexionen*, quoted on p. 61 of Paul Guyer's and Allen W. Wood's translation and edition of *CPR* (Cambridge: Cambridge University Press, 1998).

to some particular empirical concept—all that is necessary is that it should be adequate to some empirical concept or other.[16] As Kant writes:

if the form of an object given in empirical intuition is of such a character that the *apprehension*, in the imagination, of the object's manifold agrees with the *exhibition* of a concept of the understanding (which concept this is being indeterminate), then imagination and understanding are—in mere reflection—in mutual harmony . . .

(*FI*, 221)

This leaves the third characterization, which in effect merely asserts that if the imagination were not to be subject to either of two restrictions—of needing to be adequate to a particular empirical concept under which the understanding has brought the object, and of needing to produce an object of a particular form—then its activity would gravitate towards certain forms, rather than others, and a form that induces the mental state integral to finding an object beautiful is one of these favoured forms.

There is just one sense in which the *understanding* could be said to be free in judging the beauty of an object: it is free from any concern to identify the kind of object being judged, to bring it under an empirical concept, its sole aim having been accomplished in achieving the presupposition of perceptual judgement—in effecting the synthetic unity of the manifold in the concept of an object, giving it 'that unity which must be encountered in a manifold of cognition in so far as it stands in relation to an object'.

The crucial double-barrelled question is: What exactly is supposed to happen to imagination and understanding in the experience of finding something beautiful, and what is the explanation of this activity taking place when they harmonize with each other as required for cognition in general? Kant frequently asserts that the activity of both the imagination and the understanding is quickened in judging an item to be beautiful, each being quickened in virtue of the mode of operation of the other. So the imagination and the understanding do not merely harmonize but interact, reciprocally quickening each other. It is, however, difficult to know how seriously to take this characterization of each activity, for, first, the notion

---

[16] [2007] In his 'The Harmony of the Faculties Revisited', 22, Paul Guyer mistakenly represents this sentence (which he misquotes) as possibly suggesting my commitment to what he calls the multicognitive interpretation of Kant's thought. In fact, I have always regarded this interpretation as absurd. And of course the sentence he mentions is not an expression of my own interpretation of Kant, but merely an elucidation of my conclusion that Kant's second characterization takes us no further than the first.

of the quickening of a cognitive power is left undetermined, and, second, it is sometimes replaced by the idea of furthering: the mutual harmony between the two cognitive powers, their harmonious play, consists in the relation between the two cognitive powers being such that each furthers the task or the activity of the other. But whatever is to be made of this characterization, this will not itself explain why the mutual quickening takes place.

This mutual quickening, whatever exactly it is supposed to consist in, must occur in virtue of what is true of the roles of imagination and understanding in correctly judging an item to be beautiful. One distinctive feature is that each is free from a function integral to judging what kind of thing the object encountered is and it might be thought that this freedom that characterizes the activity of each of the cognitive powers is sufficient to account for their mutual quickening. But why should the activity of the understanding be quickened by the imagination's not being constrained by the requirement of being adequate to some particular empirical concept and the activity of the imagination quickened by the understanding's not being concerned to identify the kind of object being judged? Perhaps the freedom of the understanding is supposed to result in its own quickening, and the freedom of the imagination in its own quickening, each quickening further quickening the other. But why should the understanding's lack of concern to bring an object under an empirical concept result in its own quickening, animating, or enlivening, rather than its idling, relaxing, or slackening, and likewise for the imagination?

In fact, it must be a mistake to attempt to explain the mutual quickening of the two cognitive powers by reference solely to what is distinctive of the roles of the imagination and understanding in judging an object's beauty. For imagination and understanding will possess their respective freedoms in judging *any* item's beauty, but not every item will be judged to be (equally) beautiful. The solution must, therefore, lie in the relationship between, on the one hand, the constitutive functions of imagination and understanding in the assessment of an item's beauty and, on the other, the distinctive character of beautiful forms. In so far as they figure essentially in the experience of an object whose beauty is being judged, the function of imagination is to provide a representation of a manifold as a manifold and that of understanding is to give this manifold that unity that constitutes the concept of an object. In virtue of what character of a form do the imagination and understanding, in engendering a representation of it, engage in the free harmonious play that is indicative of finding the form beautiful?

There is a sense in which this question cannot be answered. For it is clear that Kant believes that it is impossible for there to be a formula or principle the application of which to objects would identify all and only beautiful forms. Accordingly, the question cannot be answered by a specification of the intrinsic nature of beautiful forms. Nevertheless, given that the reflection involved in a pure judgement of taste is reflection only on the perceptual form of the object, the spatial and/or temporal structure of its elements, the spatio-temporal manner of combination of the manifold in the object, the explanation of an object's form's engaging the imagination and understanding in the free harmonious play distinctive of the experience of beauty, of their mutually facilitating or enlivening the activity of the other in the representation of the object, is severely limited—limited to the relation between a form's complexity and unification (the nature of the elements being irrelevant). In other words, it is a function of the character of its multiplicity in unity—its manifoldness as unified in the object. Now the manifold united in an object is presented by the imagination and its unity by the understanding. But of course the mere correspondence between manifoldness and the imagination and between unity and the understanding is not itself a sufficient explanation of the free harmonious play of the two cognitive powers in the experience of beauty, for this correspondence obtains for all objects. So how, in the case of a beautiful form, might the provision of the manifoldness by the imagination and the unification of the manifoldness by the understanding endow the two cognitive powers with their mutual quickening?

The answer follows from the recognition of an ambiguity in the idea of unity or of a manifold's being unified.[17] The idea of 'that unity that constitutes the concept of an object', which is what is effected by the

[17] It is not clear to me that Dieter Henrich's unrivalled concise reconstruction of Kant's thought, 'Kant's Explanation of Aesthetic Judgment', in his *Aesthetic Judgement and the Moral Image of the World* (Stanford: Stanford University Press, 1992), steers altogether clear of this ambiguity. This uncertainty is connected with its apparent failure to accommodate the possibility of forms of varying beauty, or, at least, of identifying the crucial function at the root of differences in beauty, responsible for the variability in 'proportion' of the attunement of the imagination and understanding required for cognition in general that Kant refers to (*CJ*, §21, 238–9) and that is needed to avoid the conclusion that everything is (equally) beautiful. Cf. n. 8.

understanding, is not the same as the idea of elements of an object composing a unity in the sense of forming a unified design or shape or manifold, one in which the parts seem to fit harmoniously together, rather than constituting a mere aggregate of essentially unrelated items, as with a random set of marks on a sheet of paper. To see a manifold as united in an object is not the same as seeing the plurality of that manifold as constituting a harmoniously unified multiplicity. This makes it clear that rather than simply pairing off the imagination with manifoldness and the understanding with unity and expecting that to provide the required explanation, it must be a matter of the *manner* in which the manifold is united in a beautiful object, or the *relation* between its manifoldness and its unity, which gives rise to the mutual quickening of the two cognitive powers. This is what underlies Kant's remark that:

we can...expect that the many natural products in such a system [a system of nature] might include some that, as if adapted quite expressly to our judgement, contain specific forms: forms that are commensurate with our judgement because, as it were, their diversity and unity allow them to serve to invigorate and entertain our mental powers (which are in play when we engage in judging) and hence are called *beautiful* forms.

(*CJ*, §61)

It seems likely, then, that Kant thought of the relationship between the activity of the imagination and that of the understanding in some such fashion as this. On the one hand, the imagination feeds on and is nourished by variety and multiplicity (manifoldness), the liveliness of its activity varying in accordance with the richness or meagreness of the data on which it must operate. On the other hand, the understanding—the faculty of rules—is primed to detect regularity, and in so far as regularity is manifest in what it is faced with its activity is facilitated. Accordingly, the greater the diversity of the manifold of elements supplied by the imagination in an intuition, the harder it will be for the understanding, in the absence of any compensating manifest orderliness, to impose synthetic unity on it or detect regularity in it. And although the task of the understanding (which 'is always poring through the appearances with the aim of finding some sort of rule in them' (*CPR*, A126)) of conferring synthetic unity on the combination presented to it by the imagination is, other things equal, easier the simpler the manifold of intuition, the less rewarding will it be for the imagination to supply the understanding with that combination—at the limit, as with simple geometrical figures, its task will fail to engage it, it will find it too boring to continue with it freely (*CJ*, §22, General Comment on the First Book of the Analytic). So for an object to be beautiful its perceptual structure must have a certain complexity but this structure must be such that its elements relate to one another in a harmonious fashion, composing a highly unified whole in which each element appears to be an integral part of the design fittingly related to the other elements.[18] Given that pleasure is the feeling of the *promotion of life*, of *self-activity* according to *representations*,[19] and that an object with such a structure will in reflection on its form both be a continuing stimulus to the imagination and make easy the task of the understanding, the contemplation of such an object will be found pleasurable: an object's form will be contemplated with disinterested pleasure when the manifold combined by the imagination is both rich enough to entertain the imagination in its combinatory activity and such as to facilitate the understanding's detection of regularity within it in virtue of composing a harmoniously unified structure. Although not exactly a mutual quickening of the two cognitive powers, something very like this is what Kant appears to have had in mind.[20]

6. This leaves the question: Which concept does the reflection involved in judging an object to be beautiful make possible, and in what sense is it made possible? Now a form that is intrinsically subjectively purposive for the power of judgement is such that, reflected on independently of any particular concept under which it might be brought, 'imagination and understanding harmonize with each other on their own to make a concept possible' (*FI*, §IX). If this were to be understood as involving merely that

---

[18] As indicated earlier, no independent characterization of the intrinsic nature of the forms that satisfy this condition is possible. On the contrary, it accommodates indefinitely many different forms united by nothing other than the fact that their satisfaction of this condition is such as to engender the disinterested pleasure distinctive of the beautiful.

[19] See, for example, Immanuel Kant, *Lectures on Metaphysics*, trans. and ed. Karl Ameriks and Steve Naragon (Cambridge: Cambridge University Press, 1997), 63–4.

[20] The effectiveness of Kant's deduction of pure judgements of taste depends on his identification of the distinctive pleasure of the beautiful being a bona fide explanation, which in turn depends on the acceptability of Kant's theory of perceptual knowledge and its postulated mental mechanisms, with objects of perception being constructed out of sensory data in accordance with the forms of space and time and a priori concepts, the imagination operating on what is given in sensibility to produce, with the aid of the understanding, experience of objects. Accordingly, a soundly based assessment of the deduction requires a deep understanding of the generation of perceptual experience by the human perceptual system.

the two representational powers are so related that the understanding can impose synthetic unity on the manifold given to it in intuition by the imagination, so that the subject is aware of an object, an object that must be an object of some kind or other, then the answer to the question, 'Which concept does the reflection involved in judging an object to be beautiful make possible?', would seem to be 'No particular concept: Kant is concerned only with a form's suitability in mere apprehension to being conceptualized'. But since the harmonization requires the form of the object to be especially well suited to the joint operation of the two cognitive powers involved in the representation of it, the right answer is that the concept is that of subjective formal purposiveness (that is, beauty!), and the sense in which it is made possible by reflection on an object's form is that the form is experienced as possessing the property that the concept designates. That this is the right answer can be seen from the fact that if I am concerned with whether a given object is beautiful then, in accordance with Kant's account, I reflect on the object to determine whether the relationship between the imagination's apprehension of its form and the understanding's imposition of synthetic unity on the imagination's product is of the harmonious kind Kant indicates, that is to say, I am concerned to determine whether the object is formally purposive for the power of judgement. As Kant writes, 'our aesthetic power of judgement judges . . . the subjective purposiveness of an object', and 'our analysis of aesthetic judgements of reflection will show that they contain the concept . . . of the formal but subjective purposiveness of objects' (*FI*, §VIII, Comment, 229, 230). The crucial feature of this concept of formal subjective purposiveness is that it does not signify a perceptible property of an object, a property that an object has in its own right, independently of how it is disposed to affect human beings, detectible by cold scrutiny of the object; it is, rather, a particular kind of relational property of an object, one that involves a relation in which it stands to human cognitive powers active in perception of the world, a relation detectible only through an affect-laden contemplation of the object. In Kant's language, it is not 'a characteristic of the object, determined in it according to concepts', for 'apart from a reference to the subject's feeling, beauty [formal subjective purposiveness (*CJ*, §15)] is nothing by itself' (*CJ*, §9). So in finding an object to be beautiful I am (through the feeling of pleasure) detecting a relational property of it, its formal subjective purposiveness, and since this relational property is not 'a characteristic of the object, determined in it according to concepts' or 'a [perceptible] characteristic of the object itself' (*CJ*, Introduction, §VII), this is perfectly consistent with Kant's insistence that not only is a pure judgement of taste not *based* on a (determinate) concept, but it does not *provide* one (*CJ*, Introduction, §VII).

6

Understanding Music

1. At the heart of the aesthetics of music is a small set of connected issues: whether our musical vocabulary, by itself or in conjunction with our present non-musical vocabulary, enables us to characterize our experience of music adequately; what the relation is between technical and non-technical characterizations of music, and how important each of these is in the appreciation of music; what the understanding of music consists in and whether there are different kinds of understanding of a musical work; what it is for music to be expressive of emotion and whether, and if so why, this is a virtue of music; how the apparent discontinuity of musical experience with the rest of our experience is compatible with music's importance to us; what determines the musical value of a piece of music. Here I shall concentrate upon the nature of the experience that a listener has if he hears a musical work with understanding. This will lead me to elaborate upon other central issues to which this one is linked. And I shall begin by making two general points about the somewhat nebulous and polymorphic concept of understanding music.

2. The first is that a person's understanding of music can be assessed along a number of different dimensions. His understanding of a particular piece of music can be more or less deep and it can be more or less accurate (or precise); and his understanding of music in general can be more or less extensive and it can be more or less subtle. I shall now explain what I mean by these categories.

Someone's understanding of a musical work can be said to be superficial if, although he can follow a performance of the work without feeling lost, he fails to hear much of the significant detail or structure of the work. His understanding of a musical work can be said to be inaccurate (or imprecise) if, although he can follow a performance of the work well, he has a mistaken (or only a rather indefinite) conception of how the music should sound, and so how it should be performed. This defect in musical understanding is naturally most apparent in someone who does perform music but it is not restricted to performers. And what it comes to is that a person can experience a performance of the work with understanding and yet have an incorrect (or imprecise) understanding of the work itself, as is manifested in the way he plays the work or thinks it should be played. One form of this defect is being blind to subtle but all-important features of a composer's style and, as we say, having little feeling for the music of that composer, but there are other possible reasons. Accordingly, one aspect of musical understanding—understanding a particular musical work—is knowing how the work should sound in performance, an understanding open to someone who cannot perform the work just as much as someone who can, being an ability demonstrable either by performance or by criticism of performance. The third category of understanding is this: someone's understanding of music can be said to be narrow if it covers few kinds or styles of music, either in the sense that he is not able to follow most forms of music, or in the sense that he is not able to appreciate most forms of music, i.e. to see what there is of value in them. Finally, someone's understanding of music can be said to be primitive if he can respond only to the simplest musical relations and structures. There are, of course, connections between these various aspects of musical understanding, but I shall not elaborate them.

In some respects, the idea of understanding a work of art resembles the idea of understanding a game—a game of tennis, for example. A spectator who understands the rules of tennis can have a more or less refined understanding of any game he watches; and since the rewards of a refined understanding are not the same as, and are not essentially linked to, those of a coarse understanding, the preferences amongst games of tennis of those with a refined understanding will not be the same as those with a coarse understanding. A coarse understanding does not appreciate the finer points of a player's skill, tactics, and so on: it neither realizes that, nor understands how, a player played a certain shot (with topspin, for example), nor does it understand why the player played that particular shot—what the player was attempting to do, and why that particular thing and not something else. Consequently, the manner in which someone with a coarse understanding of the game perceives the game will not be the same as that in which someone with a refined understanding perceives the game: the concepts that inform the perceptions of someone with a refined understanding—the concepts under which he perceives various occurrences in the game—will not inform the perceptions of someone with a coarse understanding. And, hence, a game that someone with a coarse understanding finds unrewarding may be found rewarding by someone with a refined understanding, and vice versa. Artistic understanding, and musical understanding in particular, is susceptible of refinement (and so of education) in a similar fashion to the understanding of a game. The question of *which* concepts must inform someone's experience of a musical work, and the way in which they must inform it, if he is to understand the work, or to understand it in a refined manner—in particular, whether these include technical concepts of musical theory—is something I shall return to later.

3. The second general point about understanding music is this: the kinds of condition that one's experience of a musical work must satisfy if one is to experience the work with understanding vary from work to work. It follows that it would be wrong to identify the idea of musical understanding of a work with the idea of understanding a work's intrinsic, intra-musical, non-referential meaning, where such understanding consists in being able to follow the work's specifically musical development. Musical understanding does not have this as its essence. For musical works differ from one another in the kinds of aspects of music that they utilize and in the exploitation of the possibilities open to the composer. Hence, what is necessary for the appreciation of one work is not always necessary for the appreciation of any other (and not just in the trivial sense that the experience of one work will not be the same as the experience of a work that arranges tones in a different manner from that of the first work). There is no illuminating general answer to the question 'How must one hear a piece of music if one is to appreciate its appeal as a piece of music?'

It is of course easy in particular cases to specify necessary conditions of someone's understanding a musical work. The point is that in some cases these conditions will not be applicable to many other musical works, for there are features of some pieces of music which are such that their recognition or realization is essential to the music's appreciation, but which most pieces of music lack. For example, a musical work may contain a specific reference to another piece of music (as in musical quotation, for example), or it may make a specific reference to a particular composer's work (as in one kind of musical parody), or it may make an indefinite reference to music of a certain sort (as in another kind of musical parody). Thus: a phrase in the thirteenth variation of Elgar's *Enigma Variations* is a quotation from Mendelssohn's *Calm Sea and Prosperous Voyage* overture; Casella's *Entr'acte pour un drame en préparation* is a parody of Debussy; Mozart's *A Musical Joke* is a parody of the crass and mechanical application of eighteenth-century formulas to trivial and ridiculous material—it is deliberately infelicitous, as some music is non-deliberately infelicitous. In each of these cases there is a specific intention of the composer that a listener must recognize if his understanding of the work is not to be incomplete: he must realize that the quotation *is* a quotation and that Elgar intended that the listener's response to the music should be mediated by his familiarity with Mendelssohn's work; he must realize that Casella's intention was to construct a work that imitated certain features of Debussy's style of composition; he must realize that Mozart intended the listener to be amused at what would be the work's musical faults if the work were intended as a serious composition and not as a joke. And the listener is in a position to appreciate the value of these works only if he does not merely recognize the composer's intention but possesses the familiarities or responses that the works presuppose.

In each of these cases the music refers to something outside itself—to other musical works or to other kinds of music—and it is integral to the understanding of the music that it should be experienced with recognition of the composer's intention that the music should make this reference. And there are many other ways in which a musical work can make an essential reference to other music. But not all music refers (in this sense) to other musical works or to other kinds of music, or even to anything outside itself. Hence, the recognition of the composer's intention that his work should not just be music but should refer to other music is sometimes, but not always, a necessary condition of understanding the work. And of course there are many other kinds of condition that are in some but not all cases necessary conditions for understanding a musical work.[1]

---

[1] It is true that these conditions could be made universal by writing them in a hypothetical form. But this does not affect the point that the requirements imposed on understanding a musical work can be more or less demanding and can be of diverse kinds.

But the fact that musical understanding does not have an essence does not imply that it does not have a common core—the understanding of music's intrinsic, non-referential nature. It is clear that it is this specifically musical understanding that Alban Berg is referring to in the following passage from his essay 'Why is Schönberg's Music so Difficult to Understand?':

to recognise the beginning, course and ending of all melodies, to hear the sounding-together of the voices not as a chance phenomenon but as harmonies and harmonic progressions, to trace smaller and larger relationships and contrasts as what they are—to put it briefly: to follow a piece of music as one follows the words of a poem in a language that one has mastered through and through means the same—for one who possesses the gift of thinking musically—as understanding the work itself.[2]

If we wish to grasp the heart of musical understanding we must identify the basic aspects or elements of music and consider what is involved in understanding a musical work in so far as it consists of constructions or compositions of these elements or aspects.

4. Before I turn to this, I want to raise the question of the adequacy of our language for describing music. It is clear that it is no more possible to describe in detail the nature of a musical work (and so also the nature of our experience of the work) without using the vocabulary of musical theory than it is possible to describe in detail the nature of a painting without using colour vocabulary. But this does not imply that the vocabulary of musical theory is sufficient to describe all the musically relevant relations among the items for which the theory has names or descriptions or all musically relevant aspects of a composition, any more than the corresponding fact about painting implies that colour vocabulary is sufficient to describe all the aesthetically or artistically relevant visual relations among coloured items or all aesthetically relevant aspects of a painted work. Nevertheless, in each case, for any artistically relevant relation or aspect that the vocabulary in question cannot specify the vocabulary can in principle be supplemented by a name of that relation or aspect. The new vocabulary may contain terms of a different nature from those of the original vocabulary; but the inadequacy of the original vocabulary is not irremediable. It is a moot

---

[2] Alban Berg, 'Why is Schönberg's Music so Difficult to Understand?', in Willi Reich, *The Life and Work of Alban Berg* (London: Thames and Hudson, 1965).

point how adequate the vocabulary of musical theory is to its object. For example, some believe that there are important audible features of musical works that this vocabulary does not have the means to describe, and that if we are to talk about these features we must have recourse to our non-musical vocabulary used figuratively. This is the position of those who maintain that the application of emotion words to music is to be understood metaphorically, as a means of drawing attention to purely audible features of music for which we have no other more direct or more suitable means of indicating. Of course, if this were so, and if this were the sole function, or the only proper function, of emotion terms when applied to music, there would be no reason in principle why our musical vocabulary should not be supplemented by terms introduced as names of these features of music and the metaphorical use of emotion terms dispensed with. This would be an application of the general principle that mere inadequacies of vocabulary are remediable. It is an important issue whether the use of emotion words to characterize music should be understood in this eliminable way. But I do not wish to enter once again this familiar territory and I shall, except in passing, say nothing about the description of music by terms drawn from the language of the emotions. Instead, I shall consider two views, each of which maintains that extra-musical concepts are integral to the experience of listening to music with understanding, and in elucidating this thesis each assigns a crucial role to the notion of metaphor, but the two views operate at different levels and diverge considerably in the claims they make. The first of these is a remarkable view put forward by Frank Sibley.

5. What Sibley sets himself to do in his paper 'Making Music Our Own'[3] is to render plausible the supposition that when we listen to music with understanding, grasping the character or qualities of the music as it unfolds, we do so by bringing it under extra-musical concepts, hearing the music in such a manner that apt figurative descriptions of the music would be appropriate to our experience—to the way we hear the music. This supposition, if true, would, he asserts, 'lessen the "mystery" of musical understanding by questioning the supposed "isolation" or "purity" of music and the "discontinuity" between it and the rest of experience' (p. 147); and it is, at least in part, because we hear music under figurative

---

[3] In Frank Sibley, *Approach to Aesthetics*, ed. John Benson, Betty Redfern, and Jeremy Roxbee Cox (Oxford: Clarendon Press, 2001), 142–53. All page numbers in the text will be to this work.

extra-musical descriptions that music means something to us (p. 148)—that it can engage us as appreciative listeners (p. 145).

To render this supposition plausible, Sibley does three main things. First, he emphasizes the practice, common to composers, performers, and listeners of all kinds, of describing music in figurative terms, simple or complex, and argues that all music is open to apt figurative description. The practice is undeniable, as is the possibility of characterizing any piece of music in apt figurative language. Secondly, he argues that the ability to give and accept such descriptions of music, although not absolutely necessary for the appreciation of its qualities, is the primary and most conclusive indication of understanding the character of music. (There appears to be some confusion in Sibley's thought about this matter. For having stated that acquisition of certain abilities other than being able to describe music aptly or assent to proffered descriptions of it might constitute understanding a piece, he immediately proceeds to argue that the acquisition of these non-verbal abilities would not guarantee grasp of the character of the piece (pp. 151–2).) Thirdly, he counters a likely objection. The objection is that for it to be true that a certain figurative description accurately characterized the way one heard a piece of music the words of the description (or some equivalent) must have occurred to one as one listened. Sibley easily disposes of this objection and I shall leave it aside.

For Sibley, figurative descriptions include 'various non-univocal uses, "secondary senses", and obvious metaphors' (p. 144). Appropriate figurative descriptions of music are apt rather than true, so that alternative equally apt descriptions of the character of a passage may always be possible, as, for example, an 'intermingling streams' description might be as apt a description as a 'conversation' description of a trio by C. P. E. Bach, or 'aggressive, hard, and energetic' might suit the opening of Stravinsky's Symphony in Three Movements just as well as 'spiky, spare, and athletic'. Apart from programme music, there is no such thing as the right extra-musical description. And music's 'abstractness' and *sui generis* character is a matter, not of any supposed impropriety of extra-musical interpretation, but of that fact—the absence of a right figurative description.

One difficulty in assessing Sibley's position is that his class of figurative descriptions appears to be a rag-bag. Sibley does not elucidate what he has in mind by 'secondary senses' of words and, in particular, the difference between words that have secondary senses and words that are used non-univocally, and he does not indicate which non-univocal uses do and which do not fall within the class of the figurative and what grounds the distinction. Perhaps his placing the words within quotation marks shows that 'secondary senses' is intended to refer to a certain idea of Wittgenstein's. This would certainly differentiate the use of a word in a secondary sense from the use of a word that has more than one meaning, and would provide a reason for grouping secondary senses with metaphors, despite their difference. For Wittgenstein introduces his notion of a secondary sense of a word in this way:

Given the two ideas 'fat' and 'lean', would you be rather inclined to say that Wednesday was fat and Tuesday lean, or the other way round? (I incline decidedly to the former.) Now have 'fat' and 'lean' some different meaning from their usual one?—They have a different use.—So ought I really to have used different words? Certainly not that.—I want to use *these* words (with their familiar meanings) *here* . . .

Asked 'What do you really mean here by "fat" and "lean"?'—I could only explain the meanings in the usual way . . .

Here one might speak of a 'primary' and 'secondary' sense of a word. It is only if the word has the primary sense for you that you use it in the secondary one . . .

 The secondary sense is not a 'metaphorical' sense. If I say 'For me the vowel *e* is yellow' I do not mean: 'yellow' in a metaphorical sense—for I could not express what I want to say in any other way than by means of the idea 'yellow'.[4]

So a word used in a secondary sense is unlike a word used non-univocally in that it retains its familiar meaning when used in its secondary sense and it is unlike a word used metaphorically in that it is not replaceable by a non-synonymous word. But, as with a word used metaphorically in an appropriate fashion, it is not thereby used to say something true.

 But even if this straightens out one of the problems I have identified in understanding the class of figurative descriptions, it leaves untouched the other. For whatever may be meant by 'secondary senses', a word used non-univocally, 'bank', for example, is not thereby in any one of its meanings used figuratively. Furthermore, a word used non-univocally will standardly be used to assert something that is true or false, rather

---

[4] Ludwig Wittgenstein, *Philosophical Investigations* (Oxford: Basil Blackwell, 1958), II, xi, p. 216.

than merely apt, its intended meaning varying from occasion to occasion across the range of its meanings. So a criterion is needed for when a word or phrase used non-univocally (and non-metaphorically) falls within the class of the figurative. And this criterion must be such that it ensures that descriptions that satisfy it can at best be said to be apt, not true of music.

A related difficulty in understanding Sibley's class of figurative descriptions is presented by the fact that some of his own examples of figurative descriptions of music appear not to fall within the class, or do so only if taken in a tendentious manner. To murmur is, in one sense, to make a low, continued noise, like the hum of bees, a stream of water, rolling waves, or the wind in a forest. In another sense, it is to complain in a low, half-articulated or muttering voice. In the first sense, which would be the normal one, to describe music as murmuring is not to describe it figuratively and the assertion might be straightforwardly true. To describe music as silken is just to describe it as being like silk (in an unspecified respect), intimating a resemblance between how silk feels and how the music sounds, the most obvious resemblance being accorded recognition in language by different senses of the word 'smooth', so that, no matter which sense the word had originally, the description of music as being smooth can be literally correct, and, using the word 'harsh' in one of its recognized senses, the description of it as being harsh straightforwardly false.[5]

Although Sibley deliberately avoids mention of descriptions of music in terms of feelings and emotions, his discussion is, he asserts, intended to apply equally to them (p. 153). But the description of music in such terms is typically non-metaphorical, in the specific sense that it is not a metaphor, the point of which can be captured without recourse to the literal meaning of the description (as both I and Stephen Davies have argued); such descriptions do not use words in secondary senses, as Wittgenstein introduced the notion (as R. A. Sharpe has argued);[6] and there is no need

---

[5] Stephen Davies, *Musical Meaning and Expression* (Ithaca and London: Cornell University Press, 1994), 164–5, rightly maintains that many descriptions of music formulated in terms of words whose primary application is to extra-musical phenomena—such as 'high' and 'low' of tones, 'thick' and 'thin' of textures, 'metallic', 'fruity', 'hard' and 'soft' of timbres, and 'jagged' and 'spiky' of rhythms—are not metaphorical. But it is unfortunate that he refers the reader to the discussion of secondary senses in B. R. Tilghman's *But is it Art?* (Oxford: Basil Blackwell, 1984) as though this is concerned with the same topic as his own discussion of secondary meanings.

[6] R. A. Sharpe, *Music and Humanism* (Oxford: Oxford University Press, 2000), 47.

for them to make use of terms used non-univocally. Furthermore, there is no impropriety in the ascription of truth, rather than mere aptness, to the predication of sadness or joyfulness of certain pieces of music: no other description would be equally apt. Hence the typical description of music in terms of feelings and emotions falls outside Sibley's figurative class.

It might be thought that in order for Sibley's argument to go through the appropriate description of music in figurative terms must be understood in such a manner that it attributes a property to the music that makes essential reference to the extra-musical phenomenon from which the terms of the description are drawn, as a non-figurative description that attributes a relational property might do so. For otherwise the figurative description of music will not have the significance Sibley assigns to it: it will not be true that 'much that is centrally appealing about music' is 'essentially extra-musical' (pp. 146–7). If, for example, the function of a figurative characterization of music is to make salient some feature of the music, a feature that is common to the music and the phenomenon to which the description applies non-figuratively or a feature that is possessed by the music and resembles one possessed by that phenomenon, the 'purity' of music will not thereby be called into question, any more than it is threatened or compromised by the applicability of a non-figurative term that ranges outside music ('loud', say). If no essential reference to a certain extra-musical phenomenon is being made, it is unnecessary to experience the music under that description in order to appreciate the character of the music that the description draws attention to.

Now there is an entirely general problem for Sibley in meeting the alleged requirement, which is created by his acknowledgement that appropriate figurative descriptions of music are apt, not true, so that equally apt alternatives drawn from different extra-musical domains may always be possible. In fact, it is not possible for Sibley to meet the requirement. For if there are equally apt alternatives, it is not essential that a listener who recognizes the character of the music should experience it as being related to a phenomenon in one rather than another of the domains. A case in point is Sibley's example of equally apt descriptions of the C. P. E. Bach trio, one in terms of a conversation, the other using the imagery of intermingling streams: if the one is no better than the other, experiencing the music under the concept of a conversation, say, is not necessary to grasping the character of the music. If, for any figurative description of a piece of music, there is always, in principle, another, formulated in terms drawn from a different domain, that is equally apt—and although Sibley does not exactly embrace this possibility, he is not in a position to deny it and in fact is committed to it—it will never be the case that the appropriateness of figurative descriptions of music renders the corresponding extra-musical concepts essential ingredients of the content of any experience that appreciates the character of the music. And this casts doubt on Sibley's view that a listener must experience a piece of music under one or another apt figurative extra-musical description of the music if she is to hear the character of the music, and undermines the significance that Sibley wishes to assign to this fact. For the availability of equally apt figurative descriptions is most readily explained by the idea that the function of these descriptions is to draw attention to a feature of the music that, because it has nothing essentially to do with the extra-musical phenomena mentioned in the descriptions, can be recognized without being brought under any of the extra-musical descriptions. This would seem generally to be so for Sibley's highest level of figurative descriptions, so-called scenarios, such as the equally apt descriptions of the C. P. E. Bach trio. Acknowledgement of their aptness is not tantamount to one's experiencing the music under one of these figurative descriptions (or another equally apt figurative description), if this implies that an important element in the understanding of music is, as Sibley wishes to maintain, 'covertly extra-musical' (p. 153).

In fact, it is clear that Sibley would have to reject the requirement. For the possibility of equally apt figurative descriptions of the character of a piece of music, descriptions the terms of which are drawn from different domains, implies that the character of the music is not such that capturing it in words it is necessary to refer to any particular extra-musical phenomenon or to any particular domain.

Rejection of the requirement appears to leave only one way of making sense of Sibley's position. This would be to maintain that if abstraction from all the particularities of the various equally apt figurative descriptions is made, what is left is a property that is itself extra-musical, as the property of elasticity considered in abstraction from any particular substance that instantiates it or the property of spatial movement abstracted from the variety of items that move in space is extra-musical, and that the character of the music demands that one who grasps it must hear it as falling under this property, figuratively. So although the applicability of the figurative descriptions would fail to import anything extra-musical specific to one or another of the descriptions into what it is to grasp the music's character, it would nevertheless be true that the extra-musical is implicated in understanding what that character is. But there is no suggestion in Sibley's text that the sense in which the appreciation of music is 'covertly extra-musical' is that there is a property common to all the phenomena that provide the bases of equally apt figurative descriptions of a piece of music's character and that this property is extra-musical. Furthermore, this would not be a plausible general thesis across the entire range of Sibley's class of figurative descriptions.

Sibley makes this admission: 'I have said nothing about the question pursued by many theories: why or in virtue of what—resemblances, analogies, shared features—we supposedly can employ figurative language; I simply accept that we do' (p. 153).[7] But the real issue concerns, not the basis, but the function or functions of figurative language. Sibley takes the function of figurative descriptions of music to be that of describing the character of the music. It follows that in order to understand a figurative description of music it is necessary to realize what characteristic is being attributed to the music by the use of figurative language. But Sibley fails to make clear what characteristic is being attributed to music by any of the figurative descriptions he mentions.[8] And the unsatisfactoriness of his position is brought out by his confession that he is not denying the existence of 'purely musical qualities': 'the warmth or chill of music is

---

[7] In his 'Aesthetic Concepts', *Approach to Aesthetics*, 20–2, Sibley appears to accept that the metaphorical use of single words is based on the recognition of similarities.

[8] In fact, this is just one instance of a general lacuna in Sibley's thoughts about aesthetic properties. For although the aesthetic properties recognized by Sibley and the terms used to attribute them exhibit considerable variety, as early as his justly celebrated 'Aesthetic Concepts' Sibley acknowledged that it is often the case that words used as aesthetic terms are used as metaphors. And in this same essay he asserts that 'In using [words metaphorically or quasi-metaphorically] to describe works of art, the very point is that we are noticing aesthetic qualities related to their literal or common meanings' (p. 17). But neither in this essay nor elsewhere does Sibley state or examine what the relation is between the aesthetic quality noticed and the literal meaning of the metaphor. What is it about the aesthetic quality that makes the metaphorical description apt? Perhaps the question does not admit of a unitary answer covering all aesthetic qualities attributed by means of metaphors: this seems to be the meaning of Sibley's assertion that there need not 'be any general answer to why rival [figurative] descriptions [of a piece of music] may be equally apt' (p. 152). But in any particular case, without an answer to the question we have an incomplete grasp of the nature of the aesthetic property attributed by means of the metaphor. And the failure ever to specify the relation between the aesthetic property attributed by means of a metaphor and the literal meaning of the metaphor means that Sibley's consideration of aesthetic qualities leaves a fair proportion of them—all described by metaphors (and certain other kinds of figurative language)—obscure. See the discussion of Sibley in Essay 7.

only audible; it is not the warmth or chill felt in bath-water or seen in smiles' (p. 153). So a figurative description of music attributes a property to the music, but not the same property as that given by the terms of the description when used in their home domain. How, then, are the two properties related to one another, and why is it necessary to perceive the first through a description of the second (or through a description of some other property, the description of which is an equally apt description of the music)? What is the relation between the warmth of the music and the warmth of the bath-water? Without an answer to this question, it is unclear why extra-musical concepts are supposed to play a significant role in understanding music and how they are able to do so. Why is figurative language necessary to articulate the character of music? Sibley appears to believe that 'the figurative can capture what the literal cannot' (p. 150). Understood in a weak sense, this asserts only that the available range of literal uses of words in the language is not sufficient to name or describe all aspects of reality; in a strong sense it makes the absurd claim that there are certain aspects of reality that will be resistant to names or descriptions used literally no matter how rich the language may become. What Sibley needs to establish is that there are aspects of music essential to its appreciation that are such that they can be captured in any language's net only by the use of figurative language, although such an aspect does not need to be captured by any particular figurative description or one the terms of which are drawn from a particular domain. The failure to engage with the question of how figurative descriptions of music are to be understood—in what sense they describe or capture the character of the music—makes the supposition that Sibley tries to render plausible deeply problematic. For it implies that the character of a piece of music can be captured only by figurative descriptions, no one of which is needed to capture it. But how music can have a character that can be recognized only by bringing it under one or another apt figurative description is entirely unexplained.

6. I shall now examine the second of the two views I mentioned earlier that assert an essential link between understanding music and metaphor, and hereby I return to the topic of identifying, and perhaps analysing, the fundamental features of musical understanding. For my concern is the claim, articulated by Roger Scruton in his account of understanding music, that metaphor lies at the heart of musical experience and cannot

be expelled from it.[9] A consideration of this claim helps to clarify an important characteristic of musical understanding. I will present Scruton's position in a highly schematic form, but one which, I believe, does not misrepresent it.

Scruton distinguishes two modes of understanding something (a sequence of sounds, for example): scientific understanding and intentional understanding. Whereas scientific understanding is concerned with the world as material object, and attempts to explain the world's appearance to people, intentional understanding is concerned with the world as intentional object, and confines itself to the nature, not the explanation, of the world's appearance. In fact, intentional understanding of something consists in a certain kind of experience of that thing. In this experience the thing appears a particular way, and it is this appearance that provides the essence of the intentional understanding of the thing. The understanding of music—as it is realized in experiencing a (performance of a) musical work with understanding—is a form of intentional understanding. Hence, an account of musical understanding will be a description of the nature of the required or appropriate appearance: at the most general level, it will describe the kinds of experience someone has when he experiences sounds in one or another of the ways in which it is necessary he should if he is to hear the sounds as music, and, at a more specific level, it will describe the experience that someone must have if the sounds he hears are to appear to him in the way in which it is necessary that they should if he is to experience them with full understanding as (a performance of) the work they compose.

For Scruton, the fundamental distinction that needs to be clarified in an account of musical understanding is the distinction between hearing sounds only as sounds and hearing sounds as tones. This distinction can be represented as the distinction between hearing sounds only as sounds and hearing sounds as having melodic, rhythmic, or harmonic implications. Accordingly, the basic elements of musical understanding are the experiences of melody, rhythm, and harmony. Hence, if we are to have an account of musical understanding, it is necessary to describe the nature of the experiences of melody, rhythm, and harmony. Scruton maintains that these experiences can be described, but only by means of metaphors.

[9] Roger Scruton, 'Understanding Music', in his *The Aesthetic Understanding* (London and New York: Methuen, 1983).

These metaphors transfer extra-musical ideas to the experience of sound and convert the experience of mere sound into the experience of the elements of music. It is when, and only when, sounds are experienced in accordance with these metaphors that they are experienced as music. The extra-musical ideas that occur in these metaphors inform the experiences of melody, rhythm, and harmony—they form part of the content of these experiences—but only in a metaphorical sense; and it is the metaphorical incorporation of these extra-musical ideas that distinguishes the experiences of the basic elements of musical understanding from experiences that are perceptions of the same sounds but which do not involve experiencing the sounds as music. The extra-musical ideas contained within these metaphors are mainly spatial concepts. Thus: to hear a melody in a series of sounds the sounds that compose the melody must be heard as moving (in space); to hear a rhythm in a series of sounds the sounds must be heard as moving in a particular manner, namely, as if they were dancing; to hear harmony in sounds the sounds must be heard as chords, and chords must be heard as spaced, open, filled, or hollow, for example, and as involving tension, relaxation, conflict, and resolution. But the sounds in which melody, rhythm, and harmony are heard do not literally move, dance, and so on—they move and dance only metaphorically.

It is clear that we must distinguish two theses—the one uncontroversial, the other problematic—that Scruton tends to run together in his account. The uncontroversial thesis is:

(i)   There is more to the perception of melody, rhythm, and harmony in a succession of sounds than the perception of the succession of sounds.

This thesis is uncontroversial, since it is certainly not sufficient for someone to perceive melody, rhythm, and harmony in a succession of sounds that he should perceive a succession of sounds in which these musical phenomena can be heard. The problematic thesis is:

(ii)   The perception of melody, rhythm, and harmony in a succession of sounds is distinguished from the mere perception of the succession of sounds by the fact that the former perceptions involve the metaphorical transference to the sounds of the idea of movement (and so of space), the idea of dancing, and the idea of composite three-dimensional spatial entities in various conditions of stress. This metaphorical transference is an ineliminable feature of the experience of melody, rhythm, and harmony.

I believe that Scruton's problematic thesis is vulnerable in two different ways: there is an objection in principle to the kind of account he proposes—an account that assigns a crucial role to the notion of metaphor—and there are objections to the details of his account, which credit spatial concepts with an irreplaceable significance in the description of musical experience. The objection of principle is as follows. Even if the arguments Scruton advances were sufficient to establish an essential relation between the experience of melody and the concept of movement, or between the experience of rhythm and the more specific concept of dancing, and so on, to call the description of the nature of these experiences by means of the related concepts *metaphorical* is not to specify the alleged relation: the relation between the experience and the property signified by the concept, or the way in which the concept informs the experience of the sounds, is not illuminated by the metaphorical transference of the concepts or properties to the experience. For any metaphor stands in need of interpretation; a metaphor is susceptible of indefinitely many interpretations; and an interpretation of a metaphor is the injection of significance into it, not the extraction of significance from it. But not only does Scruton fail to suggest an interpretation of the metaphors that are supposed to lie at the heart of musical experience, he appears to hold that an interpretation is both unnecessary and unavailable. An interpretation is unavailable because the characterization of musical experience by means of the concepts in question is—even though metaphorical—ideally specific: they specify properties of musical experience that cannot be characterized adequately without the use of these concepts. And this position is incoherent: musical experience cannot have a merely metaphorical essence (or an essence part of which is merely metaphorical).

This conclusion might be avoided in the following way. It is often true that when someone utters a metaphor he has not already thought what its exact significance should be. Accordingly, if someone thinks in metaphor it can be true that his state of mind can be specified adequately only by means of the metaphor in the terms of which he thinks. Hence, if an uninterpreted metaphorical thought were to be embedded in some way in a perceptual experience, it would be essential to the complete specification of the experience that it should use the embedded metaphor. And if this were to be the fashion in which metaphors lie at the heart of musical experience, musical experience would have a merely metaphorical essence. But this mode of resistance to the conclusion would, I believe, be unfounded. An initial difficulty with this suggestion is that it is unclear how a metaphor could be part of the content of a perceptual experience. But even if this difficulty were to be overcome the suggestion would not be acceptable. For it is clear that it is unnecessary to think the (metaphorical) thoughts 'These sounds are moving', 'These sounds are dancing', 'This sound is hollow and tense (say)' in order to experience melody, rhythm, and harmony in the sounds heard.

It follows that if the concepts Scruton highlights are integral to musical experience, they must enter the experience of music in some other fashion than by metaphorical transference. But in fact the thesis that these concepts inform the experience of the basic elements of music, and the arguments Scruton advances in its support, are unconvincing. I shall confine attention to the case of rhythm, where Scruton's position is conspicuously weak.

The claim that the experience of rhythm must be described in terms of the concept of dancing is unattractive, if for no other reason than that the concept of dancing contains the concept of rhythm: someone dances only if she moves rhythmically. Hence, the concept of dancing, rather than being used to explain the concept of rhythm—albeit by a metaphorical use—presupposes the concept of rhythm. And the claim is unwarranted. Scruton is led to adopt it partly because he sees it as the solution to distinguishing the experience of rhythm from the experience of a temporal pattern. But this solution is desperate and unnecessary. For the experience of rhythm in a sequence of sounds and rests can be adequately characterized in the following manner: (i) it does not require that the sounds should be heard as differing in pitch, timbre, duration, or loudness, and (ii) the sequence must be heard as grouped into units in which one element is heard as accented (prominent, salient) relative to the others.[10] And the

---

[10] Compare the account of rhythm in Grosvenor Cooper and Leonard B. Meyer, *The Rhythmic Structure of Music* (Chicago: University of Chicago Press, 1960). The concept of rhythm in music can be understood in a number of ways. The account I have offered applies to the concept Scruton is concerned with. It is of course true that the nature of the rhythm we experience in a sequence of sounds that exhibit differences in one or more of the variables of pitch, timbre, duration, or loudness is

different rhythms are the different ways in which unaccented elements are heard as grouped in relation to an accented element. Hence, we can agree with the thesis that the experience of rhythm in music is (in Scruton's terminology) a form of intentional understanding of sounds, while rejecting the view that the experience of rhythm must be explained by reference to the idea of dancing and the notion of metaphor. And a similar conclusion holds, I believe, for the corresponding claims about melody and harmony.[11] In particular, the notion of movement in space is not integral to the experience of melody and the idea of composite spatial entities, hollow or filled, is not a constituent of the experience of harmony.[12]

7. I now turn to the question whether it is necessary that someone should possess specifically musical concepts, or a mastery of specifically musical terminology, if he is to be able to experience a musical work with full understanding.

The possession of a concept that applies to musical events is not the same as the ability to classify musical events on the basis of their sound by using the concept: someone can possess a musical concept and yet be quite unable to apply the concept to music as he listens to the music. Now in general neither the lack of a certain concept of a particular phenomenon nor the inability to recognize instances of the phenomenon as falling under the concept prevents a person from being sensitive to the presence of the phenomenon in a work of art and alive to the aesthetic or artistic function of the phenomenon in the work. In the case of music, a listener does not need to have the concept of, say, a dominant seventh chord, that is, the concept of a major triad plus the note which forms with the root of the triad the interval of a minor seventh—a chord that in a major scale can be built only on the dominant—in order to have a full sensitivity to the harmonic implications of such

dependent upon these differences. But the experience of rhythm does not itself require that any such differences should be heard, or should seem to be heard, in a sequence of sounds that is experienced as rhythmically organized.

[11] In fact, a relatively unified musical work is essentially a hierarchical structure of temporal groupings. It consists of phenomena grouped into units that are more or less complete in themselves, but which are combined with other units to form higher-level groupings with a more inclusive sense of completeness, thus making the work a composition of elements on different hierarchical levels. The importance of this kind of organization in music, and its significance in the understanding of music, is illustrated exceptionally well in Leonard B. Meyer, *Explaining Music* (Berkeley, Los Angeles, and London: University of California Press, 1973), ch. 4.

[12] I return to Scruton's view in Essay 8, where I examine its later development.

a chord in a work to which he is listening. And since he does not need to possess the concept, he does not need to bring the chord under the concept when he hears the chord if he is to experience the work with understanding.

The truth of the matter is that what much specifically musical vocabulary enables one to do is to name or describe phenomena that someone without a mastery of the vocabulary can hear equally well. The relation between the experience of music and the vocabulary designed to describe music is in one significant respect the same as the relation between the experience of lingual taste and the words used to describe taste. Just as someone's ability to characterize the variety and complexity of the tastes he experiences can fall far short of that variety and complexity, so someone's ability to characterize his experience of musical works can fail to do justice to many of the features of the experience. In both cases, whether through ignorance of the available words or through inability to identify instances of the phenomena they designate, a person's linguistic resources can be inadequate to the articulation of his experience. And the inarticulacy in the face of experience is of the same order: in neither case does it limit the person's experience to what he can articulate. It is true that inarticulateness is often a result of lack of vividness or delicacy of perception. And, as Collingwood insisted, a person's experience can be transformed by his coming to be able to express it. But neither of these is inevitable: an experience that someone cannot articulate need not lack strength or detail, and no transformation of the experience needs to occur if its subject acquires the capacity to render it in words.

To experience music with musical understanding a listener must perceive various kinds of musical process, structure, and relationship. But to perceive phrasing, cadences, and harmonic progressions, for example, does not require the listener to conceptualize them in musical terms. A listener can experience these phenomena whether or not he hears them under the description they are given in a correct analysis of the music. This description applies to the experience of a listener who experiences the music with understanding; but the listener does not need to recognize this fact in order to have the experience it describes.[13] Hence, the value to the

---

[13] [2007] This view has received powerful support from Mark Debellis, who has argued that, leaving aside any emotive content that music may have and concentrating solely on its structural or syntactic content, the ordinary listener, with no or little knowledge of musical theory and without the aural training concomitant with the acquisition of such knowledge, hears music largely non-conceptually, not just in the weak sense that it can be correctly described in terms of music-theoretic concepts

listener of a mastery of musical terminology is not that it enables him to have an experience that is denied to someone who lacks the mastery—the experience of listening to a musical work with understanding. It is true that the acquisition of a musical vocabulary, especially if it includes the ability to recognize by ear the phenomena that the terms designate, is likely to involve an enhancement of the understanding of music: the sensitivity of the ear to musical patterns and relationships can be increased. But the ability to articulate music in musical terms is essential, not in order to experience music with understanding, but to understand and engage in the practice of musical analysis and criticism. The task of musical analysis is to explain, first of all, what the relationships among events in a particular musical work are, and, accordingly, how they are experienced by a listener who experiences a correct performance of the work with understanding; and, secondly, why the music is as it is, what the structure and function of a particular harmonic progression is, for example, or whether a tone or harmony is structurally essential or ornamental, or why a theme is to be phrased in a certain way, or why the music must be taken at a certain tempo. And this task can be discharged only by the use of technical terms that have been developed to describe the nature of musical events in detail. Consequently, perceptive criticism of a musical work, which must be based not only upon accurate perception of the nature of the work but also on accurate and detailed description of this nature, must be technical. Hence, the musically literate listener is in a more desirable position than the illiterate listener, not with respect to experiencing music with understanding, but in his capacity to make clear both to himself and to others the reasons for his musical preferences. At a level of explanation beyond the most crude the musically illiterate listener is not only condemned to silence: he is not in a position to comprehend his own responses to music.

that the listener does not possess, so that the listener does not hear it under those concepts and lacks the corresponding music-theoretic beliefs about what he or she hears, but in the strong sense that it is not the exercise of a conceptual faculty at all, so that the experience is not informed by any concepts and does not consist in perceptual beliefs of any sort. See his *Music and Conceptualization* (New York: Cambridge University Press, 1995). (His 'The Representational Content of Musical Experience', *Philosophy and Phenomenological Research*, 51/2 (June 1991) is also of great interest and relevant to the concerns of this essay.)

7

The Characterization of Aesthetic Qualities by Essential Metaphors and Quasi-Metaphors

A neglected aspect of Frank Sibley's seminal investigation of aesthetic concepts is his account of the attribution of aesthetic qualities by the use of metaphors or 'quasi-metaphors'. This account[1] is a combination of the undeniable, the obscure, and the contestable. The first claim, which is uncontroversial, is that it is often the case that when words are used as aesthetic terms, i.e. as terms which require aesthetic sensitivity in order to apply them, their application to an object attributing an aesthetic quality to that object, their use as aesthetic terms is not their primary use. Rather, they are being used as metaphors. The second claim is largely indisputable but introduces, without explanation, the idea of the category of the 'quasi-metaphorical'. It is certain that many words that have come to be used as aesthetic terms by metaphorical transference—'dynamic', 'balanced', 'tightly-knit', 'forceful', 'melancholy', 'taut', and 'gay' are Sibley's examples—become standard critical vocabulary. But this becomes problematic when Sibley proceeds to assert that, having entered critical vocabulary as metaphors, either they are no longer metaphors or their critical employment is at most 'quasi-metaphorical' when they have become standard critical vocabulary. The difficulty is not their ceasing to be metaphors: metaphors live and die, and although they can be brought to life again, their use, as dead, is straightforward, constituting a new literal use. It is, rather, the possibility of their being 'quasi-metaphorical', which, as a contrast with 'not metaphorical', cannot mean 'apparently but not really

---

[1] See his 'Aesthetic Concepts', reprinted in his *Approach to Aesthetics* (Oxford: Clarendon Press, 2001), 1–23.

metaphorical' but must mean 'partly metaphorical', the meaning of which is uncertain.[2] William Empson has a nice observation about dead, and not so dead, metaphors:

Among metaphors effective from several points of view one may include . . . those metaphors which are partly recognised as such and partly received simply as words in their acquired sense. All languages are composed of dead metaphors as the soil of corpses, but English is perhaps uniquely full of metaphors of this sort, which are not dead but sleeping, and, while making a direct statement, colour it with an implied comparison.[3]

Perhaps Sibley's idea of the quasi-metaphorical was something like Empson's idea of words that, while being understood in their acquired sense, also suggest a comparison.

The third and vital claim emerges in his criticism of a view of Stuart Hampshire:

this view that our use of metaphor and quasi-metaphor for aesthetic purposes is unnatural or a makeshift into which we are forced by a language designed for other purposes misrepresents fundamentally the character of aesthetic qualities and aesthetic language. There is nothing unnatural about using words like 'forceful', 'dynamic', or 'tightly-knit' in criticism; they do their work perfectly and are exactly the words needed for the purposes they serve. We do not want or need to replace them by words which lack the metaphorical element. In using them to describe works of art, the very point is that we are noticing aesthetic qualities related to their literal or common meanings. If we possessed a quite different word from 'dynamic', one we could use to point out an aesthetic quality unrelated to the common meaning of 'dynamic', it could not be used to describe that quality which 'dynamic' does serve to point out. Hampshire pictures 'a colony of aesthetes, disengaged from practical needs and manipulations' and says that 'descriptions of aesthetic qualities, which for us are metaphorical, might seem to them to have an altogether literal and familiar sense'; they might use 'a more directly descriptive vocabulary'. But if they had a new and 'directly descriptive' vocabulary lacking the links with non-aesthetic properties and interests which our vocabulary possesses, they would have to remain silent about many of the aesthetic qualities we can describe; further, if they were more completely 'disengaged from practical needs'

---

[2] In fact, Sibley proposes a spectrum of words used as aesthetic terms by metaphorical transference: on the one hand, there are such live metaphors as descriptions of music as 'chattering', 'carbonated', or 'gritty', on the other, dead metaphors or 'quasi-metaphorical' uses, and in between, perhaps, words like 'athletic', 'vertiginous', and 'silken'.

[3] William Empson, *Seven Types of Ambiguity* (Edinburgh: Penguin Books, 1961), 25.

and other non-aesthetic awarenesses and interests, they would perforce be blind to many aesthetic qualities we can appreciate. The links between aesthetic qualities and non-aesthetic ones are both obvious and vital. Aesthetic concepts, all of them, carry with them attachments and in one way or another are tethered to or parasitic upon non-aesthetic features.[4]

This raises the question of what exactly the relations are between the literal and the aesthetic uses of such words.[5] Nowhere in the body of his work does Sibley appear to explicate the connection between the use of a term drawn from another domain to ascribe an aesthetic quality and its primary use within that domain—alternatively, the relation between the aesthetic quality and the reference of the term in its home domain. But if the very point in using metaphors and quasi-metaphors to describe works of art is, as Sibley maintains, that 'we are noticing aesthetic qualities related to their literal or common meanings', to understand the precise function of such an expression, or such an expression in a particular case, we need to grasp what the relation is.

Sibley proposes that the transition from the literal to the aesthetic use, the metaphorical shift, is made possible by our possession of 'certain abilities and tendencies to link experiences, to regard certain things as similar, and to see, explore, and be interested in these similarities', abilities and tendencies that can be developed and encouraged.[6] This is, I am sure, true (especially if the idea of similarities is understood as obtaining between not just individual objects but sets of objects);[7] but it falls short of what is needed to establish Sibley's position, for it does not specify the relations between the two uses.[8] Consider the words 'taut' and 'dynamic', for

---

[4] *Approach to Aesthetics*, 17.

[5] The ideas of the quasi-metaphorical and the essential connection between the metaphorical or quasi-metaphorical use of terms to ascribe aesthetic qualities and the literal references of those terms were not just constituents of Sibley's early thought but remained indispensable elements of his view of aesthetic concepts throughout his life. See, for example, the wonderful paper he worked on for a number of years, 'Tastes, Smells, and Aesthetics', but which was unpublished at his death, where, writing principally of tastes and smells, but extending the point to the arts (and most other things), he asserts that 'quasi-metaphorical descriptions link us with what are felt to be acceptable analogues between the [quasi-]metaphorical and literal references of the expressions' (*Approach to Aesthetics*, 235).

[6] Ibid. 20.

[7] See Nelson Goodman, *Languages of Art* (London: Oxford University Press, 1969), ch. II, §6.

[8] It is sometimes thought that the aesthetic use of metaphors, 'quasi-metaphors', or words employed in 'secondary senses' is sufficiently explained by the existence of a *series* of transitional uses which diverge more and more from the original or primary use and culminate in the aesthetic use, thus disclosing the aesthetic use as a natural extension of the primary use. But in itself this does not touch the vital point—the intrinsic nature of the aesthetic quality indicated by the aesthetic use.

example. For a string, rope, or wire to be taut is for it to be stretched tight, not slack, and for a player's performance to be dynamic is for it to be powerfully energetic. But what aesthetic quality is being assigned to a poem by calling it taut or to a painting by calling it dynamic? If Sibley's claim about the use of metaphors and quasi-metaphors is given the strong interpretation that it invites, this quality must be not just 'related' to the literal meaning, which imposes little, if any, restriction, but related to it in such a manner that a word with a different meaning would not be suitable as a description of the quality: the claim is that the non-aesthetic concept of tautness or dynamism is essential to capturing the character of the aesthetic quality—it is intrinsic to its identification. Whatever exactly the notion of the 'quasi-metaphorical' is supposed to be, if it is to have any force at all it is essential that it should imply that a 'quasi-metaphorical' use of a word is not attached to the straightforwardly literal use of the word only historically or by means of resemblances that do not need to be recognized by one who fully grasps what is said by it. For when a word is extended from one domain to another on the basis of recognized similarities between properties of items in the two domains—and then, perhaps, to further domains—if this use becomes standard then it is characteristic for a new sense of the word to be distinguished, one that is not parasitic on the original meaning, so that this sense of the word can be grasped independently of an understanding of what at one time was the word's (only) literal meaning. To understand what is meant by a jagged rhythm it is unnecessary to think in terms of some material's edge being irregularly indented with projecting points. And at least some of Sibley's examples seem to fall into this class and so fail to meet the required condition. Consider the expression 'tightly-knit'. For a garment to be knitted it must be composed of interlocking loops of some material (wool, say), which loops can be more or less tight or close together. By a thoroughly understandable extension, 'tightly-knit' (or 'close-knit') is now applied to items that are not composed of interlocking loops, such as groups of people, and someone who lacks the concept of a knitted garment is not thereby denied a full grasp of the idea of a tightly-knit group. It is easy to express the extended sense or senses in which something can be said to be tightly-knit without resort to the concept of interlocking loops of material; and it is in one of these extended senses that a poem might well be said to be tightly-knit. I am not aware of an aesthetic use of 'tightly-knit' which meets the requirement imposed by the strong reading of Sibley's position.

It is clear that not every metaphorical use of an expression to ascribe an aesthetic property, even an expression that has become standard critical terminology, accords with the strong reading. How would it be possible for an aesthetic term, introduced into critical vocabulary by metaphorical transference, to satisfy the requirement imposed by the strong reading, indicating an aesthetic quality the intrinsic nature of which can be captured only through the non-aesthetic meaning of the term? There is more than one possibility. I shall consider just two, one arising directly from Sibley's account of the metaphorical shift in the use of a word to designate an aesthetic quality, the other being more radical and, I believe, encompassing a wider range.

The importance Sibley assigns to our recognition of and interest in similarities between items of different kinds immediately suggests one possibility. If the point of a metaphor of the simple form 'X is P' is to intimate that X has a P-like character, an intimation that might encourage people to experience X as having such a character, this character might or might not be such that its intrinsic nature must be specified in terms of P. If the sense in which a 'quasi-metaphor' used as an aesthetic term retains a metaphorical element is cashed out in terms of an intimated resemblance, this could be done in two ways. A weak reading of Sibley's position would represent it as maintaining that an aesthetic quality ascribed by a 'quasi-metaphor' is merely a quality that resembles the property the expression stands for when used literally. But if the quasi-metaphorical use signals an analogy between the metaphorical and literal references of the expression, it will always be possible that an expression with a different meaning will provide an equally acceptable analogy. Accordingly, the aesthetic (use of the) term does no more than call attention to this aesthetic quality through its resemblance to the original property, the character of the aesthetic quality not being ineluctably tied to but being specifiable independently of this property. However, to accord with the strong reading it would be necessary to substitute for this idea of an intimated resemblance a different idea, the idea that the aesthetic term is used precisely to signify a resemblance between what it is applied to in its aesthetic use and what it is applied to in its non-aesthetic use—that is precisely what it announces. In other words, the aesthetic quality it ascribes is the relational property of resembling what is designated by the word used literally. A natural extension of this idea would allow the relational property to be that of resembling what is designated by the literal use of some complex expression containing the word, as, for example, 'sorrow' occurs in '(inarticulate aspects of) a vocal expression of sorrow', so that, as some have suggested, to call a piece of music sorrowful is to liken it to (inarticulate aspects of) a vocal expression of sorrow, this likeness being integral to the attribution.

I propose now to approach the issue from a different direction by focusing on the nature of the canonical basis on which a judgement that a certain item possesses an aesthetic quality is made, which is to say, the perceptual or imaginative experience of the item as possessing that quality. The strong reading of Sibley's view requires that, for an aesthetic quality for which a metaphorical or quasi-metaphorical use of a word with a particular literal meaning is essential to the quality's description, the specification of the intrinsic nature of the canonical basis on which a correct ascription of that quality is made must incorporate a term with that meaning: in other words, that concept must figure in the intrinsic nature of the experience of the item as possessing the quality. The two accounts of aesthetic qualities distinguished above, one satisfying the strong reading of Sibley's position, the other only the weak reading, are both formulated in terms of the idea of resemblance. But this idea would figure in the specification of the intrinsic nature of the perception of aesthetic qualities only in the case of the account that satisfies the strong reading: in each case the perception is of a property that (supposedly) resembles another, but only when the strong requirement is satisfied is the experience the perception of the property *as* resembling the other.

There is, of course, a question as to how exactly this idea of a perceived resemblance is to be understood, and whether there are any aesthetic qualities—and if so which—for which the idea of perceived resemblance figures in the specification of the intrinsic nature of the canonical basis of a judgement that a certain item possesses that aesthetic quality. However, there is another question, which I prefer to address here, and that is whether, instead of the idea of a perceived resemblance, a related notion might be a much better choice, or at least a viable alternative, to introduce into the canonical bases of many judgements that ascribe aesthetic qualities.

In *The Brown Book* Wittgenstein considers a variety of cases in which the same word is applied across a variety of seemingly heterogeneous instances, where we are inclined to justify the application of the term to such different things by appeal to there being something in common to or some similarity between the various instances.[9] What I want to take from Wittgenstein's discussion (which includes examples of what he later described as words being used in secondary senses) are these two points: (i) even if similarities between or something common to the instances can be pointed out to someone who does or is inclined to apply the term to these very different things, the person need not be aware of these similarities or the common element that binds them together (in the sense of being able to specify them), and (ii) experiencing a variety of items as being similar in some respect may consist partially or wholly in being prompted to use the same term in that variety of cases. And I want to add to these another point taken from Wittgenstein, this time from his brief consideration in *Philosophical Investigations* of a word that might be said to be being used in a secondary, rather than its primary sense (meaning), as when someone is inclined to describe Wednesday as being fat or says that for him or her the vowel *e* is yellow.[10] In cases such as these, you can use the word in a secondary sense only if you know its primary meaning, and this is so precisely because you would not be able to say what you want to say in any other way, i.e. by using another word with a different (primary) meaning. It is for just this reason that Wittgenstein declares that the secondary sense is not a 'metaphorical' sense, understanding by a metaphorical use of an expression a use which is such that you could say what you want to say without using that expression (an expression with that [primary] meaning), as when, if you use the expression 'cutting off someone's speech', the use of 'cutting off' (as in 'cutting off a piece of thread') is inessential.[11] Since it is not mandatory to use the notion of metaphor in this restricted manner and Sibley did not do so, although I am sympathetic to Wittgenstein's use, I shall here ignore it.

A radical position about the experience of an item as possessing an aesthetic quality flows from Wittgenstein's insights and, if Sibley had

[9] Ludwig Wittgenstein, *The Blue and the Brown Books* (Oxford: Basil Blackwell, 1960), 129–41.

[10] Ibid., *Philosophical Investigations* (Oxford : Basil Blackwell, 1958), pt. II, §xi, p. 216.

[11] See Ludwig Wittgenstein, *Last Writings on the Philosophy of Psychology*, i (Oxford: Basil Blackwell, 1982), §799.

embraced it,[12] it would explain, at least to a certain extent, his silence about the connection between, on the one hand, the use of a term drawn from an alien domain to ascribe an aesthetic quality and, on the other, its primary use within that domain, or the nature of the relation in which the aesthetic quality stands to the reference of the term in its home domain. The view could be refined in a number of ways, but a simple version is sufficient for my present purpose. This maintains that for at least some aesthetic qualities commonly ascribed by an expression used metaphorically (or quasi-metaphorically) nothing more, but nothing less, is needed for someone to perceive an item as possessing that quality than for the person, in perceiving the item, and triggered or confirmed by that perception, to regard that expression (or some synonymous expression) as being well-suited to capture an aspect of the item's character.[13] This suggestion receives support from the following line of thought. When people look at a picture or building, read a poem or novel, or listen to a piece of music, usually they do so without attempting to articulate aspects of the work's aesthetic character and often without any characterization of a particular aspect simply occurring to them. Many of them would in fact struggle to come up with anything other than a highly general characterization of a certain aspect, a characterization which satisfies them. Others might be at a complete loss as to how to capture that character of the work in words, if they were asked to do so. Now suppose a characterization in metaphorical terms is offered to someone who experiences difficulty in coming up with an adequate description of the aspect, and this characterization seems to them to fit the character of the work well, perhaps exactly: it seems to them to hit it off, perhaps perfectly.[14] When she now looks at, reads, or listens

[12] In a footnote to 'Tastes, Smells, and Aesthetics' Sibley indicates that some such idea as Wittgenstein's notion of 'secondary sense' is fundamentally involved in the metaphorical use of terms to characterize tastes, smells, works of art, and much else, a use that is inevitable if we are to capture the qualities these things possess, but he does not mention it in the main text in order not to get involved in exegesis of Wittgenstein's remarks. See *Approach to Aesthetics*, 236 n. 45.

[13] One possible refinement would be to substitute the idea of being disposed, or being ready, to regard a characterization as being well-suited to capture the aspect for the idea that the regard is triggered or confirmed by the perception. The crucial issue is, of course, how best, consistent with the leading idea of the view in question, to describe the notion, as it might be put, of perceiving an item under a metaphorical description.

[14] This covers two kinds of case. Just as there might be nothing amiss with a description of an item's colour, and yet the colour can be specified more precisely, so there might be nothing amiss with a metaphorical characterization of an aesthetic quality of an item, and yet the characterization can be made more specific.

to the work, regarding this characterization as being well-suited to convey the work's character, without anything else needing to happen, she thereby experiences the work as having that character. Her experience of the work has changed: previously it was inchoate, the character being obscure; now it is distinct, the character apparent. There will, of course, be non-aesthetic features of the work in virtue of which she regards the metaphorical characterization as being well-suited to capture the work's character: alter these features in certain ways and the appropriateness will disappear. But it is not necessary that she should be able, without help, to support her view that the characterization fits the work by identifying these features: there will be something about the work that makes her regard it as well-suited to convey the work's character, but she may not be able to put her finger on what this is. Moreover, it is not necessary that whenever someone regards the characterization as well-suited to capture a work's character, her regard is founded on the same non-aesthetic features: the foundational features are likely to exhibit very great variety. Furthermore, it does not follow from the fact that someone perceives an item as possessing a certain set of non-aesthetic features—perhaps exactly the set of non-aesthetic features that the item actually displays—that she will, or that she will not, regard a particular term with a certain meaning, when used metaphorically, as being well-suited to capture an aesthetic quality of the item. (It will be noticed that these two facts mirror two crucial aspects of Sibley's account of the relation between aesthetic and non-aesthetic properties.)

If Q is an aesthetic quality for which this minimalist account is correct, the experience of perceiving an item as possessing Q is, in brief, just the experience of perceiving the character of the item as being well-caught by 'T' (let us say).[15] Now there are two possibilities. If you perceive an item as possessing Q, either (i) although you regard 'T' (or a synonymous term) as being well-suited to convey Q's character, you are not so attached to it as to rule out the possibility that you might regard an expression with quite a different literal meaning, 'S', say, drawn from a different domain, as being equally well-suited, or (ii) you regard 'T' (or a synonymous term) as being uniquely well-suited. But if you are a certain kind of person, the first possibility is likely to resolve into the second. For, if 'S' occurs to

---

[15] This is not to rule out the possibility that our readiness to regard 'T' as a fitting characterization of Q might partly be a product of our being affected by Q in a way similar to some way in which T affects us.

you then, given the equal claims of 'S' and 'T', you are likely to find the situation unsatisfactory, neither expression seeming to you to hit off the character perfectly, and you will strive to find a term that is better-suited than 'S' or 'T' to convey it. And if you persevere, then by reflection on the work and the meanings of the two terms—by combining different aspects of the two meanings, by abstracting from the details in which they differ while retaining the common element, or by the importation of additional features—you might well arrive at an expression, 'R', say, that seems to you uniquely well-suited to convey Q's character, one that does full justice to it, that hits it off precisely: for you it is the *mot juste*. In any case, there is, for any aesthetic quality that conforms to the account sketched above, a simple answer to the question that arises about an aesthetic quality for which a metaphorical or quasi-metaphorical use of a word with a particular literal meaning is essential to the quality's description, the question, namely, 'How does that concept figure in the intrinsic nature of the experience of the item as possessing the quality?' For the experience is just one in which the act of perceiving the item is informed by the subject's regarding some part of the item's character as being uniquely well-caught by the concept: in perceiving the item the person regards the concept as being uniquely well-suited to convey an aspect of the item's character.

There is, of course, a correlative account of what it is for something to possess an aesthetic quality for which a particular metaphor or quasi-metaphor is essential to the quality's characterization, an account the exact details of which must be sensitive to the kind of item that is being considered, whether it is a natural thing or a work of art, for example. I shall illustrate the account with a single example. If a painting's dynamism, say, is such an aesthetic quality, what it is for a painting to be dynamic—to be a dynamic painting—is just for it to be such that 'dynamic' is uniquely well-suited to convey an aspect of it, considered as the painting it is (with all that that entails), and, accordingly, what all paintings have in common in virtue of their being dynamic is just that their constellation of non-aesthetic features, when perceived under the appropriate artistic category, and in light of the context of the work's creation (and so on), is such that 'dynamic' (or a synonymous term) is best-suited to capture the common character.

It will be clear that, if Sibley were to have held something like this kind of view for a large range of aesthetic qualities, it would explain, to a greater or lesser extent determined by how inclusive he took that range to be, why we fail to find in his work any attempt to explicate the connection between, on the one hand, the use of a term drawn from an alien domain to ascribe an aesthetic quality and, on the other, its primary use within that domain, or, in other words, what the relation is in which the aesthetic quality stands to the reference of the term in its home domain. For in the case of an aesthetic quality for which the metaphorical use of a term with a certain meaning is regarded as being uniquely well-suited to capture that quality, and for which the minimalist account holds, the only interesting question is whether it really is so suited in any particular case and what it is about the item that makes it so. But since what might make it so will vary from case to case, the question is to be resolved by criticism, not philosophy.

I am sure that this view is liable to attract the criticism that it fails to characterize the phenomenology of the perception and appreciation of aesthetic qualities. It will, of course, be readily conceded that agreement or disagreement about the aesthetic qualities of an item may well be expressed in agreement or disagreement about the appropriate metaphorical characterization of the item, but this agreement or disagreement is usually thought of as arising from the distinctive phenomenology of the perception of an item as possessing a certain aesthetic quality, agreement being founded in sameness, disagreement in difference, of phenomenology. However, for those aesthetic qualities for which it is offered as the right account—a wide range, I believe—this criticism seems to me to misfire. For I believe that there is less to the phenomenology of the perception of many aesthetic qualities than traditionally there has been thought to be (and which aestheticians have struggled to specify): agreement or disagreement is not a consequence of sameness or difference in phenomenology but constitutive of it. And there is no difficulty in accommodating what might be involved in the appreciation of such aesthetic qualities, if this is intended to capture, not just their recognition, but, as they are realized in an item, their contribution to the item's aesthetic value, or the positive or negative responses the qualities are liable to evoke, considered in themselves. A highly attractive feature of Sibley's view is his anchoring every kind of aesthetic quality in non-aesthetic qualities. He claims that both words the aesthetic use of which is 'quasi-metaphorical' and words which have no standard non-aesthetic use are linked to non-aesthetic features and are learned by the use of certain natural abilities, the former by noticing similarities, the latter 'by our attention being caught and focused in other ways', certain outstanding, remarkable or unusual phenomena 'catch[ing] the eye or ear, seiz[ing] our attention and interest, and mov[ing] us to surprise, admiration, delight, fear, or distaste'.[16] Furthermore:

most of the words which in current usage are primarily or exclusively aesthetic terms had earlier non-aesthetic uses and gained their present use by some kind of metaphorical shift. Without reposing too great weight on these etymological facts, it can be seen that their history reflects connections with the responses, interests, and natural features I have mentioned as underlying the learning and use of aesthetic terms. These transitions suggest both the dependence of aesthetic upon other interests, and what some of those interests are. Connected with liking, delight, affection, regard, estimation, or choice—*beautiful, graceful, delicate, lovely, exquisite, elegant, dainty*; with fear or repulsion—*ugly*; with what notably catches the eye or attention—*garish, splendid, gaudy*; with what attracts by notable rarity, precision, skill, ingenuity, elaboration—*dainty, nice, pretty, exquisite*; with adaptation to function, suitability to ease of handling—*handsome*.[17]

Now the literal references of terms that are used metaphorically (or quasi-metaphorically) to describe the aesthetic qualities of things are, of course, phenomena fit to interest us and to which we respond in a multitude of ways. And since these interests and responses are reflected in our interests in and responses to the aesthetic qualities for which we find these terms, used metaphorically, the indispensable characterizations, the appreciation of such qualities is no more problematic than the appreciation of aesthetic qualities of other kinds.[18]

---

[16] *Approach to Aesthetics*, 22.   [17] Ibid. 22 n. 18.

[18] This essay complements my examination of Sibley's essay 'Making Music Our Own' in my Critical Study of his *Approach to Aesthetics* and of Emily Brady and Jerrold Levinson (eds.), *Aesthetic Concepts: Essays after Sibley*, in *The Philosophical Quarterly*, 52/207 (April 2002). (The relevant part of this Critical Study is contained in Essay 6, §5.)

8

Musical Movement and Aesthetic Metaphors

1. The notion of metaphor (or the metaphorical) can be understood in a number of ways; there are different kinds of metaphor; and metaphors can serve a variety of functions. The function I am concerned with is that of characterization. For my present purpose, a characterization will count as metaphorical if it satisfies the following two conditions. The first is that it indicates a feature of something by using a term or phrase the primary application of which is restricted to a different domain. The second is that no secondary application to the domain referred to by the characterization has so established itself as to constitute a different sense, another (literal) meaning of the term or phrase, one that could in principle be fully mastered without a grasp of the primary application informing that mastery. By an aesthetic metaphor I mean a metaphorical characterization of some item that is intended to indicate some aesthetically significant feature or aspect of the item, the experience of which constitutes part of the aesthetic appreciation of the item.

It has often been stressed that the non-technical characterization of the materials of music (the sounds of instruments), the principal kinds of musical process (rhythmic, melodic, harmonic), and musical works themselves, is mostly in terms the primary application of which is to non-audible sensible and other qualities, and the ordinary language of musical description is rife with metaphor and other forms of figurative language. Now the first issue in the aesthetics of music concerns the nature of the principal kinds of musical process: What is the nature of these phenomena, the intentional objects of musical experience, and how far and by what means is it possible to capture their essence in language?

My question in this essay is somewhat narrower: what is the relevance of spatial aesthetic metaphors—metaphorical characterizations drawn from the language of space—to understanding the phenomena of rhythm, melody, and harmony? And my target is the view that spatial aesthetic metaphors are located at the heart of music. This kind of view has been championed, above all, by Roger Scruton, whose work I shall focus on.[1]

2. Scruton argues that 'the ways of hearing *sound* that we consider to be ways of hearing *music*, are based in concepts extended by metaphorical transference ... and this means that the ability to hear music is dependent upon the capacity for metaphorical transfer' (UM 79). The argument is founded on a claim about the nature of the basic perceptions involved in hearing music, a claim that concerns the concepts that inform these perceptions. The claim arises from a consideration of the difference between the experiences of hearing a pitched sound and hearing a tone, hearing temporal sequence and hearing rhythm, hearing change of pitch and hearing movement (of a melody, theme or phrase) from one note to another, and hearing aggregates of sounds (tones) and hearing harmony. The difference is alleged to be this: in the case of each of these pairs, a certain kind of metaphor, a different one in each case, is integral to the intentional object of the second member (but not the first). The reason that it is necessary to hear sounds under a certain concept (or set of concepts) understood metaphorically in order to hear a tone, rhythm, melody, and harmony is that this constitutes the very essence of the experience. It is the imaginative transference of these concepts to sounds—concepts the sounds cannot literally fall under—that renders the experience of hearing a sound that of hearing a tone, and so on. It is for this reason that it is impossible to eliminate from the description of the experience of music the complex system of metaphors that is built into it.

So 'sounds become music only when organized by concepts taken from another sphere' (333). What are these concepts? Briefly, for rhythm they are those of action, for melody those of movement, space, height, and depth, and for harmony, first, those of spaced, open, filled, hollow

[1] The majority of page references will be to his *The Aesthetics of Music* (Oxford: Clarendon Press, 1997), which is the definitive statement of his position. These references will consist of bare page numbers. References to the early version of his view, 'Understanding Music', in *The Aesthetic Understanding: Essays in the Philosophy of Art and Culture* (London and New York: Methuen, 1983), will have page numbers preceded by 'UM'.

(for chords), and second, those of geometrical relations between parts, the coming together and separating of movements, oppositions and agreements, tension, relaxation, conflict and resolution (for harmony in the structural and dramatic sense).[2] To hear a tone is to hear a sound with rhythmic, melodic, and/or harmonic implications, the implications being informed by the concepts integral to these processes. Accordingly, '[Tones] have properties that no sound could have: for example, they occupy positions in an acousmatic[3] space; they attract and repel one another; they point towards and away from one another, and carry the mysterious movement that flows through music' (161).[4] So, in short, Scruton's claim is that the object of musical experience cannot be described without using metaphors of space, movement and animation, and the reason is that the intentional content of the experience of hearing sounds as music is partly constituted by the concepts of these phenomena: to hear sounds as music is to hear 'unreal movement in imaginary space' (239): 'sounds are transfigured into tones—into metaphorical movements in metaphorical space' (364).

How convincing is this account of the nature of the basic perceptions involved in hearing sounds as music? What is it to hear sounds under these concepts understood metaphorically? Is there an alternative account of the differences between the members of each of the above pairs (i) which dispenses with the notion of metaphor, (ii) which makes no reference to the concepts Scruton identifies? To evaluate the claim that the basic perceptions of music are informed by spatial concepts understood metaphorically, it is necessary to grasp Scruton's theory of metaphor, which has largely been neglected.

3. The conception of metaphor that Scruton puts forward does not issue in a crystal-clear account of what it is for the experience of music to 'involve' the metaphors he identifies. It is therefore unsurprising that nobody has yet managed to extract such an account from Scruton's text and to evaluate

---

[2] In the course of his magnificent discussion of tonality, Scruton allows (I simplify somewhat) that the ideas of 'attraction and repulsion', or 'saturation and unsaturation', or 'pain and soothing', might be as fitting as 'tension and release' (266).

[3] To hear a sound acousmatically is to attend to it as it is in itself, independently of whatever its cause may be.

[4] This 'mysterious' movement is implicated in each of rhythm, melody, and harmony. Moreover, the organization of music effected by the concept of movement 'is perceived not merely as movement, but as gesture' (333). The upshot is that 'we hear music as life' (339), as (self-)conscious life: 'In hearing the movement in music we are hearing life—life conscious of itself' (353).

it. The basic idea is that a metaphor—one that is being used 'to describe how the world seems, from the point of view of the active imagination', rather than 'to convey a truth about the material world' (91)—is the verbal expression of a fusion of two experiences, that is to say, the verbal expression of an experience with 'double intentionality', the intentional content of the fused experience consisting of one asserted and one unasserted thought, the experience being one that is directed towards two 'appearances' simultaneously, the subject's response to each appearance being fused with his response to the other. This experience is deemed one of imaginative perception, 'the coming-together in a single perception of asserted and unasserted thought' (90). It follows that the crux of Scruton's view of the nature of musical experience, which is sometimes expressed as music's being the object of a metaphorical perception (e.g. 342, 353), can be elucidated without reference to the notion of metaphor.[5] The essential claim is that the experience of hearing sounds as music has two intentional objects, on the one hand, sounds and silences, on the other, life and movement (for short (96)), the intentional content of the experience at any time being composed of an asserted thought, concerning the sounds and silences, and an unasserted thought, concerning life and movement (*in* the sounds and silences).

4. But before I continue, I want to distance myself from a common criticism of Scruton's use of the notion of metaphor in the articulation of the nature of musical experience. Jerrold Levinson is among those who have expressed sympathy with this criticism.[6] While appearing to accept the idea that the experience of hearing music is an experience of imaginative perception of the kind Scruton indicates, Levinson objects to Scruton's characterizing the experience in terms of metaphor, on the ground that Scruton has failed adequately to justify the claim that the basically *linguistic* idea of metaphor illuminates the experience. But this criticism is shallow and fails to engage with the substance of Scruton's position. Scruton claims that what we experience in hearing rhythm, melody, and harmony has to be described in metaphorical terms, by which he means terms known not to apply to the material object of perception (sounds). If this claim, which Levinson does not oppose, is true, it *would* throw light on the experience, despite its being a linguistic matter—as long as we understand the point of the metaphors.

---

[5] This is one reason why it is fruitless to contest Scruton's conception of metaphor.
[6] See his review of *The Aesthetics of Music*, in *The Philosophical Review*, 109/4 (October 2000), 608–14.

Scruton's original version of his view was hamstrung by the lack of an interpretation of the metaphors.[7] But this defect is remedied in the later version (which is the one Levinson is responding to), where Scruton is well aware that he must provide an interpretation of the metaphors he regards as essential to the description of musical experience: 'To say that a given usage is metaphorical is to say nothing definite, without some theory of metaphor' (52). However, to do justice to Scruton's view it is necessary, not just to interpret it in accordance with the theory of metaphor he proceeds to outline, but to acknowledge his reason for considering the system of metaphors he identifies to be ineliminable: this yields the interpretation he intends. And what the criticism that Levinson embraces fails to recognize is that, on the conception of metaphor Scruton puts forward, the nature of the basic perceptions involved in hearing sounds as music *is* illuminated by the idea of metaphor precisely because the metaphors required to characterize rhythmic, melodic, and harmonic processes are the linguistic expressions of these perceptions. So the insistence that metaphor is basically a linguistic idea fails to undercut Scruton's position. Furthermore, if spatial (and other) concepts figure in the experience of music in the manner Scruton claims, then the description of music in terms of those concepts will indeed be metaphorical. But it is misguided to focus on the idea of metaphor and leave untouched Scruton's introduction of spatial concepts into the heart of music: the real issue is the viability of Scruton's claim that the intentional content of musical experience is partly constituted by these concepts.

5. To return to the main line of thought: What is the content of the unasserted thought involved in the fused experience of hearing (i) rhythm, (ii) melody, (iii) harmony in a succession of sounds?[8] Scruton's theory of metaphor will provide an elucidation of the basic perceptions of music only if there is a viable answer to this question. What is Scruton's answer?

---

[7] See Malcolm Budd, 'Understanding Music', *The Aristotelian Society*, Supplementary Volume 49, 1985 (nearly all of which is included in Essay 6).

[8] In fact, if an imaginative perception possesses double intentionality, there will always be *two* questions that need to be answered if the character of that perception is to be understood fully: first, the *nature* of the unasserted thought, and second, the *way in which* it occurs in the perception and so the *form* of the double intentionality. Kendall Walton indicates with exemplary precision the form of double intentionality integral to pictorial perception, as he understands it, when he characterizes the experience as one of imagining *of* one's seeing of the picture surface *that it is* the seeing of the pictured scene.

I propose to engage with this question by considering, first, melody. But melody involves sounds of different pitch. So a prior question is this: How are pitched sounds heard? What kind of characteristic of a sound is its pitch—its pitch as heard? What is the intentional content of the perception of pitch?

Before attending to these questions about pitch, it will be helpful to consider timbre. For here the matter seems clear. The timbre of a sounded note has a distinctive character, in the same sense as that in which the hue of a patch of material does (hence the expression 'tone colour'). Lacking terms the specific function of which is to stand for such characters (simple or complex), we refer to them in one or another of the following ways. The first is by specifying the instrument that produces the sound.[9] Of course, this will be a rough and ready characterization in two respects. First, the same note played in the same manner on different instruments of the same kind, different violins, for example, will not have exactly the same timbre (nor—to continue with the violin—will the same note played on two different strings of the same violin, or the same note played in different manners or at different places on the same string). Secondly, different notes played on the same instrument are liable to vary not just in pitch but also in timbre. The second way in which we describe timbres is by having recourse to terms drawn from other domains which strike us as appropriate: 'dull', 'brilliant', 'mellow', 'rich', 'thin', 'clear', 'lean', 'piercing', 'penetrating', 'sweet', 'dark', 'dry', 'crisp', 'round', 'soft', 'sparkling', 'sharp-edged'. Typically they will strike us as appropriate because of an apparent isomorphism between some aspect of the domain of timbre and the domain from which the characterizing terms are taken, the relations between the phenomena signified in the primary domain being

[9] The situation is much the same as with tastes and smells, for which we have few terms whose primary application is to those domains, and which, accordingly, we frequently refer to as 'the taste (smell) of . . .', or which we characterize in terms drawn from elsewhere. The case of colours is rather different in that we possess a set of general colour words covering the visible spectrum. But if we want to specify a hue more precisely than by using one of the general colour terms, most of us, lacking a mastery of a wide range of more specific colour terms, are reduced to indicating the colour by reference to something of that colour, which, if the reference is not to a particular but a kind of thing (lily/milk white, salmon pink, heliotrope—which can refer to the scent, as well as the colour of the flower), will itself in general be susceptible of greater precision. The idea that the exact qualitative character of colours, tastes, or smells cannot be expressed in language used literally—so that recourse to metaphor is essential—has no plausibility: colours, for example, *can* be given as determinate names as is required (as by the colour charts of paint manufacturers); and any detectible difference between two hues, smells, or tastes can be marked by the assignment of distinctive names to them.

similar in some manner to those of the features of timbre at which the terms are directed—any particular term used metaphorically to characterize a timbre deriving its significance from the relations between its referent in its primary application and the referents of other terms of its ilk.[10] If we use a term drawn from another domain, the phenomenon referred to in the primary application of the term constitutes no part of the nature of the character of the timbre described by the use of that term, and it is not necessary to hear the sound under that metaphorical description in order to hear the timbral character of the sound.[11] Of course, this does not rule out the possibility of applying a term taken from elsewhere to a timbre precisely in order to relate that timbre to the phenomenon referred to in the primary application of the term. The point is just that its being heard as standing in that relation is not essential to hearing its distinctive character. So the relation between the nature of a particular timbre and the extra-auditory phenomenon in terms of which it is characterized is not that the concept of that phenomenon is included in the concept of that timbre. Put differently: the specification of the intentional object of the experience of a sound's timbre does not require, of necessity, a reference to that phenomenon.[12]

6. Now to pitch. I begin with the nature of the experience of pitch *as such*, rather than the nature of the experience of pitch when sounds are heard as constituents of music, or when sounds are heard as elements in melodic and harmonic processes. The distinctive character of the experience of hearing difference of pitch is that sounds of different pitch are experienced as ordered along a continuum where the ordering is not effected by the varying strength of some feature heard in the sounds—by the degree of some quality that the sounds are heard to possess—the two directions along the continuum usually being characterized as 'up' and 'down', a sound of one pitch being said to be 'higher' or 'lower' than a sound of another pitch.[13]

[10] Compare Nelson Goodman, *Languages of Art* (London: Oxford University Press, 1969), 71–2.

[11] I am leaving aside those terms that have been taken from the realm that was the extension of their primary application, have been applied to a new realm, and over time have acquired a new (literal) sense, or terms that now have a univocal sense extending over two realms: their original realm and the realm of timbre. The use of such ambiguous or unambiguous terms to characterize timbres does not change the picture.

[12] Compare the metaphorical use of colour terms, for example, as with 'blue mood' and 'black heart'. What holds for timbre I consider to be true of many other metaphorical descriptions of music—of musical textures (itself a metaphor) as 'thick', 'thin', 'transparent', 'luminous', or 'dissolving', for example.

[13] See Malcolm Budd, *Music and the Emotions* (London: Routledge and Kegan Paul, 1985), 41–3.

For pitch as such, it seems clear that the terms 'high' and 'low', 'higher' and 'lower', do not import an essential reference to relative spatial height. Even when these terms first came to be used (as metaphors) to characterize the pitch of sounds they were doing duty for predicates—predicates we lacked—standing for a specifically audible characteristic of sounds; and now, when these terms are used to characterize the pitch of sounds, we no longer lack the predicates, for 'high' and 'low', in this use, have become them.

Scruton appears to maintain *of pitch as such* that 'we hear the pitch continuum as though it were a dimension', 'up' and 'down' indicating 'a movement up and down, towards and away from, in two-dimensional [?] space' (20–1). This cannot be right: it is clear that the pitch continuum is not *constituted* by sounds being brought under spatial concepts (really or imaginatively); on the contrary, sounds have a character, *pitch*, that can be heard, recognized, discriminated, without this character being brought under spatial concepts. In fact, unless this were so, it would not be possible to hear sounds of different pitch as constituting different tones. But I take Scruton to intend, not the over-strong claim, but the weaker thesis that when sounds are heard as tones they are heard as located along a spatial dimension—which requires that sounds are heard as having a character, *pitch*, that does *not* consist in their being thought of under spatial concepts. In other words, to hear sounds as the materials of music it is essential to hear (imaginatively) sounds of different pitch as falling under concepts of relative height. The question is whether there is good reason to embrace this view.

7. If there is such a reason it must stem from the musical implications implicit in hearing a sound as a tone. Of these, only the melodic and harmonic are relevant, rhythm not being dependent on difference in pitch. Scruton's principal consideration arises from his conception of melody: 'tones, unlike sounds, seem to contain movement. This movement is exemplified in melodies, and can be traced through a "musical space", which we describe in terms of "high" and "low"' (UM 80). For Scruton a melody is a particular kind of temporal *Gestalt*, one that has a beginning and ending, which moves on through changes of pitch, and functions as a 'reidentifiable particular' (40) or 'musical individual' (71 ff.) in the sense, not of something that cannot be in two places at the same time (73), but of something that can 'reappear in another context, and undergo change' (72). In hearing a melody we hear a *movement* (which is still

going on in any silences that compose the melody) (47–8): 'what we hear in melody is not just change but *movement*' (49)—melody 'is change of a particular kind—the change that we know as movement' (49); and movement involves 'a spatial frame, an occupant of that frame, and a change of position within it' (49)—it requires 'both a spatial dimension, and objects that occupy positions within it' (50). Now Scruton recognizes, of course, that 'a tone . . . is inseparable from the pitch at which we hear it', so that no tone moves from one pitch to another and no tone is ever heard as doing so (50–1). And Scruton emphasizes that 'Musical space, and musical movement, are not even *analogous* to the space and movement of the physical world', everything 'that constitutes space as a frame *in* which objects are situated as occupants [being] absent from the pitch continuum' (51). So if when we hear a melody we hear a movement taking place, what constitutes it? What exactly do we imagine when we hear a melody? More precisely, what is the content of the unasserted thought integral to hearing a melody in a sequence of sounds?

It is here that we encounter a difficulty. For if we study Scruton's texts, in places we find him asserting that we hear the sounds (93, UM 94) or the tones (19) as moving. In both 'Understanding Music' and *The Aesthetics of Music* we find the assertion that if reference to space were to be eliminated from the description of (the experience of) music, 'tones would no longer move towards or away from each other' (93, UM 85). And he states:

It is true that the terms used to describe music *refer* to material sounds. But they refer to them under a description that no material sound can satisfy. Sounds do not move as music moves . . . Nor are they organized in a spatial way, nor do they rise and fall. Yet this is how we hear them when we hear them as music.

(93; cf. UM 86)

But this is not a viable view, if the movement is supposed to occur along the pitch continuum. For given that the identity of a tone is tied to its pitch level, to hear tones as moving towards or away from one another along the pitch continuum would be to hear something *that lacks sense*, an impossible accomplishment.[14] Accordingly, the unasserted thought, which gives the

---

[14] The 'virtual causality' that Scruton attributes to tones—'each note of a melody being heard as the effect of the one preceding it' (79)—does not give rise to a comparable problem (at least where this causality is not the 'causality of reason' (76)), for there is nothing inherently absurd in imagining one

movement component of the intentional content of the experience of hearing a melody, could not be 'This tone is moving up to this one, which is moving down to this one . . . '.[15] In other words, my perception of a melody is not one in which I imagine *that* tones (sounds heard in a certain manner) are moving from place to place.

What other possibilities are there? One idea would be to exploit the possibility of imagining a sound to be something other than it is: to hear a melody in a sequence of sounds we imagine *of* the tones we hear that they are (two-dimensional)[16] spatial items, items other than sounds, located not in physical space but in a space of their own, a 'phenomenal' space.[17] But this suggestion does not go far enough. For, as it stands, it would not introduce the movement we are supposed to hear a melody performing. So it would need to be supplemented. Are we supposed to imagine these spatial items moving along a spatial dimension from position to position? Or are we to imagine another occupant of this 'phenomenal' space that moves along a spatial dimension from the position of the first of these items to the position of the last?[18] Neither of these is a plausible supplement: in listening to a melody we do not hear tones as moving along some (indeterminate) spatial dimension, nor do we hear something other than the tones moving in this manner. So whichever of these additions were to be made to the proposed act of imagination, it is clear that this act would not be a necessary condition of undergoing a perceptual experience the intentional object of which is a melody. Furthermore, it would not do to represent the

sound to be the cause of another. Nevertheless, I am sceptical about the frequency with which tones are heard to possess virtual causality, to be the immediate causes of their successors. Characteristically, our perception of music is informed by our awareness of the notes as being produced intentionally by some external cause or other—which is consistent with the 'acousmatic' experience of sound, since the listener may well not be concerned to *identify* the cause. (This is not to acquiesce in the idea that the appreciation of music requires the adoption of the acousmatic posture: on the contrary, our perception of music is properly often coloured by our awareness of the nature of the cause—the range of the instrument and the degree of difficulty of producing on it such a realization of the music, for example.)

[15] The natural understanding of the notion of an unasserted thought requires the thought to be a complete proposition.

[16] 'A tone has *volume*: it seems to fill another dimension of musical space, a dimension of "thickness", quite independent of that established by the pitch continuum' (75). (In fact, of course, volume, unlike thickness, implies *three* dimensions.)

[17] There is perhaps a hint of this suggestion in the cloudy discussion at *The Aesthetics of Music*, 74–5.

[18] This additional occupant could not be the melody itself, which is not an entity over and above the sounds and silences that compose it: when a melody is said to move from one tone to another, the melody is not an individual that moves its location from position to position.

unasserted thought in the imaginative perception of a melody to be the mere thought of movement in space taking place, of something changing its spatial location, without the moving item being definitely conceived. For the mere imagination of movement—movement unattached to the basic constituents of music—concurrently or somehow 'fused' with hearing a series of sounds of different pitch as having a beginning and an ending would not yield the idea of melody as consisting of movement in the sense Scruton desires.

Scruton's emphasis on hearing movement (and other phenomena)[19] *in* sounds and the parallel, in certain respects, with pictorial perception[20] that he draws, might suggest that we hear music as having a representational (depictive) content—a content concerning movement (amongst other things). That is to say: we hear movement in sounds in the same sense that we see scenes in marked opaque surfaces. But this is not Scruton's position.[21] (If it had been, it would have been wrong to represent musical movement as being a metaphor.) And the view cannot be right, for the analogy between musical and pictorial perception (whether of still or moving pictures) fails to hold in crucial respects. In pictorial perception we perceive objects as lying in some physical space (no matter how the appearance of its spatial features diverges from that of the physical space that surrounds us), and a picture can depict (immediately) only something that has a visual appearance. But Scruton locates tones in an acousmatic, phenomenal space, and movement, as such, has no audible appearance, and so cannot be heard in the relevant (immediate) sense.[22] Hence, the

---

[19] The prime phenomenon is *movement*: 'Musical movement . . . is exemplified in all musical organ-ization' (55). But musical movement is heard, not just as movement, but as action.

[20] Scruton prefers to call representational seeing 'aspect perception' (86–7). In his *Art and Imagination* (London: Methuen, 1974) he maintains that it is impossible to give an independent specification of the thought involved in the seeing of an aspect (pp. 118–19). But the supporting reasoning is defective, and I have ignored the possibility that a similar claim might be made about the unasserted thoughts of movement and life supposedly involved in the experience of rhythm, melody, and harmony.

[21] 'If we hear movement in sounds this is not because the sounds convey to us the thought of a fictional world, in which things are moving. The experience of movement is here *primitive*, and depends on no representational thought' (139). 'I have argued that music is not representational, since thoughts about a subject are never essential to the understanding of music' (138). And: 'Although musical understanding involves the perception of imaginary movement, it is a movement in which nothing moves. Understanding requires no recuperation of a fictional world, and no response to imaginary objects' (211).

[22] We can hear a sound moving and we can hear something moving by means of hearing the changing positions of the various sounds it makes. But neither of these is to the point. To hear a

unasserted thought is not 'This (i.e. the item depicted by these sounds) is moving from one position to another . . . '.

Scruton draws a distinction between

the sequence of sounds and the movement of the tones that we hear in them . . . When we hear music . . . we hear something *in* the sound, something which moves with a force of its own. This intentional object of the musical perception is what I refer to by the word 'tone'. . .

(19–20)

But, as we have seen, the movement of a melody is not a matter of tones moving. Moreover, there is no imagined spatial movement of anything *between* tones—from one tone to another: when we hear a melody in a sequence of sounds this does not consist in our imagining something moving up and down a spatial dimension, as a bird might hover over a spot, descend towards that spot, move a little higher and so on, or as a yo-yo moves up and down its string, or something moving in two spatial dimensions, in a constant direction, say, while also changing height, as when a leaf is carried by the wind, or as the point of a pencil moves when drawing an undulating line across a page.

There is, of course, an obvious alternative to Scruton's view: a melody is a temporal *Gestalt*, with a beginning and end, and functions as a reidentifiable particular or musical individual, in the sense Scruton indicates, but to hear a melody is not to have a perception one part of the intentional content of which is a thought about *spatial* movement. A melody does move from one tone to another, but this movement is merely *temporal*, not spatial, progress in time, not space: the movement of a melody is constituted by the succession of the tones of different pitch that compose it, the relations amongst these tones being a matter of their positions on the pitch continuum, which is not itself a spatial dimension, although to a limited extent analogous to one, rendering terms that indicate relative positions along that dimension suitable as descriptions of relative positions along the continuum and terms indicating movement along the dimension suitable as descriptions of change of position along the continuum. Scruton dismisses this view (UM 84–5), claiming that it erases the distinction

---

melody is not to hear the constituent sounds as depicting a moving sound or to hear them as depicting the successive positions of other sounds.

between a sound and a tone. But to hear a tone is to hear a sound with rhythmic, melodic, and/or harmonic implications, and it is only on Scruton's spatialized conception of what these implications are that the distinction would vanish.[23]

In *The Aesthetics of Music*, he considers as an alternative to his view the suggestion, founded on the Kantian idea of a 'unity of the manifold' which is 'given' preconceptually, that a melody should be thought of as a temporal *Gestalt* organized preconceptually and argues that this would not be sufficient to hear a series of sounds as a melody (94–5). Now it is not necessary to embrace the idea of a temporal *Gestalt* organized preconceptually to have a conception of melody different from Scruton's: it suffices that the organization should be effected conceptually, but not by means of the concepts of space and movement in space. But in any case Scruton's argument consists merely in emphasizing the necessity of hearing in a series of sounds *direction*, upward and downward movement understood spatially, rather than progression from part to part of the (non-spatialized) pitch continuum, in order to hear a melody in the series. Without a plausible account of the unasserted thought about spatial movement that is supposed to be partly constitutive of hearing a melody in a series of sounds, this insistence is unconvincing.[24]

The fact is that 'movement' is not restricted to mean change in spatial location, but can be used to mean change along a non-spatial continuum or with respect to some discrete variable, no reference to spatial movement being intended or implicated. If there is no reason to insist that we hear a melody move from one tone to another in some spatial sense, then the idea of melodic movement should not be thought of as an aesthetic metaphor. If melodic movement consists in a melody's progression from one tone

[23] In the early articulation of Scruton's view, the feature of 'orientation' is taken to be definitive of space, orientation being 'present whenever there is "incongruity", of the kind displayed between an object and its mirror image' (UM 82). And Scruton asserts that if the experience of space were to be removed from the experience of music, we would cease to hear orientation in music, and so would no longer hear musical movement, with the consequence that we would no longer be hearing sounds as music. I take it that the reason this consideration has been dropped from *The Aesthetics of Music* is that Scruton came to recognize that it is not compelling.

[24] There is one puzzling remark that Scruton makes which, reflected upon, appears to draw back from the idea that the notion of melody involves the concept of spatial movement: 'Music shows us movement without the thing that moves; it can therefore present us with a reality that we know otherwise only through the workings of consciousness—movements outside physical space' (341). But the workings of consciousness are not spatial movements outside physical space.

to another of different pitch, then, given what I have said about pitch, it follows that it is *literally* true that a melody moves up and down.[25] But since the literal/metaphorical distinction is liable to cloud the issue, it is better not to insist on this point but to reiterate that there is no plausible content for the unasserted thought of spatial movement that is alleged to transform a perception of change of pitch into a perception of melodic movement.

8. The nature of chords, which, for Scruton, 'provide the primary experience of a spatial (as opposed to a temporal) *Gestalt* in music' (71), fails to advance his position.[26] For if the phenomenon of melody fails to support the view that when sounds are heard as tones they are heard as located along a spatial dimension, what reason is there to accept the idea that when we hear tones sounding concurrently as a chord, we hear the tones (imaginatively) as arranged along a spatial dimension ('vertically'), rather than spread out along a non-spatial continuum—the pitch continuum? Scruton suggests that the existence of such *musical individuals* as chords, motifs, and melodies, the 'true objects of musical understanding', 'compel[s] us to think of music as spread out in acousmatic space' (32). But, as he himself emphasizes, musical individuals are not concrete particulars (73), and their ability to reappear in other contexts and undergo change is shorn of the implications that are carried by the corresponding ability of concrete particulars.

9. What about rhythm? Scruton identifies a number of variables in the rhythmic organization of music: 'A rhythm is not one process but many (measure, division, stress, and accent), organized and overlaid by grouping. To hear a rhythm is already to hear a simultaneity of coalescing movements, in a placeless and transparent medium' (338).[27] But his conception

[25] Compare Stephen Davies, *Musical Meaning and Expression* (Ithaca, NY and London: Cornell University Press, 1994), 235–6.

[26] I leave harmony aside for two reasons. First, as far as the idea of movement is concerned, Scruton's account of harmony introduces no new considerations. Secondly, the notions of tension, relaxation, conflict, and resolution, which are integral to harmony, raise different issues from the ones I am concerned with in this essay.

[27] In fact, Scruton identifies nine 'variables in rhythmic organization' (24–31). But these so-called 'variables' are of categorially different kinds, not all of them being essential elements of the 'objective correlate' of the experience of rhythm, essential constituents of the intentional object of the experience of rhythm, i.e. essential elements or constituents of rhythm itself—as with the distinction between simple and compound rhythm, or the idea of cross-rhythm.

of rhythm—'In hearing rhythms, we are hearing a kind of animation' (30)—appears to be based above all on the phenomenon of beat: 'The beat in music is comparable to the heartbeat—the regular, but flexible, throbbing upon which our life depends' (24): 'To hear rhythm is to hear a kind of animation. Rhythm involves the same kind of virtual causality that we find in melody. Beats do not follow one another; they bring each other into being, respond to one another, and breathe with a common life' (35) ['life conscious of itself as life' (35)]. So we experience rhythm 'as a form of life' (50): 'Even so basic a phenomenon as rhythm turns out, on examination, to be a multivalent ordering of pulses, in which life and rationality are miraculously fused, as they are fused in the human person' (337). Scruton does not elaborate the notion of movement as it is supposed to figure in rhythm. But if we take the comparison with the heartbeat as our guide, the idea would be, not that of something moving along a dimension from one spatial location to another, but that of something contracting and dilating, as with the systole and diastole. However, to build this idea of movement into the experience of rhythm in music represents the intentional content of this imaginative perception as (always) involving the unasserted thought of three-dimensional space, which is an extravagant misrepresentation; and no other form of movement would fare better, for to hear rhythm—acousmatically—is not to hear imaginatively any kind of spatial movement. Furthermore, it is mistaken to attribute virtual causality to rhythm as an essential component: at the basic level, we hear rhythm in music, not as beats causing one another to come into being, but as an intentionally designed process in which sounds and silences are grouped into units in which an element is heard as accented relative to the others, patterns of stressed and unstressed moments. This is not to say that we never hear rhythm as a form of animation, imagining the tones to be the expression of pulsations of life, perhaps imagining the tones 'from within' as the expression of the pulsations of our own life. But what is possible is not what is necessary, and this kind of imaginative perception is not (partly) constitutive of the experience of rhythm.

10. The view that spatial aesthetic metaphors (understood as indicating unasserted thoughts about spatial movement as essential components of imaginative perceptions) are integral to the perception of rhythm, melody,

and harmony is, I believe, wide of the mark. Spatial aesthetic metaphors do not figure in the experience of music at this foundational level. On the one hand, it seems that there is no viable account of the contents of the unasserted thoughts about spatial movement that are postulated constituents of the perception of rhythm and melody, and, on the other, that the character of the intentional objects of melodic and rhythmic perception can be specified without making use of the concept of movement in space. Accordingly, the intrinsic natures of rhythm, melody, and harmony are not owed to concepts the primary application of which is to space and its occupants and which are applied metaphorically to the basic musical processes, capturing their essence: the concept of movement in space is not implicated in them.[28] This means that, as far as the concept of spatial movement is concerned, neither an extreme 'purist' view of music, which considers the perception of music to be free of all concepts of extra-musical phenomena, nor a purist or 'formalist' conception of musical value—that the musical value of 'abstract music' is always 'specifically musical', never a function of the way that any extra-musical phenomenon is 'realized' ('figures') in the music—is at once ruled out by the very nature of music. But it does little or nothing to establish either of these positions. For, first, it does not follow from the fact that the concept of movement in space is not integral to the perception of rhythm, melody, or harmony that this perception is devoid of all concepts of extra-musical phenomena. If it is not, the extreme purist view will collapse immediately, whatever these phenomena may be. But the effect on the purist conception of musical value will depend on the character of the phenomenon (or phenomena), as can be seen from the fact that the inclusion of the idea of bare spatial movement in the content of the perceptions of rhythm, melody, and harmony would be less threatening than would be the case if the spatial movement were to be heard as gesture and music were to be heard as life conscious of itself, as Scruton maintains. Secondly, even if no concept of an extra-musical phenomenon is an essential element of the perception of the most basic musical processes—if their nature is 'specifically musical'—a work composed of rhythmic, melodic, and harmonic processes might well be such that its value as music is dependent

---

[28] The fact that the idea of movement in space is not built into the experiences of rhythm, melody, and harmony does not imply that music never invites or encourages the imagination of spatial movement. On the contrary, it frequently does—as it does other kinds of imagination.

upon a relation in which it stands to phenomena outside music. Moreover, the possibility would remain that this must be so if a musical work is (i) valuable as music, or (ii) rightly thought of as having a value comparable to that of the greatest works in other art forms, the representational arts in particular.[29]

[29] I am grateful to David Landells, Hallvard Lillehammer, and Peter Lamarque for their insightful comments on a draft of this essay.

9

Aesthetic Realism and Emotional Qualities of Music

1. Aesthetic Realism and Anti-Realism

The primary philosophical issue about aesthetic properties is not whether attributions of them can properly be thought of as being genuine assertions which are, at least in some cases, true or false (given minimalism with respect to truth and assertoric content, it is clear that they can be) nor whether their truth-value can be evidence-transcendent (it cannot) nor whether the properties they attribute are response-independent (at least some are not) nor whether they claim and, at least in many instances, are such as to allow the possibility of intersubjective validity (they do). It is, instead, an issue about the nature of the canonical basis on which judgements of an item's aesthetic properties are made. This canonical basis is a perceptual or imaginative experience of the item as possessing the property or properties. The question is what this canonical basis includes, in addition to a representation of the item's non-aesthetic properties in which the aesthetic property is realized. Does it include a further representational state or aspect or some non-representational element (or perhaps a combination of the two)? By a representational state I mean, not just a state that possesses intentionality, but one that represents the world as being a certain way: the possession of a thought-content is not sufficient for a psychological state to be representational. Both desire and pleasure are intentional states, but neither is representational: desire wants the world to be a certain way (but does not represent it as being that way) and pleasure, whether propositional or not, is not itself a representation but a reaction (of delight) to the way the world is represented as being. It is sometimes maintained that the most important philosophical issue about aesthetic properties is whether the claim to intersubjective validity built into attributions of them is warranted. This may well be true: I believe it is. Nevertheless, the nature of the canonical basis for making such attributions is the primary issue, for without an understanding of this it will remain unclear how scepticism about the claim to intersubjective validity might be removed by establishing the credentials of a judgement that attributes an aesthetic property to an item.

'Aesthetic realism' can mean many things. One sense that might be given to the idea of aesthetic realism can be expressed in terms of the canonical basis for a judgement about an aesthetic property: a realist about aesthetic properties construes the experience that is the canonical basis for the attribution of an aesthetic property to an item as being through and through representational, the representational content of the experience not being such that nothing in the world can answer to it; an anti-realist maintains that the experience essentially involves a non-representational element—pleasure or displeasure, an emotion, feeling or attitude, for example.[1] If the canonical basis for the attribution of an aesthetic property is solely representational, then disagreement between two observers, each of whom has the appropriate cognitive stock, will indicate a representational failure in at least one of them[2] and the intersubjective validity of attributions of the property will be, not just possible, but an unproblematic notion; if it is not, and disagreement arises from a difference in the non-representational element, the idea that attributions of the property can nevertheless possess intersubjective validity, which idea is built into our understanding of judgements about the aesthetic properties of an item, will depend on sense being given to the idea of a fault of some other kind. An exceptionally clear case of how a canonical basis that is not representational might allow of the possibility of the intersubjective validity of judgements based on it is provided by Kant's theory of free beauty. The canonical basis for the attribution of what Kant called free beauty is disinterested pleasure in the contemplation of the object's structure, and this exhausts the perception of it as being beautiful, which does not represent it as having any non-relational

---

[1] I ignore error-theoretic anti-realism, which, on this representational construal of realism, maintains that the canonical basis is representational, but the representation is of such a nature that nothing can answer to it.

[2] I ignore the possibility that representations of aesthetic properties might faultlessly differ, as is perhaps the case with some of the colour-representations of human beings and honey bees.

property not included in the perception of its structure. And yet, although the canonical basis is a disinterested pleasure, rather than a representational state, if Kant's deduction of judgements of free beauty were to be sound, properly founded judgements would rightly claim intersubjective validity. Furthermore, the fault underlying disagreement between two observers, if each is really attempting a judgement of free beauty, would lie in one judgement not being supported by the proper basis.

Leaving aside the question of how the idea of an aesthetic property is best defined,[3] it is clear that the properties commonly recognized as aesthetic are of different kinds and grouped together they form a somewhat heterogeneous class. For example, the canonical basis for the attribution of aesthetic affective properties includes an emotion, the attribution expressing or implying a judgement of the emotion's appropriateness as a response to the item; but it is clear that an affective state is not always a component of the canonical basis for the attribution of an aesthetic property and it is doubtful whether some other kind of non-representational state must be a component. It follows that there may be no general solution to the primary issue and so to the question of aesthetic realism (understood in this representational manner).[4]

Although the characterization of aesthetic realism that I have offered is unexceptionable, its usefulness depends on the provision of an accurate description of the experience that constitutes the canonical basis of the attribution of an aesthetic property and a criterion for determining whether an experience that satisfies this description should be deemed represent-ational. Nevertheless, this characterization as it stands does identify the

---

[3] 'Aesthetic property' is a term of art associated with the work of Frank Sibley, who offered no definition of his notion of an aesthetic concept, although there is a certain confluence of opinion on the best way of defining the notion. If we consider the list Sibley gave to introduce the idea of aesthetic concepts, aesthetic properties are those properties the detection of which displays aesthetic sensitivity, which is to say those properties of an item relevant to an assessment of the item's aesthetic value, which are dependent upon lower-order properties of the item, and which a subject can experience the item as possessing—in many cases (but not all) by perceiving the item to possess the property. But perhaps there is no good reason to think that Sibley's examples pick out a well-defined class. However, for the principal concern of this essay—the attribution of emotion qualities to music—any indefiniteness of or heterogeneity within the class of aesthetic properties is immaterial.

[4] An alternative conception of realism, founded, not on the canonical basis of a judgement about an item's aesthetic properties, but on the content of the judgement itself, might discriminate against realism about aesthetic properties if the content of a judgement that attributes an aesthetic property to an item—or the commitment of one who makes the judgement—includes the idea of the item's meriting a certain response.

crux of the issue whether the predicates of sentences that, taken at face value, attribute aesthetic properties, really do stand for properties that an observer can detect or fail to detect by scrutiny of an object—a view associated above all with Frank Sibley. For Sibley, the features attributed by the predicates of substantive aesthetic judgements are aesthetic properties, 'emergent' properties detectible in objects, properties that are dependent on the first-order properties of objects, aesthetic appreciation of an item essentially involving the gaining of knowledge of its aesthetic properties by means of ordinary perception and intelligence allied with the exercise of 'aesthetic perception' or 'taste'.

2. An Argument Against Realism

I begin by considering an argument that Roger Scruton has directed against 'any realist interpretation of emotional [and affective] qualities in works of art',[5] its target actually being the form of aesthetic realism and cognitivism embraced by Sibley. The argument is based on a crucial characteristic of a certain kind of metaphorical characterization of works of art.[6] Metaphorical characterizations of this kind are ones that are in a certain sense ineliminable or irreplaceable. Scruton tends to deploy the argument by a consideration of the use of emotion terms to describe works of art, pieces of music, in particular, and I shall follow him in this respect.

The argument runs as follows.[7] If the sadness attributed to a piece of music by describing it as sad is a property of the music, a property that we hear by hearing *that it is there*, this sadness must either be the same property

---

[5] *The Aesthetics of Music* (Oxford: Clarendon Press, 1997), 160. Scruton brings the argument I consider against a realist construal of emotional properties only, not affective properties. Although he does not make this clear, the argument he refers to in the quotation in the text consists of two parts, the first part being the argument I consider. The second part concerns affective qualities and maintains that in describing a work by using an affective term I am not merely expressing my own emotional reaction to the work but also recommending my response (*The Aesthetics of Music*, 154). I would prefer to put the point by saying that in describing a work in this way I commit myself to the work's being such as to merit or call for an emotional response of the kind in question.

[6] By metaphor Scruton understands 'the deliberate application of a term or phrase to something that is known not to exemplify it' (*The Aesthetics of Music*, 80). (I ignore the fact that as it stands this turns many lies into metaphors, which is not Scruton's intention.) Since not all aesthetic properties are attributed through words being taken from one context and applied in a context known not to exemplify them, the argument has a limited scope.

[7] *The Aesthetics of Music*, 153–4. See also p. 372.

as that possessed by a sad person or another property. But it cannot be the same property, the sadness of a person, which can be possessed only by a conscious organism. However, it cannot be another property, since:

it is precisely this word—'sad'—with its normal meaning that we apply to the music, and that is the whole point of the description. To say that the word ascribes, in this use, another property, is to say that it has another sense—in other words that it is not used metaphorically but ambiguously. If that were so, we could equally have used some other word to make the point . . .

Hence:

It follows that the word 'sad' attributes to the music neither the property possessed by sad people, nor any other property. It therefore attributes no property at all.

How forceful is this argument?

The obvious response to it is that the aesthetic property indicated by the metaphor, although different from the non-aesthetic property, might nevertheless be definable in terms of it.[8] The aesthetic property might be a relational property, the definition of which makes essential reference to the non-aesthetic property: the property attributed to a piece of music by describing it as sad might be the property of representing sadness, or that of resembling an expression of sadness, for example. So as it stands the argument is invalid. But the effectiveness of this response depends on whether a plausible definition of the required kind is (always) forthcoming. It is Scruton's view that it is not;[9] and if this is right and the point is added to the argument, the adorned argument is not open to the obvious response to the bare argument. I take it that Scruton did not intend the bare argument to stand alone (although in *The Aesthetics of Music* he invites misunderstanding by passing over the necessity of the supplementary point). I propose to assume, for the moment, that the aesthetic property indicated by the metaphor is not definable in terms of the non-aesthetic property signified by the metaphor taken literally. How else might the argument be countered?

[8] As Gary Iseminger in his review of *The Aesthetics of Music* (*The Journal of Aesthetics and Art Criticism*, 57/3 (Summer 1999)) has pointed out.
[9] See the arguments Scruton gives in his earlier work *Art and Imagination* (London: Methuen, 1974), 46 ff. against construing the meaning of aesthetic descriptions paronymously. (Contrast the view of W. Charlton, *Aesthetics: An Introduction* (London: Hutchinson, 1970), 94–5.) *Art and Imagination* contains the same argument against a realist interpretation of aesthetic properties: see pp. 38, 44.

3. A Realistic Alternative

Consider the following view of aesthetic descriptions that are metaphorical. The words used in these metaphors have their normal (literal) meaning, but such a metaphor expresses a thought, the content of which must be specified by a different concept from the one given by the normal meaning of the word that is used metaphorically. The connection between the concept embedded in the thought and that associated with the sentence is that the acquisition of the first concept is causally dependent on the possession of the second (so that it is not a mere coincidence that the same word is used, in the one case metaphorically and in the other literally, for the two concepts). And it is not possible to express the concept embedded in the thought—the aesthetic concept—in non-metaphorical terms. In other words, the view maintains that it is necessary to distinguish two concepts, one of the aesthetic property, the other of the non-aesthetic property; it claims that the thought expressed by the aesthetic metaphor employs the first concept, and the thought expressed by the non-metaphorical sentence employs the second; it asserts that the acquisition of the aesthetic concept is causally dependent on the possession of the non-aesthetic concept; and it maintains that the only way that the content of the thought can be expressed in language is by the use of language metaphorically. This is the view of Nick Zangwill, who has directed it against Scruton's anti-realist argument.[10]

This is not an adequate response to Scruton's argument. But first, it is important to recognize the exceptional strength of the modal claim that the aesthetic concept cannot be expressed in non-metaphorical terms (or the aesthetic property cannot be described non-metaphorically). The claim is not that *we* possess concepts (or are aware of properties) that we do not possess the means to express (or describe) non-metaphorically, but that can in principle be so expressed (or described), and which (perhaps) could be captured non-metaphorically by us, if only we were able to construct the means. Rather, the claim is that these aesthetic concepts (or properties) are

---

[10] Nick Zangwill, *The Metaphysics of Beauty* (Ithaca and London: Cornell University Press, 2001), ch. 10. I have expressed the position in one of the ways Zangwill does—in terms of concepts—rather than the other—in terms of properties. Zangwill directs his criticism against the argument as it is formulated in *Art and Imagination*: as I have previously indicated, the argument is the same in the two works.

such that it is *logically impossible* that they should be expressed (or described) non-metaphorically.

Zangwill's defence of the modal claim consists of two parts. In the first place, he appeals to the existence of a 'companion in guilt'. Secondly, he argues that there is an essential connection between the two culprits, so that given what is true of its non-aesthetic companion, it is unsurprising that the same holds true for the aesthetic subject. The companion in guilt is alleged to be the phenomenological properties of 'inner experience'. The essential connection is the fact that aesthetic descriptions are based on inner experiences. His case rests on the idea that the exact phenomenology of an inner experience can be described only metaphorically: although we are aware of the intrinsic features of inner experiences, these features are such that it is impossible that they could be captured in non-metaphorical terms. He concedes that it is possible to classify inner experiences non-metaphorically, but maintains that such classifications will inevitably fail to capture the precise natures of inner experiences. Now it would certainly be a very curious fact, one demanding explanation, if there were items in the world that are amenable to non-metaphorical classification but that are such that beyond a certain level their precise character, of which we can be well aware, resists non-metaphorical but allows metaphorical specification. For if we can be aware of the properties of items of a certain kind, but lack names of them, it seems that nothing can stand in the way of our coining such names;[11] and if we can indicate a property by using a word metaphorically, what is to stop us from replacing the metaphor with a word designed precisely for the task for which the metaphor was being used? But it is not necessary to engage with this strange idea, for Zangwill provides no reason to accept, and offers no explanation of the alleged fact, that although inner experiences are such that they allow of non-metaphorical classification, there will inevitably come a point beyond which their exact phenomenology evades the use of terms understood literally.

So far I have said nothing about the claim that the acquisition of the aesthetic concept that forms part of the content of the thought alleged to be expressed by a metaphorical description of an aesthetic feature is causally dependent on the possession of the non-aesthetic concept which the word

---

[11] Compare colour descriptions, which, like aesthetic descriptions, are based on inner experiences: colours can be given as determinate names as are required (as by paint manufacturers).

used metaphorically signifies. Here Zangwill's position encounters a twofold difficulty. For, first, what is needed is an explanation of why the only causal route to the acquisition of the aesthetic concept is through the possession of the corresponding non-aesthetic concept. Not only does Zangwill fail to explain why it is that one cannot grasp the aesthetic concept without possessing the non-aesthetic concept, but no plausible line of thought seems available, certainly not one based on a conceptual connection between the contents of the two concepts (since there is not supposed to be one). The second difficulty is that the alleged causal connection would not give a satisfactory explanation of the use of the same word for the aesthetic property and the corresponding non-aesthetic property. Zangwill believes that it does: 'we can see why it is natural to use the same word to pick out aesthetic and nonaesthetic concepts of delicacy: given the ineliminability of aesthetic metaphor, there is no other'.[12] But the conclusion does not follow. For what the supposed ineliminability of aesthetic metaphor that Zangwill has argued for comes to is that, for aesthetic properties of the kind with which he is concerned, no such property can be specified in non-metaphorical terms; and this is much weaker than what is needed if the conclusion is to follow, which is the implausible thesis that for any such property there is only one metaphor that can indicate it. Furthermore, recourse could not be had to the alleged fact that the possession of one concept is causally dependent on the possession of another, for this does not make the word for the second concept an apt metaphor for the other, let alone the most appropriate or natural one.

However, whatever force the above considerations might be thought to have—they seem to me decisive—there is a more important consideration: Scruton's argument is not properly met by distinguishing two concepts, one of the aesthetic property, the other of the non-aesthetic property, and by asserting both that whereas the thought expressed by the aesthetic metaphor employs the first concept, the thought expressed by the non-metaphorical sentence employs the second, and that the acquisition of the aesthetic concept is causally dependent on the possession of the non-aesthetic concept. For the force of Scruton's argument is not adequately captured by the fact that an understanding of the aesthetic metaphor is based on an understanding of the literal use in the sense that understanding the literal use

---

[12] *The Metaphysics of Beauty*, 175.

is a causal condition of understanding the metaphorical use. His point is the stronger one, that an understanding of the metaphorical use must be *guided* by an understanding of the literal use of the sentence: the meaning of 'sad' used literally *informs* the correct interpretation of its aesthetic metaphorical use, for the point of using the term 'sad' is precisely to indicate or express a connection between the music and sadness—it is precisely to relate the music to sadness.[13] It seems to me clear, as I have argued elsewhere, that this stronger claim is true of the indispensable emotive metaphors that are Scruton's concern and therefore that the position Zangwill argues for is not a viable realistic alternative.[14]

4. Abandoning the Argument Against Realism

But, as we have seen, Scruton's argument for anti-realism needs more than the fact that the point of using the term 'sad', in the cases he has in mind, is to invoke a connection between the music and sadness. He must rule out the possibility that the aesthetic property ascribed by the metaphor is a relational property, the definition of which makes essential reference to the non-aesthetic property. Unless this can be done, the view that the canonical basis for the attribution of an emotional quality to a work of art is representational remains viable.[15]

How forceful are the arguments that Scruton marshals against the possibility of defining the aesthetic property attributed by an emotive metaphor

[13] This is plain enough in *The Aesthetics of Music*. See also *Art and Imagination*, 38–40. Frank Sibley had himself made a generalization of this point long ago in his ground-breaking 'Aesthetic Concepts'. Discussing the aesthetic use of such words as 'forceful', 'dynamic', 'tightly-knit', 'melancholy', 'balanced', 'taut', 'gay', which is at most quasi-metaphorical, he wrote: 'We do not want or need to replace them by words which lack the metaphorical element. In using them to describe works of art, the very point is that we are noticing aesthetic qualities related to their literal or common meanings. If we possessed a quite different word from 'dynamic', one we could use to point out an aesthetic quality unrelated to the common meaning of 'dynamic', it could not be used to describe that quality which 'dynamic' does serve to point out.' See 'Aesthetic Concepts', as reprinted in Sibley's *Approach to Aesthetics* (Oxford: Clarendon Press, 2001), 17.

[14] To readers of my *Music and the Emotions* (London: Routledge & Kegan Paul, 1985), ch. II, §13, it will be clear that Zangwill in effect embraces what I there called 'the purely sensible description thesis'—a thesis I take myself to have given compelling reason to reject.

[15] Note that an anti-realist does not need to deny that an aesthetic property ascribed by an emotive metaphor can be explicated by means of a definition that makes essential reference to the emotion. For the definition might be such that it yields the result that the canonical basis for the attribution of the emotional quality is not representational.

in terms of the property that the metaphor, understood literally, signifies? It is not easy to see how there could be a successful general argument against this possibility. According to Scruton's theory of metaphor, to explain a metaphor—an indispensable metaphor—is to explain the experience that it is designed to convey,[16] which experience must be characterized in terms of the phenomenon the metaphor designates when used literally. And this, he believes, rules out the possibility of defining the metaphorical use, any definition breaking the connection with its central use.[17] But not every definition breaks this connection and it is an open question whether a definition can capture the experience that a description of music in emotional terms is intended to convey. If no general argument is available, the best that might be done would be to draw up an exhaustive list of definitions which have at least some plausibility, and show each of them to be unviable. Scruton, understandably, does not attempt this somewhat nebulous task. In *Art and Imagination* the focus is again on sadness predicated of music, but the arguments have a very restricted scope and so, even if successful, do not achieve the goal.[18] For Scruton rejects two straightforward paronymous suggestions for what 'M is sad' means ('M makes me sad', 'M makes (or tends to make) people sad'), one suggestion that invokes a resemblance between the music and something that is sad paronymously ('M resembles a sad gesture'), and one that offers a definition in terms of the appropriate response to the sadness of a work of art, whatever this might be supposed to be (Scruton is sceptical whether there is any such thing). In *The Aesthetics of Music* it is unclear that any purported definitions of what it is for a piece of music to possess an emotional quality are examined and dismissed, for Scruton there targets, not various attempts to define the possession by music of an emotional quality, but certain attempts to define what it is for music to be expressive of emotion, which he distinguishes from mere possession.[19] But even if these are included along with the ones rejected in *Art and Imagination*, it is clear that Scruton's critique is not comprehensive enough to rule out the possibility of defining what it is for a piece of music to possess an emotional quality in terms of that emotion.

Scruton's adorned argument against a realistic interpretation of aesthetic properties ascribed by means of indispensable metaphors may well be sound.

---

[16] *The Aesthetics of Music*, ch. 3.   [17] Ibid. 153–4, 352–3.   [18] *Art and Imagination*, 46–8.
[19] On the distinction between expression and (mere) possession, see *The Aesthetics of Music*, 155ff., 344–5.

But I believe that the attempt to rule out the possibility that the aesthetic property ascribed by the metaphor is a relational property, the definition of which makes essential reference to the non-aesthetic property, either by some general argument or by the elimination of all candidates, should be abandoned: in advance of a positive account of the attribution of emotional qualities to music, there is too little to work on.

5. Anti-Realism and Evaluative Attitudes

Anti-realists about aesthetic properties standardly emphasize the alleged evaluative, rather than descriptive, nature or function of words that stand for aesthetic properties, this characteristic being thought of as being definitive of a sincere attribution of an aesthetic property, someone who sincerely attributes an aesthetic property having a favourable attitude to the instantiation of a positively evaluative property and an unfavourable attitude towards the instantiation of a negatively evaluative property. There are problems with this view,[20] but I shall not pursue them here, for as far as the emotional qualities of music are concerned, the view that their sincere attribution is expressive of an evaluation is wide of the mark: that I credit a piece of music with an emotional quality by itself implies nothing about whether or not I favour it. It is sometimes thought that the issue of realism arises only for those aesthetic properties, if any, that are evaluative in the sense that the sincere attribution of them expresses an evaluative attitude of the subject. But the distinction between those aesthetic properties that are in this sense evaluative and those that are not does not coincide with the distinction between those aesthetic properties for which the question of realism arises and those for which it does not. For the fact that an aesthetic property is not evaluative does not entail that the canonical basis for its attribution is through and through representational: non-evaluative aesthetic properties ascribed by means of indispensable metaphors admit the question of realism as readily as do evaluative aesthetic properties. It is one of the great merits of Scruton's work that he recognized this long ago.

---

[20] The most serious criticism is Jerrold Levinson's 'Aesthetic Properties, Evaluative Force, and Differences of Sensibility', in Emily Brady and Jerrold Levinson (eds.), *Aesthetic Concepts: Essays after Sibley* (Oxford: Clarendon Press, 2001).

6. Imagination and the Canonical Basis

The form of aesthetic realism that Scruton opposes maintains that the features attributed by the predicates of aesthetic judgements are aesthetic properties, 'emergent' properties detectible in objects, properties that are dependent on the first-order properties of objects, aesthetic appreciation of an item consisting in the gaining of knowledge of its aesthetic properties by means of ordinary perception and intelligence allied with the exercise of 'aesthetic perception' or 'taste'. Now Scruton does not insist on the compelling nature of the bare argument that he brings against this view and he is content, instead, to emphasize the special nature of emotional (and affective) qualities of works of art, which, following well-established usage, he is happy to describe as 'tertiary' qualities.[21] Given that there are no ordinarily perceptible, lower-level features that one who does not perceive an aesthetic property of some item is thereby blind to, it is understandable that Scruton likens the 'perception' of an aesthetic property to the perception of aspects or 'seeing-as' (aspects being paradigms of tertiary qualities). His position might be represented in this way: hearing the music's sadness is a matter not of hearing *that*[22] but of hearing *as*—hearing the music as sad. It is a form of imaginative hearing.

Now in *The Aesthetics of Music* Scruton does not present an account of the nature of the canonical basis for the attribution of sadness (or any other emotion) to music. This is because, as I have already indicated, he wishes to distinguish a piece of music's being sad from its being expressive of sadness and his preoccupation is with the musical expression of emotion, rather than the mere possession by music of emotional qualities, a musical work that expresses emotion necessarily being expressive, the expression of emotion by a musical work necessarily constituting success in communication. But if a piece of music's being sad is a necessary condition of its being expressive of sadness, as Scruton seems to hold,[23] an explication of the canonical basis for the attribution of the musical

[21] *The Aesthetics of Music*, 160.
[22] See Scruton's opposition to the idea that 'We hear the sadness [of the music] by hearing *that it is there*' (*The Aesthetics of Music*, 153).
[23] Ibid. 155. It is hard to be sure, since Scruton does not hold in general that music is qualified by what it expresses. See also ibid. 344–5.

expression of emotion requires an account of the canonical basis for the attribution of an emotional quality. The application of his theory of metaphor, while it does not deliver a full description of the canonical basis for the attribution of an emotional quality to music, yields this outline account: the concept expressed by the non-aesthetic use of the emotion term is a constituent of the intentional content of the experience of perceiving an item as possessing the aesthetic emotional property—a constituent that figures in an 'unasserted' thought, one of the two thought components of the experience. It is for this reason that only the non-aesthetic concept can serve as the right metaphor to characterize the item and why metaphor, that particular metaphor, is indispensable. Note that the fact that the experience possesses double intentionality does not imply that its representational content is twofold. The concept expressed by the non-aesthetic use of the term occurs in the content of a thought that is unasserted: the world is not represented as containing an item that falls under the concept—that is not how, in his or her experience, the world actually seems to the subject to be. Hence Scruton's view of aesthetic properties ascribed by an indispensable metaphor is anti-realist (by the representational criterion), in whatever way the description of the canonical basis might be filled in.

This outline account of the canonical basis for the attribution of an emotional quality to a piece of music is compatible with any number of imagination-based accounts that have been given of the experience of hearing music as having an emotional quality. It is compatible with the account Scruton offers in *Art and Imagination*, which represents the experience of hearing sadness in music as being 'in some irreducible way analogous to hearing the expression of sadness—say, in another's voice'.[24] It is, indeed, compatible with two that I have suggested: imagining of the experience of hearing the music that it is an experience of undergoing the emotion and imagining the music to be an occurrence of the emotion.[25] In so far as any imagination-based conception captures what is at issue in the attribution of emotional qualities to music, I am at one with Scruton in embracing an anti-realist view of the emotional qualities of music, although I prefer a different form of anti-realism from Scruton's.

---

[24] *Art and Imagination*, 127.
[25] Malcolm Budd, *Values of Art* (London: Allen Lane, The Penguin Press, 1995).

7. An Alternative Version of Anti-Realism

The essence of Scruton's anti-realism about aesthetic qualities of works of art attributed by metaphor is, as he presents it, that an aesthetic description of an object expresses and recommends a particular response to the object: the acceptance or sincere assertion condition for an attribution of an aesthetic property is not a belief but an experience. He defends an anti-realist theory of aesthetic description in *Art and Imagination*: in *The Aesthetics of Music* he develops an anti-realist account of musical expression but is not concerned to defend his anti-realist theory.[26] But in both works he expresses his anti-realism in terms of the idea of the acceptance or sincere assertion condition for an attribution of an aesthetic property to a work, requiring a person to have undergone a certain experience of the work in order to be in a position to accept or sincerely assert that the work possesses the aesthetic property, the acknowledgement or assertion being an expression of the experience.[27] This signals Scruton's commitment to what Richard Wollheim referred to as the Acquaintance Principle—a commitment I take to be unwise.[28] But this commitment is not essential to his view of aesthetic properties, which can easily be freed from it. For if the canonical basis of the attribution of an aesthetic property, which is an experience, is not through and through representational, it does not follow that the sincere assertion or acceptance condition is an experience, an actual response to the object of the attribution. And there is an attractive alternative to its being an experience: the sincere assertion or acceptance condition is a commitment to the object of the attribution being such as to require or merit a certain kind of non-representational response or to its being such that this kind of response is an appropriate one.

---

[26] *The Aesthetics of Music*, 367.

[27] See, for example, *Art and Imagination*, 49; *The Aesthetics of Music*, 367.

[28] See Essay 3, 'The Acquaintance Principle'.

10

On Looking at a Picture

1. When you look at Monet's *The Seine in Thaw*,[1] you are looking at a marked surface. But if you see it as Monet intended it to be seen, as a depiction of a river with melting ice drifting along it, you do not see it merely as a surface marked in a specific way, as you might see a puzzle picture or a Chinese character as a mere configuration of lines which means nothing to you. Yet neither do you see it as you would see the Seine if you were actually to see the Seine in thaw and were to recognize what you saw as a thawing river: your experience in front of the picture is not an experience of the same intrinsic nature as one of seeing and recognizing a thawing river. Nevertheless, your experience of the picture as a depiction of a river in thaw does appear to involve both an awareness of the marked surface and an awareness of what a thawing river looks like. For if it did not involve any awareness of the marked surface, you would not be taking yourself to be seeing a *depiction*, and if you were unaware of what a thawing river looks like, you would not see Monet's picture as a depiction *of a river in thaw*. The problem is to explain in what way your experience of Monet's picture involves a visual awareness of a marked surface and also a visual awareness of a river in thaw; and unless this problem can be resolved, the distinctive artistic values of depiction and the value of the experience of seeing a depiction of reality rather than the reality itself must remain uncertain.

[1] I was fortunate to have the opportunity of looking at this picture with Richard Wollheim when we attended a colloquium at Ann Arbor in March 1988. The painting is in the University of Michigan Museum of Art, Ann Arbor, and it is one of the two pictures reproduced in Wollheim's *Painting as an Art* (London: Thames and Hudson, 1987) that he had not seen when the book was published. In the essay I use Monet's picture only as an example of a river-picture (in Goodman's sense) and ignore the fact that it is a picture of a particular river, the Seine. I believe that the concept of an F-picture is more fundamental in the theory of pictorial representation than the concept of a depiction of a particular thing, and I am concerned only with the first concept.

But the idea of a visual awareness of a river is ambiguous. It covers both experiential and dispositional forms of visual awareness—experiential, as when you see a river or visualize one in the mind's eye; dispositional, as when you possess the capacity to recognize a river if you see one or to recall in your mind's eye how a river looks. Accordingly, a visual awareness of a river can be introduced into the experience of seeing Monet's picture either in an experiential or in a dispositional form, and in whichever way the visual awareness is recruited to the experience, this can take place in more than one way. If it is introduced in a dispositional form, the general idea is likely to be that the intrinsic nature of the experience of seeing Monet's picture as depicting a thawing river consists in the visual awareness of its surface, which is interpreted as a depiction of a thawing river on the basis of the spectator's awareness of how a river in thaw can look. But if it is introduced in an experiential form and it is also recognized that the experience of seeing Monet's picture involves an awareness of the picture's surface, then the experience will be credited with a complex intrinsic nature, containing an experiential awareness, presumably of different kinds, both of the marked surface and also of a river.

The outstanding advocate of the view that the experience of depiction should be understood in the second of these two ways was Richard Wollheim. He argued persuasively against certain alternative conceptions of the nature of pictorial experience, and in his book *Painting as an Art* he constructed an exceptionally rich and illuminating account of the art of painting founded upon his own conception of the experience of seeing what a picture depicts. His principal claim is that the experience of depiction is grounded in, and can be defined in terms of, a particular kind of visual experience, one which has a distinctive phenomenology involving a visual awareness not only of the marked surface, but also of what is depicted. What exactly is this special kind of seeing, and does it form a secure basis for the impressive structure erected upon it?

2. It will be helpful first to take a step backwards and reconsider the question of whether the experience of seeing Monet's depiction of a thawing river can be assimilated to the experience as of really seeing a thawing river. For there is a persistent tendency to construe pictures, especially those that are to some degree or in a particular respect realistic, as being in some way illusionistic. Can such an equation be so lightly dismissed? The natural

place to look for an answer to this question is the work of E. H. Gombrich, the most powerful advocate of the view that pictorial experience involves illusion; moreover, a consideration of his claims will be doubly useful, for Gombrich's position is one of the most important against which Wollheim defined his own.

One of Gombrich's principal contributions to the understanding of pictorial representation is the emphasis he placed upon the fact that any artist works in a medium and so is restricted in his representational ambitions by the limitations of his material, the ways in which the material—tapestry, lace, mosaic, pencil, oil paint—can be used artistically. But used to what purpose, if the purpose is to represent the world? Not, of course, to reproduce the subject; that is to say, to produce a replica or facsimile of it. Nor to reproduce the exact appearance of the subject. For—apart from certain exceptional cases in which the nature of the subject fits the medium perfectly—it is not possible to create a picture which looks exactly like what it depicts, except from a point of view that denies the spectator the normal visual access to the picture. It is because an artist's medium precludes the matching of his picture with its subject that, in Gombrich's words, 'no artist can copy what he sees'.[2] What, then, can the representational artist achieve? Gombrich's answer is that he can render his subject in terms of his medium; which is to say that he can transpose some of the relationships in his subject into the terms of the medium.

Now it might be thought to follow from the fact that there is in general no possibility of match between picture and subject that a picture must deliver to the spectator a different visual experience from one of the kind he would have if he were actually seeing what is depicted. But Gombrich is right to resist this conclusion, and he goes further when, in one of the accounts of realism or naturalism that he presents in *Art and Illusion*, he elucidates realism in terms of illusion. According to this account, in front of a realistic picture the spectator experiences the illusion that what is depicted is before his eyes, in the sense in which he might experience the illusion of seeing someone when looking into a good mirror. Gombrich repeatedly emphasizes that he rejects the equation of

[2] Gombrich makes this claim a number of times in *Art and Illusion* (London: Phaidon Press, 1962); see p. xi.

illusion with false belief, and also the weaker view that someone who experiences an illusion thereby has a false belief about his environment.[3] By an illusion he means a perceptual experience that is caused by a seen object but that represents the world differently from the way the object is. A visual illusion of a river is a visual experience as of seeing a river—a visual experience whose representational content is that there is a river before the subject—but one which is not actually the perception of a river. Making use of the convenient ambiguity of the notion of representational content, Gombrich's claim is therefore that the spectator of a naturalistic picture undergoes a visual experience whose representational content is identical with the representational content of the picture: if the picture depicts a certain state of affairs, the spectator's experience represents that state of affairs as really obtaining.

It is his theory of perception that allows Gombrich to combine the two claims that, first, no artist can copy what he sees and, second, realistic pictures induce illusions of what they represent. He concedes that if the spectator attends to the marked surface of the picture, he will be able to detect any number of differences between the picture and what it represents, so that his experience of the picture will not be an illusion of what it depicts. But there is another way in which the spectator can look at the picture, and he is required to adopt this different approach if he is to experience the picture as being a realistic depiction. Rather than attending to the nature of the marked surface of the picture, he must project onto it an image of what is absent, the subject it depicts. He is encouraged to do this by the picture in so far as it is realistic; and it is possible for him to do this because perception is not the passive receipt of information about the environment, but is grounded in the mechanism of projection. Since what image will be projected is underdetermined by the nature of the perceptual stimulus and is dependent upon the character of the subject's visual system, his mental set, and various other factors, disparities between the nature of the marked surface of the picture and the nature of what it depicts, which affect the light transmitted to the eye, do not preclude the possibility that the picture will create the illusion of seeing what it depicts. When the spectator's attention is not directed to the marked surface of the

[3] See, for example, E. H. Gombrich, 'Illusion and Art', in R. L. Gregory and E. H. Gombrich (eds.), *Illusion in Nature and Art* (London: Gerald Duckworth, 1973).

picture, differences are overlooked, gaps are completed, and the mechanism of projection operates to produce the intended illusion: the depicted scene apparently lies before the spectator, who 'sees' what is not there.

It is unnecessary to examine this theory of perception, for Gombrich's position, although consistent, is inadequate, as can most easily be seen by considering the qualifications he is forced to introduce. For in normal perception of a picture, information will be presented to the spectator's eyes which will affect his visual experience in such a manner that its representational content will not be just what it would be if the spectator were actually seeing the state of affairs depicted. Accordingly, Gombrich recognizes that the illusions he believes realistic pictures to be capable of inducing will rarely be complete, and in fact they will be complete only for a stationary eye whose field of vision is within the boundaries of the picture surface.[4] And this is sufficient to undermine the force of his claim that a picture is realistic to the degree that it is effective in inducing an illusion of what it depicts. For if it is only under highly artificial conditions that a realistic picture will induce an illusion of its subject-matter, a spectator who looks at such a picture in a normal manner will not experience the illusion it is capable of producing. And if, as will be the case, a spectator experiences a picture as being realistic when he looks at it in a normal fashion, his finding it realistic is not the same as his being induced by it to undergo an illusion of seeing what it depicts.[5]

It would be fruitless to insist that illusion is a matter of degree[6] and to retreat to the thesis that the experience a spectator has in front of a realistic picture is *similar* to an illusion of seeing what is depicted. For the issue is not whether the spectator's experience is more or less like an experience of seeing the item depicted, but in what ways it is like or unlike such an experience. If it had been shown that the only way in which the visual experience of looking at the surface of Monet's picture differs from an experience of seeing a river is of the same kind as that in which the experiences of seeing similar shades of colour differ, Gombrich's position would be viable. But if one of the experiences contains a visual awareness

[4] James J. Gibson, *The Ecological Approach to Visual Perception* (Hillsdale, NJ: Lawrence Erlbaum Associates, 1986), 281.
[5] For other criticisms, see Richard Wollheim, 'Reflections on *Art and Illusion*', in his *On Art and the Mind* (London: Allen Lane, 1973).
[6] Gombrich, 'Illusion and Art', 196.

of the presence and character of a marked surface and the other does not, the concept of illusion is misplaced in a description of the first experience.[7]

If a spectator of Monet's picture were to experience an illusion of seeing what is depicted, it would not be possible for him to be concurrently visually aware of the marked surface as a marked surface. For it is not possible for his visual experience to possess incompatible representational contents of the kind that such concurrent awareness would require: the world in front of his eyes cannot be represented to him as being an opaque marked surface and also as being a river in thaw. Now Gombrich's account of seeing a realistic depiction is buttressed by a more general claim about pictorial experience, which applies to all pictures, not just those that are experienced as being realistic. This maintains that it is *impossible* for a spectator to attend to the character of the marked surface of a picture and simultaneously see what is depicted. If this claim were correct, Gombrich's thesis about the experience of a realistic picture would gain plausibility, although it would not thereby be established. For one explanation of the alleged impossibility would be that the visual awareness of a marked surface as a marked surface has a representational content incompatible with the representational content of seeing what is depicted, and one way in which this could be so in the case of a realistic picture would be for the second experience to be an illusion. But Gombrich's argument for the alleged impossibility of a dual awareness of the presence and character of a marked surface and the nature of what the surface depicts has been shown to rest on a false analogy;[8] accordingly, his illusionistic account of realistic pictures can derive no support from this source.

It is impossible to resist the conclusion that Gombrich has failed to provide a good reason for the view that the experience of a depiction, even a depiction experienced as being realistic, essentially involves an illusion of seeing what is depicted. So he has given no reason for the assimilation of the experience of seeing a thawing river depicted in Monet's picture

---

[7] Gombrich was prepared to concede that a spectator's visual experience characteristically reveals to him that he is face to face with a picture. But he appears not to have recognized the difficulty this creates for his emphasis on the idea of visual illusions in the experience of pictures. See his 'The Sky is the Limit: The Vault of Heaven and Pictorial Vision', in *Perception: Essays in Honor of James J. Gibson*, ed. Robert B. MacLeod and Herbert L. Pick, Jr. (London: Cornell University Press, 1974).

[8] See Wollheim, 'Reflections on *Art and Illusion*'; 'Seeing-as, Seeing-in, and Pictorial Representation', in his *Art and Its Objects*, 2nd edn. (Cambridge: Cambridge University Press, 1980), 213–14, and *Painting as an Art*, 360; also Michael Podro, 'Fiction and Reality in Painting', *Poetik und Hermeneutik*, 10 (1983).

to the experience as of seeing a thawing river. Neither has he shown that it is impossible to see the character of the marked surface of the picture and at the same time see what is depicted therein. The possibility of a dual awareness—a dual visual awareness—of a marked surface and what is depicted forms the foundation of Wollheim's technical notion of 'seeing-in', in terms of which he elucidates the idea of pictorial representation. It is now time to return to the question: What is it to see one thing in another?

3. Wollheim's explanation of the concept of seeing-in exists in two forms, early and late, the first of which construes the dual visual awareness as a duality of experiences, the second replacing this with a duality of aspects of a single experience. I begin with the early account, certain features of which carry over into the more recent theory.

This original explanation of the notion of seeing one thing in another consists of two parts.[9] The first assigns to the experience of seeing-in three basis characteristics, which endow the experience with a distinctive phenomenology. The second specifies the perceptual project associated with seeing-in, and uses this association to explain the possession by seeing-in of all three of the features from which its distinctive phenomenology arises.

The first property assigned to seeing-in concerns the range of items that can be seen in something, and this range is said to cover both particulars and states of affairs. Now if seeing-in is to be used to elucidate pictorial representation, this must indeed be its range, for both particulars and states of affairs can be depicted, and, accordingly, a spectator of a picture can see depicted either a particular or a state of affairs. Looking at Monet's picture, you can see a river depicted, and you can see that depicted ice is depicted as drifting down the depicted river. But this characteristic of seeing-in is not especially helpful, for it does not distinguish seeing-in from certain other species of seeing, and in particular from seeing face to face (to use Wollheim's favoured locution).

---

[9] Wollheim, 'Seeing-as, Seeing-in, and Pictorial Representation'. Wollheim develops his account by drawing a contrast between seeing-in and seeing-as (his original candidate for the experience involved in seeing a depiction as the depiction it is). Here I ignore the contrast with seeing-as and extract the analysis of seeing-in. I am sure that Wollheim was right to reject any analysis of pictorial representation in terms of the particular concept of 'seeing-as' that he articulates. For what would a picture be seen as? There are two possibilities: either as the item it depicts or as a depiction of that item. But to see Monet's painting as a picture of a river is not to see it as a river. And although Monet's painting should be seen as a picture of a river, this concept of seeing presupposes the concept of depiction and cannot be used to elucidate it.

The second characteristic assigned to seeing-in is that it does not need to meet the so-called requirement of localization. The requirement of localization demands that there must be an answer to the question of whereabouts in something another thing is seen. Hence the stipulation that seeing-in does not need to meet this requirement means that there need not be any answer to the question of whereabouts in one thing another is seen, so that the reason why a spectator may be unable to specify where in the first item he can see the second is that there is no such place. But the assignment to seeing-in of this characteristic is, I believe, problematic, as is clear from a consideration of the cases Wollheim introduces in support of the view that seeing a picture as a depiction of something does not require localization.

These cases fall into two classes: depictions of particulars and depictions of states of affairs. Now the instances of the first kind are unpersuasive. Wollheim cites two depictions of a crowd in which only some members of the crowd are depicted: in the first, the other members are hidden by a fold in the ground; in the second, they are cut off by the frame. The claim that seeing what is depicted in these pictures does not meet the requirement of localization exploits the fact that someone can be said truly to see a collection of items or a discontinuous aggregate, even though there are members of the set that he does not, perhaps cannot, see. This runs parallel to the fact that a picture can be said truly to contain a depiction of a set of items even though not all the members of the set are depicted. It is unsurprising that if a picture depicts a collection, but not every member of the collection, the whereabouts of the collection in the picture cannot be precisely specified and, accordingly, a spectator cannot identify exactly the location of the collection he sees depicted. What the spectator can do is specify the location in the picture of each depicted member of the collection. It would be specious to maintain that seeing a depiction of a continuous item (a person, say) need not meet the requirement of localization on the ground that parts of the item might not be depicted; and there is no relevant difference concerning localization between the depiction of such a discontinuous aggregate as a crowd and the depiction of a continuous item, part of which might be obscured by another depicted item or cut off by the frame. The requirement of localization must be met by each depicted part of a depicted particular.

If we now turn to the instances of the second kind—depictions of states of affairs—there is a simple explanation of the fact that they do not satisfy the requirement of localization, but this explanation undermines the significance of that fact. The reason why a spectator is under no obligation to specify whereabouts in a picture he can see the state of affairs depicted by that picture—the gathering of the storm, that the stag is about to die, the degradation of the young rake—is that a state of affairs, unlike a particular, lacks a location (or at least a circumscribed location that would allow the satisfaction of the requirement of location). And since it is an immediate consequence of the inclusion of states of affairs in the range of seeing-in that seeing-in does not need to meet the requirement of localization when what is seen in something is a state of affairs, nothing is added to the characterization of such cases of seeing-in by the stipulation that they do not need to meet the requirement.

So the requirement of localization has an unproblematic application to the perception of a depiction of a particular, but it must be applied at the level of depicted parts; and its failure to apply to the perception of a depiction of a state of affairs is a direct consequence of the nature of a state of affairs. The characterization of seeing-in by reference to the fact that it does not need to meet the requirement of localization therefore does not align it perfectly with the seeing that takes place when a spectator sees a depiction as a depiction of its subject. But in any case it is unilluminating to characterize seeing-in by reference to this requirement, for, as in the case of the assignment to seeing-in of its proper range, it does not enable seeing-in to be distinguished from face-to-face seeing: a spectator can see, not only depicted but also in reality, a crowd some members of which are out of view, that a stag is about to die, the gathering of a storm, or the degradation of a young rake. And hence only the third feature assigned to seeing-in can define a distinct species of seeing.

This third feature is that seeing-in permits simultaneous visual awareness of the surface in which something is seen and that which is seen in it.

Wollheim argues that there is a thesis, 'the twofold thesis', which is true of pictorial representations and which ensures that seeing a marked surface as a depiction of something allows simultaneous visual awareness of the marked surface and what is depicted in it. This twofold thesis maintains that the visual attention of a spectator who sees what is depicted in a picture *must* be distributed between the marked surface and the item depicted; and Wollheim advances three considerations in support of the twofold thesis.

The first is that the twofold thesis provides an account of the distinctive phenomenology of seeing something as a depiction. But even if we concede that the experience of seeing something as a depiction has a distinctive phenomenology, this is an inconclusive reason, as Wollheim admits, since it does not follow that the experience has the phenomenology assigned to it by the twofold thesis.

The second maintains that the explanation of the fact that perspectival distortion of what is depicted is not necessarily brought about by changes in the spectator's viewing point that would cause perspectival distortion if what were seen were the object itself is that the spectator is, and remains, visually aware not only of what is depicted, but also of the marked surface of the picture. This is unconvincing, however, for there is a much better explanation of the fact that in general the depicted object maintains a relatively constant appearance when the spectator changes his position in front of the picture: the object itself is not being seen, and changes in the viewing point do not reveal hitherto unseen parts of the object, but only the same disposition of marks on the surface. The argument will appear plausible, I believe, only if it is tacitly assumed that the spectator sees the actual object, not a depiction of it.

The third consideration claims that a spectator's admiration for the way in which an artist has created a depiction by marking the surface of his picture in a particular manner would not be possible if the spectator had to alternate his visual attention between the marked surface and what is depicted in it. However, if this claim were correct, it would not establish the twofold thesis, because the possibility of twofold visual attention would not imply that it is an essential feature of the experience of depiction. But in fact the claim is unfounded, for no reason has been given for accepting the conclusion that the only way in which artistry in marking a picture's surface to create representational effects could have received recognition is through simultaneous twofold visual awareness. An alternation in the spectator's visual attention would seem to be sufficient for the recognition of and consequent admiration for the artist's artistry.

These considerations fail, therefore, to establish the twofold thesis about pictorial representation, and, without its support, the definition of seeing-in in terms of a dual visual awareness does not place seeing-in securely within the domain of the perception of depictions as representations of their subjects. Seeing-in permits simultaneous visual awareness of a surface and what is seen in it, but seeing what a picture depicts has not been shown to require, and so to allow, simultaneous visual awareness of the surface and what is depicted therein.

It should be noted that seeing-in is characterized as permitting simultaneous *visual* awareness of the surface in which something is seen and that which is seen in it. It is essential to Wollheim's claim that seeing-in is a distinct species of perception with its own phenomenology that it should receive such a characterization. Hence, the appropriateness of seeing-in as a candidate for the experience of seeing what is depicted is not secured by the plausible thesis, which is weaker than the twofold thesis, that it is possible (perhaps mandatory) for the spectator to be simultaneously aware of the nature of the marked surface and what is depicted. For such a dual awareness might not be a twofold visual experiential awareness, but a single visual awareness (of the marked surface) combined with a non-experiential awareness (of what is depicted), as in the case of reading with understanding a handwritten sentence, which allows the reader's attention to be distributed between the handwriting and the meaning of the sentence. The comparison that Wollheim seeks to exploit between the appreciation of poetry, which is grounded in a simultaneous awareness of the sound and the meaning of words, is therefore not to the point.

4. As yet, we have seen no reason to accept seeing-in as the seeing that takes place when a spectator sees what is depicted in a picture. But perhaps this is because we do not fully understand the concept of seeing one thing in another, and especially the idea that seeing-in involves a visual awareness not only of the surface before the eyes, but also of the item seen in it, which is not before the eyes; and if we were to understand the concept of seeing-in better, it might recommend itself as the seeing involved in seeing a depiction as a depiction. To achieve this deeper understanding we must turn to the second part of Wollheim's account, which seeks to fill out the notion of seeing-in by specifying the perceptual project that underlies it and that explains the possession by seeing-in of all three of the characteristics assigned to it in the first part of the account. This further elucidation underscores Wollheim's commitment to a double visual awareness in the analysis of pictorial experience.

We are told that seeing-in derives from a special perceptual capacity. This special perceptual capacity presupposes the normal capacity to see things present to the eyes, but it also includes the capacity to undergo visual experiences of things that are not present to the eyes—things absent or non-existent. When this special capacity operates, Wollheim writes, 'visions of things not present...come about through looking at things present'.[10] And these visions or visual experiences of what is not present to the eyes are not merely caused by the visual awareness of what is present, which dies at the moment it gives birth to its progeny, but are sustained in existence and derive their character at least in part from a continued visual awareness of what is before the eyes, so that the subject undergoes two experiences, one of seeing what is present and one of seeing what is not. Seeing-in, Wollheim writes, 'is the cultivation of a special kind of visual experience, which fastens upon certain objects in the environment for its furtherance';[11] what seeing-in consists in is the union of the cultivated experience with the visual awareness of what supports this experience.

Now, as I have indicated, Wollheim uses the elaboration of the idea of seeing-in to account for the fact that seeing-in has precisely the set of characteristics he has already assigned to it. But if what I have said about these characteristics is correct, it is not to be expected that his explanation will be entirely successful, and I am going to pass over it in silence. For there is a fundamental weakness in the elucidation of seeing-in, and this weakens whatever force his explanation might be thought to possess. The general idea is clear: seeing-in consists of two experiences, one of which—the visual awareness of the features of the item before the eyes—generates and sustains the other—the vision of something not present to the eyes. But there is an obvious lacuna: the nature of this second, cultivated experience has been left blank, and it is difficult to see how it could possibly be filled in. It is certain that this experience is not intended to be one indistinguishable by the subject from a corresponding instance of face-to-face seeing, for this would have the consequence that when seeing-in is appropriately exercised upon a depiction, it yields an illusion of seeing the item depicted. This interpretation would be inconsistent with Wollheim's long-standing opposition to illusionistic accounts of seeing what a picture depicts, and it would render his conception of seeing-in

---

[10] Wollheim, *Art and its Objects*, 218.   [11] Ibid. 223.

a mere substitution for Gombrich's oscillating illusion account—the view that the spectator's experience is an alternation of an illusion of seeing the item depicted and a visual awareness of the qualities of the picture surface—a mere substitution for this of the simultaneous occurrence of the same two experiences. Moreover, this suggestion would be absurd, for it would involve the ascription of incompatible qualities to a spectator's visual experience, as we have already seen. But if the cultivated experience contained within seeing-in is not intended to be an illusion of seeing what is not present to the eyes, what kind of visual experience is it supposed to be? It would seem that the only alternative to an experience as of face-to-face seeing is the second principal form of experiential visual awareness—visualizing what is not present to the eyes. The possibility that the experience of seeing a picture as depicting its subject has as a constituent the experience of visualizing, rather than the experience of seeing face to face, has one advantage. For there is no longer an incoherence in the addition of the experience to the core experience, the visual awareness of the marked surface, for you can visualize one state of affairs at the same time that you see another, as when in reading a novel you visualize the incident being described. But there are a number of objections that count decisively against this approach to the problem of depiction.

First, there is the fact that your capacity to visualize a complex state of affairs is likely to be extremely limited, and in so far as you succeed in visualizing the state of affairs your image is likely to be infected by a considerable degree of vagueness. Yet normally you have little if any difficulty in seeing what a picture depicts and the content of your experience can be as detailed as the state of affairs depicted. Perhaps it will be thought that this objection overlooks a crucial difference, the difference between the aided and the unaided use of the visual imagination. Undoubtedly, the response concedes, there are narrow limits to your capacity to visualize unaided the state of affairs depicted in Monet's picture; but, so the response continues, when you visualize it in looking at the picture your imagination receives strong support from the coloured expanse of the picture-surface, which has been designed with the intention that it should be such as to encourage the spectator to visualize what it depicts. But this response is unconvincing. For what is supposed to be the precise relation between the experience of seeing the opaque marked surface that confronts you and the content of your visualization? If the suggestion is that the picture-surface merely triggers your imaginative visual experience, the relation between visual image and picture-content will be much too loose for it to be plausibly maintained that you see what the picture depicts even in a case where the character of your image matches what is depicted. Any correspondence between picture-content and what you visualize will be merely coincidental. But even if the idea is that there is a one–one correspondence between features of what is visualized and features of the picture-surface, there is a problem about the basis of the alleged correspondence, whether it is supposed to exist in virtue of conventions or a natural, non-conventional relation.

Consider first the possibility that the correspondence between one item and another is conventional, so that it is in virtue of your understanding of these conventions that your visual image assumes the character it does. Then it is clear that the theory fails to engage with a salient feature of your capacity to visualize. For even if you have a thorough understanding of what you are on some occasion meant to visualize, it will rarely be the case that you can immediately form a detailed and stable image of the required kind. Yet in general you will immediately see and continue effortlessly to see what a picture depicts. The reason the theory is inadequate, therefore, is that it cannot explain the control that pictures are alleged to exercise over your power to visualize their subjects. The postulation of a conventional relation in virtue of which the spectator is supposed to visualize the depicted state of affairs greatly exaggerates the likely success, specificity, and stability of any spectator's involvement in the imaginative project the theory requires.

If we now introduce a related disanalogy between pictorial experience and visualizing it is clear that the theory would not be substantially improved by the substitution of a natural for a conventional relation. Except for such special cases as ambiguous pictures, your pictorial experience is not subject to your control in the way your visualizing is. When you look at a picture you cannot in general switch from seeing it as a depiction of one state of affairs to seeing it as a depiction of another, as you can switch from visualizing Jack to visualizing Jill. Even in the case of ambiguous pictures, there is a lack of analogy between your capacity to switch, not only from visualizing one state of affairs to visualizing another, but also from visualizing one to visualizing none, and your capacity, which may be minimal, to switch from seeing the picture as a depiction to seeing it non-pictorially. The postulation of a natural relation as the basis of a point-for-point correspondence between features of your image and features of the picture-surface is intended to tie together capacities that are not otherwise perfectly suited to each other, with the result that the normal freedom of the imagination should come into line with the lack of freedom that characterizes pictorial experience. But this is a desperate manoeuvre forced on the theory by the assumption that the experience of seeing what a picture depicts is a combination of the visual awareness of the picture-surface and an additional visual experience. This assumption, and so the theory itself, is perhaps most easily exposed as baseless if we contemplate subtracting the visual awareness of the picture-surface from the experience of seeing what the picture depicts. For the subtraction would not leave any experience behind, and in particular it would not result in an experience of visualizing the depicted subject.

So it seems impossible to give a plausible answer to the question of what the cultivated visual experience contained within seeing-in is. But without an answer it is not possible to understand the idea of seeing-in, for it has been incompletely characterized.

5. Perhaps it will be thought that the weakness in this first account of seeing-in stems from the conception of seeing-in as consisting of two visual experiences, and that this weakness has been repaired in Wollheim's later account.[12] For in this more recent account the idea that seeing-in involves two experiences is replaced by the idea that it is a single experience, but one that possesses two aspects. I shall argue, however, that this merely conceals, and does not remove, the weakness, and that this second conception of seeing-in not only inherits the weakness of the first, but develops weaknesses of its own.

In this new account seeing-in is credited with a distinctive phenomenology, 'twofoldness', which now refers to the possession by a single experience of two aspects, a 'recognitional aspect' and a 'configurational aspect'. So in this later conception seeing-in not only permits, but demands, a dual visual awareness, and this duality is one of aspects, not experiences.

---

[12] Wollheim, *Painting as an Art*, ch. 2, B 1–11; 'Imagination and Pictorial Understanding', *Proceedings of the Aristotelian Society*, Supplementary vol. 60 (1986), §§2–3.

The configurational aspect is a visual awareness of the marked surface facing the spectator, and the recognitional aspect is an awareness of depth in which one thing is seen in front of another—a boy in front of a darker ground, for example. And neither of these aspects can have a separate existence: an instance of the one can occur only in combination with an instance of the other. For although each aspect of a seeing-in experience can be described as though it were a case of face-to-face seeing—a simple visual awareness of a marked surface or an experience of seeing a boy—this is not what it is. Moreover, it is illegitimate to enquire about the experiential resemblance between either aspect of the complex experience and the simple face-to-face experience after which it is described; for 'the particular complexity' of the seeing-in experience makes its phenomenology incommensurate with the phenomenologies of the two simple experiences.

Now the reason given for deeming it illegitimate to raise a question about the experiential resemblance between the recognitional aspect (for example) of a seeing-in experience and the face-to-face experience after which it is described is unconvincing. For whatever the particular complexity of the twofold experience is supposed to be, why should it render the phenomenology *of its recognitional aspect* incommensurate with that of the face-to-face experience? If we accept the thesis, however, it is clear how this new conception of seeing-in protects it against the objection brought against the original conception—the objection that seeing-in is under-characterized, because the nature of the cultivated component experience is left blank and there is no indication as to how it should or could be filled. For if it is illegitimate to ask how experientially like or unlike the recognitional aspect of a seeing-in experience is to the corresponding or analogous face-to-face experience, and yet it is this face-to-face experience which provides the model for the description of the recognitional aspect, then the nature of the recognitional aspect cannot be elucidated in any way, and it is therefore inappropriate to press for an elucidation. But I believe that this apparent strength of the new conception is nothing but a veil drawn over the original weakness, which cannot be repaired by fusing the two experiences of the first account. For the blankness of the original cultivated experience is passed on to the recognitional aspect of seeing-in, with the result that the twofoldness of the single seeing-in experience is rendered incomprehensible. The insistence that the recognitional aspect and the corresponding face-to-face experience are experientially incomparable undermines the force of the idea that for any recognitional aspect there is an analogous face-to-face experience after which it can be described. The recognitional aspect cannot properly derive the only description it can be given from an experience with an incomparable phenomenology: the alleged experiential incommensurability prevents the description of the one from being modelled on the description of the other—or, if it is so modelled, makes it inappropriate, indeed mistaken. Hence, the so-called recognitional aspect of seeing-in merely masquerades as an analogue of a face-to-face experience; and when the description it has wrongly borrowed is stripped from it, it not only has no other description to clothe itself in, but is revealed as having no nature of its own.[13]

The problematic nature of the double aspect account of seeing-in is exacerbated by Wollheim's thesis concerning the relative prominence of the two aspects of the experience. He claims that either aspect can be more prominent than the other, and that when one aspect becomes overwhelmingly prominent, the recessive aspect evaporates and seeing-in is replaced by an experience of a different kind. At one extreme, the configurational aspect evaporates and seeing-in is succeeded by an experience of visualizing the object of the preceding recognitional aspect; at the other, the recognitional aspect evaporates and seeing-in is replaced by an experience of seeing face to face the object of the preceding configurational aspect.[14] But there are two problems with this idea. The first and less serious is this: if the evaporation of the configurational aspect

[13] An unwelcome consequence of the denial that the phenomenology of the recognitional aspect of a seeing-in experience can be compared with the phenomenology of an experience of seeing something face to face is that it becomes impossible to make sense of the application to pictures of the property of realism, naturalism, lifelikeness, or truth to nature. Wollheim puts forward (*Painting as an Art*, ch. 2, B 10) the unusual view that this property must be elucidated in terms of a particular kind of reciprocity which obtains between the recognitional and the configurational aspects of a seeing-in experience when this experience prompts the spectator to regard the picture as realistic. But in whatever manner realism is best understood and whatever kind of reciprocity this is supposed to be, there can be no question of a depiction capturing well or badly an appearance of reality unless the recognitional aspect is allowed to possess a content comparable to that of a face-to-face experience. And this is denied to the recognitional aspect by the insistence that its phenomenology is incommensurate with that of a face-to-face experience.

[14] Wollheim's unsatisfactory double aspect conception of seeing-in seems to have come about in the following way. Realizing the inadequacy of his original double-experience conception, which, although this was not spelled out, represented seeing-in as the concurrence of a visual awareness of the picture-surface and a visualization of the object or state of affairs depicted, he reconceived seeing-in as a fusion of the two experiences in which some of the character of each experience was retained, the rest being transformed by the merging of the two experiences.

leads to an experience of visualizing the object of the former recognitional aspect, why should this recognitional aspect be described as though it were a case of face-to-face seeing, rather than visualizing? The second is this: if the gradual recession of one aspect does not transform the other aspect into something of a different kind—and what could this be?—the two aspects must be two experiences, the configurational aspect an experience of seeing face to face and the recognitional aspect one of visualizing. For at the moment when one aspect drops right away, on one side there is the other (untransformed) aspect and on the other side an experience which is either an instance of face-to-face seeing or an instance of visualizing. Why should the recognitional aspect, say, be thought to vanish at the very moment when it has become so prominent that the configurational aspect slips away?

The foundation of Wollheim's thought about pictorial representation is the belief that the awareness or recognition of what is depicted is both experiential and specifically visual; it involves the awareness of depth in the sense that something is seen as being in front of something else;[15] and yet it is neither an illusory experience of seeing face to face nor an experience of visualizing in the mind's eye. My claim is that this finally led him to the construction of an elusive amalgam of two will-o'-the wisps. For it is not only the recognitional aspect of seeing-in whose nature is problematic: an equal difficulty arises for the configurational aspect. Wollheim's thesis is that the phenomenology of the configurational aspect of an experience of seeing-in is likewise incommensurate with that of the analogous face-to-face experience. But if we now consider the nature of this face-to-face experience, it is apparent that the thesis of incommensurability deprives the configurational aspect of a nature of its own. The face-to-face experience is one of seeing a flat[16] differentiated surface without seeing anything in it (in Wollheim's sense). This face-to-face experience therefore does not involve a visual awareness of depth in what is seen and it must consist in the visual awareness of a two-dimensional coloured expanse, at a definite or indefinite distance from the subject. If the phenomenology of the configurational aspect of a seeing-in experience is incommensurate with

---

[15] This feature is present as early as 'On Drawing an Object' (§§24–6), reprinted in *On Art and the Mind*. See also *Art and Its Objects*, §13.

[16] It is certainly unnecessary that the surface should be flat, but the stipulation rules out irrelevancies. It is not essential to the recognition of the subject of a picture that its surface should look uneven.

the phenomenology of such a face-to-face experience, the configurational aspect cannot be the visual awareness of a two-dimensional coloured expanse. But it cannot involve a visual awareness of depth, which is confined to the recognitional aspect of the seeing-in experience. Hence it consists of nothing at all.

Perhaps it will be thought that this is too easy a dismissal of the double aspect conception of seeing-in. But the problem created by the thesis of incommensurability cannot be evaded, and it arises in a stark form in the application of seeing-in to the perception of a class of pictures that Wollheim countenances, pictures which are *abstract* representations.[17] An abstract pictorial representation is a picture that represents a non-figurative or abstract item, and the recognitional aspect of an appropriate seeing-in experience directed at such a picture might involve just the awareness of planes of colour being in front of other planes. If the configurational aspect of this experience is restricted to the visual awareness of a two-dimensional coloured expanse, the two aspects of the experience would appear to be incompatible with each other. But if it is not restricted in this fashion, then there will be two awarenesses of the relative distances of (the same) coloured planes, one in the configurational the other in the recognitional aspect; and the only way in which this could be accommodated is by the specification of different senses of the expression 'visual awareness of depth', which would need to be definable independently of the concept of depiction.

6. The collapse of seeing-in should, I believe, lead to the rejection of the assumption upon which it is based, that the awareness of what is depicted in a picture is both experiential and specifically visual, its heart consisting in a visual awareness of something lying in front of something else. It is unclear what Wollheim supposes this visual awareness of depth to be, and in the absence of any explanation, the suspicion must arise that it is nothing other than the experience of seeing something *as if it were a depiction* of one thing lying in front of another, the idea of which presupposes, and so could not be used to analyse, the concept of depiction.

But if this assumption is rejected, what should take its place? I believe that the way to capture the experience of seeing a picture as a depiction of its

---

[17] Wollheim, *Painting as an Art*, ch. 2, B 7; 'On Drawing an Object', §25.

subject is not by adding any other visual experience to the visual awareness of the picture-surface—either as a separate experience or by fusing it with the visual awareness of the picture-surface—but by specifying the nature of the visual awareness of the picture-surface when you see what the picture depicts. The visual awareness of the picture-surface must assume a certain form if what is depicted in it is to be seen, and what needs to be done is to characterize how the surface is seen when you see what it pictures. But what form must this visual awareness take? A consideration I introduced at the beginning of this essay will play a crucial role in determining the right answer. The consideration is that you would not see Monet's *The Seine in Thaw* as a depiction of a river in thaw if you were unaware of what a thawing river looks like. This consideration can be generalized: whatever a picture depicts, you would not see it as a depiction of that thing if you were unaware of what that thing looks like. And since, first, depiction is always from a point of view and, second, the appearance of something changes in accordance with the point of view from which it is seen, the condition can be expressed more precisely in this way: whatever a picture depicts, you would not see it as a depiction of that thing if you were unaware of what that thing looks like from the point of view from which it has been depicted. It is a short step to the conclusion that it is in virtue of your knowledge of how something looks that you are able to see a picture as a depiction of that thing.

I believe this conclusion is correct if it is interpreted in the right manner. It must not be interpreted in such a way as to rule out the possibility of learning what a certain kind of thing looks like from a depiction of something of that kind. If you have no idea what an aardvark looks like, you can acquire knowledge of its appearance from a depiction of one, and thereby gain the capacity to recognize an aardvark if you see one. But this is possible only if you are in some way informed that the animal you see depicted is an aardvark or you somehow work out that this is what it must be. Unless this is so, although you may be able to see an aardvark depicted, you cannot see that one is depicted. Furthermore, if you have no idea of what an animal, a tongue, an ear, a tail, or a leg looks like, then, although you may be able to see one depicted, again you cannot see that one is depicted. Interpreted in this manner, therefore, it is true that you are not in a position to see a picture as a depiction of its subject unless you are aware of the visual appearance of what it depicts. Moreover, if you possess the capacity to see pictures as depictions, your awareness of something's appearance enables you to see what is depicted by a picture of that thing. Hence a constraint on a viable theory of pictorial experience is that it should respect, and be such that it can explain, the fact that a spectator who is unaware of how a certain kind of thing looks is not able to experience a depiction of that kind of thing as such a depiction, whereas in general someone familiar with its appearance suffers from no such disability.

It is clear that an account of depiction in terms of seeing-in fails to satisfy this constraint. For it is stipulated that the phenomenology of the recognitional aspect of a seeing-in experience directed at Monet's picture cannot legitimately be compared with that of a face-to-face experience of seeing a river. Accordingly, there is no reason why a spectator should be familiar with, or possess an awareness of, the phenomenology of such a face-to-face experience to undergo a seeing-in experience the recognitional aspect of which is supposed to deliver to the spectator what is depicted in Monet's picture.

Now there are many approaches to the topic of depiction that are not based on the assumption that underlies Wollheim's. I shall consider just three. First, it might be suggested that the awareness of what a picture depicts, unlike the visual awareness of the picture's surface, is not itself experiential, but instead a matter of understanding or interpreting the marks on the surface in the right manner. This suggestion can assume two significantly different forms. One of these does not build into the manner of interpretation any reference to the spectator's awareness of the visual appearance of what it depicted—as in Nelson Goodman's theory[18]—and it is thereby disqualified in virtue of violating the constraint that a spectator sees that a river is depicted in Monet's picture only if he is aware of the visual appearance of a river. The other does build in such a reference and is therefore compatible with the acknowledgement of this constraint—as in Flint Schier's theory, according to which a depiction is interpreted by engaging with the spectator's capacity to recognize with his eyes something of the kind depicted.[19] In my view, however, such an account is misconceived, because the awareness of what a picture depicts is

[18] Nelson Goodman, *Languages of Art* (Indianapolis: Hackett Publishing Co., 1968).
[19] Flint Schier, *Deeper into Pictures* (Cambridge: Cambridge University Press, 1986).

experiential, as can perhaps be seen most economically in the switching of awareness that can take place in the perception of ambiguous figures.

The second kind of approach is based on the imagination. What it seeks to do is to add the imagination to the visual awareness of the picture surface in such a manner that it generates the experience of seeing what is depicted. This addition can take place in a number of ways. In its simplest form, the suggestion is that the spectator imagines of his visual awareness of a picture that it is an instance of seeing what is depicted, so that the surface of the picture is imagined to be a transparent plane through which what is depicted is seen. But this primitive form of the proposal is certainly inadequate, for it ties the spectator's awareness of what is depicted too loosely to the character of the picture surface, and—a related point—it does not capture the experiential nature of the awareness of what is depicted, reflected in the characteristic inability of the spectator to see a picture in any other way than the one which imposes itself on him and which the artist intended. The most sophisticated version of this approach is Kendall Walton's, which overcomes the weakness of the simple form, but only at the cost of requiring that if there is to be such a thing as seeing a depiction as a depiction, there must be rules of make-believe in accordance with which the imagination is exercised upon the awareness of the picture surface.[20] It is important to recognize that a spectator's engagement with a depiction will usually involve much more than what is barely constitutive of the experience of seeing the picture as a depiction of its subject; but while the imagination plays an essential role in the richer experience, it is mistaken, I believe, to attempt to build it into the unadorned experience. Hence the fact that this kind of theory satisfies the constraint that I have identified as governing a viable account of pictorial experience is insufficient reason to recommend the theory.

The third approach to the topic of depiction has its roots in Wittgenstein's consideration of the heterogeneous collection of experiences that he grouped under the heading 'noticing an aspect'.[21] This includes contemplating the face of someone whom you have not seen for a number of years and suddenly seeing his former face in his new one, contemplating the expression on someone's face and suddenly seeing it as a malicious smile,

---

[20] Kendall Walton, 'Pictures and Make-Believe', *Philosophical Review*, 82 (1973), 283–319.
[21] Ludwig Wittgenstein, *Philosophical Investigations* (Oxford: Basil Blackwell, 1953), II. xi.

and seeing the duck-rabbit figure first as a picture of a duck's head and then as a picture of a rabbit's head. In each case, a certain concept is integral to the specification of the intrinsic nature of the perception. This concept is the concept of that which is seen in the item in question, or what the item is seen as—the concept of how the person's face formerly looked, the concept of a malicious smile, the concept of a picture of a duck's (or rabbit's) head, and so, derivatively, the concept of a duck's (or rabbit's) head. It is for this reason that Wittgenstein asserts that what you see in the dawning of an aspect is an internal relation between the seen object and others. Now you cannot see this internal relation unless you are familiar with the look of whatever you experience the seen object as being related to, so that this account, applied to the perception of pictures, perfectly satisfies the requirement of an acceptable theory of pictorial experience. Regrettably, Wittgenstein does not characterize the nature of the internal relation that is perceived to hold between a depiction and what it depicts.

Christopher Peacocke represents the required relation as an experienced resemblance between the shape of the appearance of the depiction in the spectator's two-dimensional visual field and the shape that would be presented in the spectator's visual field by the depicted item if it were to be seen from a certain point of view.[22] Although this is not the place to evaluate Peacocke's proposal, it is instructive to place it correctly in relation to Wollheim's, especially since this relationship has been doubly misrepresented, first by Peacocke, subsequently by Wollheim. Peacocke suggests that his account can be seen as an attempt to remove any obscurity from Wollheim's idea of seeing one thing in another. But his proposal cannot properly be thought of as an elucidation of Wollheim's original double experience conception of seeing-in (which Peacocke is referring to), since his proposal does not analyse the seeing appropriate to depictions in terms of two simultaneous visual experiences. Wollheim acquiesces in the description of Peacocke's proposal as an attempt to analyse further the notion of seeing-in, although he is sceptical of its success.[23] But it could not be thought to elucidate Wollheim's later double-aspect conception of seeing-in (which Wollheim has in mind), for it conflicts with this conception in at least two significant ways. First,

[22] Christopher Peacocke, 'Depiction', *Philosophical Review*, 96 (1987), 383–410.
[23] Wollheim, *Painting as an Art*, 360.

Peacocke's conception, unlike Wollheim's, does not credit a spectator's visual awareness of the picture surface when he sees a picture as a depiction with a nature that is experientially incommensurate with that of the relevant face-to-face experience and which disallows its separate existence. Second, the experience of visual field shape similarity is not a visual awareness of depth, but an awareness of a resemblance between the intrinsic properties of two two-dimensional visual fields, one actual, the other hypothetical.

7. I have argued that Wollheim's account of pictorial representation in terms of seeing-in is an unsure basis for his theory of painting as an art. But, happily, much of the theory of painting developed in *Painting as an Art*—the account of the practice of painting as an art, the analysis of expression in painting, the elucidation of the idea of the unrepresented spectator in the picture, the discrimination of the various kinds of meaning paintings can possess, and the attributions of particular meanings to the works of certain artists—survives the collapse of one of its foundation stones. It remains an outstanding contribution to the subject.

Postscript [2007]

My essay did scant justice to Kendall Walton's account of depiction, my only excuse being that I wrote it before the publication of his magisterial book *Mimesis as Make-Believe*,[24] in which he develops a general theory of what he calls representations, and uses it both to distinguish the main kinds of artistic representation (e.g. linguistic, dramatic, pictorial) and to elucidate the various factors in, and forms of, the appreciation of representational works of art. In particular, his account of the concept of pictorial representation (depiction) is founded on this general theory of representations. The minimal essence of this general theory is this: for Walton, a representation is something that possesses the social function of serving as a prop in a game of make-believe. A prop mandates imaginings by virtue of principles or rules of generation that prescribe what is to be imagined in what circumstances. Props in games of make-believe can

---

[24] Kendall L. Walton, *Mimesis as Make-Believe: On the Foundations of the Representational Arts* (Cambridge, Mass.: Harvard University Press, 1990). All page number references are to this work, unless otherwise indicated.

prescribe either propositional or non-propositional imaginings or both. Propositional imagining is merely imagining *that* such-and-such is the case. An example of non-propositional imagining would be *visualizing* a scene. According to Walton, a *depiction* is something that has the function of serving as a prop in *visual games of make-believe* of a certain kind, participation in such games involving an experience that is both *imaginative* and *visual*. When I look at a picture and see what it depicts, I must, Walton maintains, imagine 'from the inside' seeing the scene depicted. Imagining from the inside is imagining doing or experiencing something, as opposed to merely imagining *that* one acts or experiences in a certain way or is in a certain condition (forms of [merely] 'propositional imagining'). But it is not sufficient that my seeing the picture should prompt me to imagine from the inside seeing the scene depicted. Rather, I must imagine *of* my perception of the picture that it is a perception of what the picture depicts (and this game of make-believe must be both reasonably rich and vivid). So, Walton writes, the spectator of Hobbema's *Water Mill with the Great Red Roof*

imagines that [he sees a red-roofed mill]. And this self-imagining is done in a first-person manner: he imagines seeing a mill, not just that he sees one, and he imagines this from the inside. Moreover, his actual act of looking at the painting is what makes it fictional that he looks at a mill. And this act is such that fictionally it itself is his looking at a mill; he imagines of his looking that its object is a mill. (p. 293)

Imagining of my act of looking at the picture that it is an instance of looking at the scene depicted is a specific form of imagining from the inside seeing the scene depicted, and it is this specific form of imagining from the inside that needs to take place in front of the picture for me to see the picture as a depiction of its subject. This, Walton claims, endows the experience of seeing what a picture depicts with a distinctive phenomenology. For, so he maintains, the perceptual and imaginative aspects penetrate one another in such a manner that they are inseparably bound together. My experience of looking at a picture and seeing what it depicts contains, is penetrated by, both my imagining that my seeing the picture is my seeing the scene depicted and also my awareness that what I am really seeing is the picture, not the scene depicted. I am—and I am aware of—seeing a picture and I am imagining myself undergoing a different visual experience—one of seeing the scene depicted—and my seeing the picture as a depiction of the scene consists of my imagining this different experience by imagining of my experience of the picture that it is this different experience.

Walton's theory, of which I have extracted the bare bones, is extraordinarily well defended, both in *Mimesis as Make-Believe* and in later writings. For example, it is integral to Walton's make-believe approach that there are rules or principles that determine what it is that a spectator must imagine seeing when looking at a picture, and that a spectator must have a mastery of these rules if she is to see what is depicted. But it would be fruitless to express scepticism about the existence of such rules on the grounds that nobody has ever devised rules for the kind of imaginative project postulated by Walton, nobody has ever drawn up a list of them, and nobody has ever been taught to govern what she might imagine in looking at a picture by reference to what these rules require. For, in the first place, Walton distances himself from the view that games of make-believe always depend on stipulations and he refrains from specifying the supposed principles governing depictive representation because, in addition to its not being necessary to know what they are in order to know that they exist, he believes that the concept of depiction does not require that these rules should be of any specific kind, the rules governing different kinds of picture, pictures in different styles, with different systems of perspective, for example, varying. Furthermore, a spectator does not need to consult or think of the principles of depiction in order to act in accordance with them and imagine of her perception of a picture what these principles dictate that she should imagine. For it is unnecessary that engagement with the right imaginative activity should be a deliberative act and, apart from exceptional cases, a spectator does not decide what to imagine in perceiving a picture but just finds herself imagining what she should imagine when triggered by perception of the work. Accordingly, in one place, distancing himself from the view that games of make-believe always depend on stipulations, he is happy to make the following suggestion:

One might think of the principles of generation for our games with pictures as consisting, in part, in something like the prescription that, on observing a picture, we are to imagine seeing whatever the visual design naturally inclines us to imagine seeing, provided that circumstances are 'normal' in certain respects and that we have had suitable background experiences, are suitably familiar with other pictures, etc.[25]

So the analysis of depiction requires only that there are principles that mandate what is to be imagined and that a spectator has a mastery, an understanding, an internalized awareness, of these rules which allows her to imagine appropriately without conscious appeal to the principles that underpin her activity.

Nevertheless, there is room for doubt, if not, perhaps, reason for outright rejection. My doubt is two-pronged, each doubt being directed at one of the crucial elements of Walton's account of pictorial perception, the first being aimed at the (propositional) *content* of the imagining, the fixity of it, the second at the imaginative element (the *imagining* of the content), its nature and effect.

In the first place, there is one conspicuous fact about our perception of pictures that appears to count heavily against the imagination's figuring essentially in an elucidation of the very nature of pictorial depiction. This fact is what might be called the resistance of pictures to perceptual depictive reinterpretation. A depicted state of affairs may be simple and minimal, but it may be complex or highly detailed with very subtle gradations of distance and colour, for example, which, often, we see immediately as our eyes scan back and forth across the canvas. The crucial point is that, given that we do not misperceive the picture and that we give it the attention it deserves, it will usually be the case that we cannot see it differently, i.e. as a depiction of a different state of affairs. Of course, there are exceptions, ambiguous figures, for example, such as Jastrow's duck-rabbit figure, which can be seen either as a picture of a duck or as a picture of a rabbit, or a schematic drawing of a cube, which can be seen as depicting different kinds of thing, and even when seen as depicting the same thing, a cubical wire framework, for example, it can still be seen in different ways, the framework being seen on one occasion as having one orientation and on another as having a different orientation. If we are familiar with these exceptional cases, we may well have the ability to switch at will between one perception and another. But in general what we see a picture as depicting is not within our control. Now our imagination is not always within our control, but

[25] Kendall Walton, 'Reply to Reviewers', *Philosophy and Phenomenological Research*, 51/2 (June 1991), 426.

usually it is, and it is in general easy to switch between making-believe one thing and making-believe another. So if our imagination plays the role assigned to it by Walton in the perception of pictures it needs to be capable of more or less instantaneous, highly stable, and detailed content,[26] triggered to imagine just the same objects of vision on looking at the same surface from the same distance and point of view, constrained by the nature of the surface and the more or less internalized rules of depiction to be unable to imagine of our perception that it is anything other than the seeing of one particular (complex) state of affairs. Walton denies that imaginative acts must be deliberate or under a person's control, citing dreams as obvious counter-examples, and also many of the imaginings that make up day-dreams.[27] This may be so. But what we are concerned with is wide-awake persons with equal vision looking at pictures, each of whom, whenever he looks at a certain picture from a normal distance in normal conditions and focuses on the picture, is supposed to imagine in exactly the same manner, as his eyes traverse the same course, each being unable to imagine differently. And this is supposed to hold across the entire range of pictures (depictions of all kinds), from those with minimal depictive content to those however great their depictive content may be. This sort of constancy and irresistibility of imaginings does not appear to hold with any other subject matter. It would be a curious fact if our imaginations were so tightly constrained in the manner Walton's theory requires them to be in the case of depictions, but were always free elsewhere to vary from person to person and from time to time.[28] If we now consider that

[26] The condition that Walton imposes on the visual game of make-believe definitive of something's being a picture that it must be sufficiently *rich*, which requires the game to allow for the make-believe performance of a large variety of visual actions (such as noticing or overlooking a feature of the depicted scene, looking for one or another feature it may contain, gazing intently or casually at part of it) by virtue of the actual performance of various visual actions on the work (p. 296), implies a certain richness in the depicted content, and so in the propositional content delivered by the imagination in its engagement by the work.

[27] Kendall Walton, 'Seeing-in and Seeing Fictionally', in Jim Hopkins and Anthony Savile (eds.), *Psychoanalysis, Mind and Art: Perspectives on Richard Wollheim* (Oxford: Blackwell, 1992), 285.

[28] What I am concerned with is the demand on our imaginations for the production of (often highly detailed) *propositional content* and the severe constraint imposed on the imaginations of each of us always to produce the same content (to put it roughly). In no other operations of our imaginations do our imaginations produce a fixed, determined, propositional content as they are required to do by Walton's theory of depiction. Consider, for example, the reading of fiction. It would, of course, be wrong to think of this as a counter-example, for it is clear that it is not our imagination, but our ordinary linguistic understanding, that gives us the basic propositional content of what we might imagine to be true.

what we see a picture as depicting is no more in our control than our ordinary perception of the world—in general, I can no more see an object as being different from what it clearly presents itself to me as being than I can see a picture as depicting something different—then it might seem that the resistance of pictures to perceptual depictive reinterpretation, as with the analogies Walton draws attention to between the process of inspecting pictures to see what is depicted and the process of inspecting reality to see what is there (pp. 304f.), are most easily explained by the engagement of just our ordinary visual recognitional capacities in the perception of what is depicted (as resemblance theories of depiction maintain), not our ability to imagine one thing to be something else, in particular, a certain experience to be a very different one. But this is not a decisive consideration. So it is necessary to look elsewhere.

Walton's theory is anchored in the notion of the imagination and is only as secure as its foundation. Although he makes many excellent observations about various forms of imagining, he confesses that he is unable to unify these activities by providing an account of what it is to imagine. He is, however, unworried by this lacuna, believing that an intuitive understanding of the notion sharpened by his observations is sufficient for his purposes. But an unanalysed notion of imagining cannot really bear the weight that Walton's theory of depiction places upon it. In fact, what makes it difficult to assess his account of pictorial experience is the notion of imagining it incorporates. Consider his claim that the perceptual and imaginative aspects of the experience of seeing what a picture depicts penetrate one another in such a manner that they are inseparably bound together, endowing the experience with a distinctive phenomenology. What exactly does this interpenetration come to? Walton adverts to the common view that visual experiences contain thoughts, and—imaginings being a kind of thought (pp. 295, 300)—claims that they also can be constituents of visual experiences. Now if we take the relevant case of complete thoughts, propositions, Walton's view is that (propositional) imagining is *doing* something *with* a proposition one has in mind (p. 20). Although the imagining supposedly integral to pictorial perception is not *merely* propositional, it does consist in a proposition that is imagined to be true of its object, which is the seeing of the picture. If one sees a picture as depicting a woman, the proposition is: I am seeing a woman (pp. 296, 300). But without an account of what imagining is, we do not know what is being done with this proposition, and what effect the imagining might have on its object—in what ways it might transform it, if that is what it is supposed to do.[29] And if it is not supposed to transform the unadorned perception, the interpenetration of the visual and the imaginative aspects of the experience comes to nothing more than that my perception of a picture is the *object* of my imagining: I am imagining *of* my seeing the picture that it is my seeing the scene depicted. Accordingly, a description of what it is like for me to see the picture in the way I do must mention both seeing and imagining, the contents of which are different. Either way, we do not have a real grasp of the phenomenology attributed by Walton's theory to the experience of seeing something depicted, which we can then hold up against the actual phenomenology to determine whether they match.[30]

This doubt about the ability of Walton's theory, as it stands, to capture the distinctive phenomenology of the perception of pictures is strengthened by Walton's representing his foundational idea—the idea of a perception of one thing being suffused with the imagining of it as being the perception of another thing—as having a wide application, covering the perception of sculptures and theatrical performances, for example. But, first, before I deploy this aspect of his view, I want to defuse any scepticism that might be directed at my introducing the idea of an unadorned perception of a picture—the perception of a picture unadorned by the imagining of it that, according to Walton's theory, is intrinsic to its constituting seeing what is depicted. For such scepticism would be misplaced: even with good eyes, in good conditions, focusing on the picture from a distance from which its depictive content can be seen, it is certainly possible in the case of *some* pictures to fail to see their depictive content—to see them as depicting anything at all. And now I can make the point: given my own grasp of the notion of imagining (of one experience that it is another), the transition from seeing a depiction non-depictively, e.g. seeing a puzzle picture as

---

[29] Another way of bringing this out is to focus on Walton's requirement that the imagining involved in pictorial perception must be *vivid*: one must vividly imagine seeing a woman (p. 296). Since thoughts themselves cannot be vivid, an account of what one is doing with a thought when one imagines it to be true of a perceptual experience is necessary to make applicable the notion of vividness.

[30] Walton is in fact well aware that his account is not fully satisfactory as it stands. His view is that three things are true of one who looks at a picture and sees a woman depicted in it, the first two combining in such a way as to make the third true: one is seeing the picture, one is imagining of one's seeing the picture that it is a seeing of a woman, and one is imagining seeing a woman (in a first-person manner). The problem is (personal communication) to explain how exactly the combination of the first two makes the third true.

just a tangle of lines, to seeing it depictively, i.e. as being a depiction (or containing depictions) of such-and-such (e.g. various animals), does not seem to be of the same order as either (i) the transition from just seeing a stick (as being a stick) to imagining (from the inside, in a first-person manner) of one's seeing the stick that it is a seeing of a snake, or (ii) the transition from seeing a person on a stage as an actor playing a certain role to imagining of one's seeing the actor that one is seeing the character the actor is playing. For example, if, when attending a school play, I imagine of my seeing a child that it is my seeing an angel, my perception of the child does not acquire a markedly distinct phenomenology which it lacks when I drop the imagining. So imagining (from the inside, in a first-person manner) of a visual experience I am actually undergoing that it is a different visual experience—one that I am not actually undergoing—although it introduces a thought-content into the imaginative experience that is absent from the non-imaginative experience and in that sense effects a new phenomenology, does not always alter the phenomenal character of the experience, at least to any great extent, perhaps hardly at all. But if the phenomenal character of seeing a picture depictively is markedly different from that of seeing it non-depictively, what good reason is there to believe that Walton's imagining captures the phenomenology of seeing a picture depictively?[31]

[31] I am grateful to Hallvard Lillehammer, Rafael de Clercq, Derek Matravers, and Rob Hopkins for their comments on this Postscript.

11

The Look of a Picture

1. Pictures are a distinct kind of representation: it is definitive of a picture that it represents what it depicts by depicting it, and depiction is a form of representation different from any other.[1] What distinguishes pictorial representation (depiction) from non-pictorial representation? An obvious and familiar idea is that a picture is a variety of iconic representation, representing its subject by means of the properties it shares with it. These properties are visual properties, so that the distinctive mark of a picture is that it represents its subject in virtue of looking like what it depicts. Now it is clear that this naive idea is inadequate as it stands. Perhaps its most important defect is that it operates with the concept of one thing's looking like another, and this is too loose a notion to bear much weight. It is, indeed, the vagueness of this concept that renders analyses of depiction based on it vulnerable to counter-example and at the same time allows them a further life when a different aspect of the concept is turned to face the objection. The resilience of the intuition that a picture looks like what it depicts is therefore partly due to the intuition's flexibility. The question is whether there is a stable form of the intuition upon which a correct theory of depiction can be founded. Is there a specific way a picture looks when it is seen as a depiction of its subject, and which is not shared with other kinds of representation? Or are pictures distinguished from non-pictorial representations on some other ground?

But there is an ambiguity in the idea that a picture depicts something. When an item is said to be a picture of a woman, a landscape, or any other

---

[1] The *pictorial* content of a picture is what a picture depicts. What a picture represents on the basis of its pictorial content can exceed what it depicts, and what it represents may not be a state of affairs that could be seen, as when a picture represents a man dreaming a certain scene by depicting a bubble attached to his head within which the scene is visible. In what follows I am concerned to elucidate the perception of a picture's pictorial content, not any additional content the picture may have.

kind of thing, there are two different ways in which the remark can be understood: it can be understood to license existential generalization or not to license it. If the remark is intended to license existential generalization, it follows from the fact that something is a picture of a woman that there is or was a woman of whom it is a picture; if the remark is understood otherwise, this conclusion does not follow (although it may in fact be true). The first concept of a picture can be called the relational sense and the second the non-relational sense. In the relational sense, a picture must stand in a certain relation to an actual thing, which it depicts; in the non-relational sense, this is not required. Now the fundamental concept in a theory of depiction is the concept of a picture in the non-relational sense. The reason this is so is not so much that, whereas every relational picture is at the same time a non-relational picture, the converse does not hold. The vital consideration is that what is constitutive of something's being a picture is its being a picture in the non-relational sense, and that this is what distinguishes pictorial representation from all other kinds of representation. The relations in which objects stand to relational pictures of them are not distinctive of, specific to, pictorial representation, as opposed to other kinds of representation. Relational pictures refer to what they depict; pictorial reference is not different in kind from other forms of reference; and, as with other forms of reference, it is the artist's intention or the causal role of the object in the production of the picture that determines reference. So an account of what is distinctive of depiction does not need to characterize the relation in which a relational picture stands to its subject. That is a task for a general theory of reference and representation. The primary task of a theory of depiction is the characterization of what it is to be a picture, that is, a picture in the non-relational sense. The question is whether the non-relational sense is rooted in the fact that a picture presents a distinctive visual appearance to the beholder.

If there is one thing that the most impressive recent philosophical theories of depiction are in agreement about it is precisely the rejection of the idea that depiction should be elucidated in terms of one thing's looking like another.[2] What I propose to do in this essay is to develop what seems to

---

[2] See Nelson Goodman's semiotic theory in his *Languages of Art* (London: Oxford University Press, 1969); Roger Scruton's seeing-as theory in his *Art and Imagination* (London: Methuen and Co. Ltd., 1974); Richard Wollheim's seeing-in theory in his *Art and its Objects*, 2nd edn. (Cambridge: Cambridge University Press, 1980), Supplementary Essay 5, 'Seeing-as, Seeing-in, and Pictorial Representation', and his *Painting as an Art* (London: Thames and Hudson, 1987); Flint Schier's natural generativity

me the only viable form of this currently heretical idea by specifying the species of likeness perception it must invoke. If this version of the idea that a picture depicts its subject in virtue of looking like it is unacceptable, a theory of depiction cannot be founded on the relation *looking like*.

2. First, I want to arm myself against a brusque dismissal of the idea. Consider the following argument.[3] If one thing looks like another, then the second thing also looks like the first: *looking like* is a symmetrical relation. *Looking like* is also a reflexive relation: anything that has a look looks (exactly) like itself. But depiction is neither reflexive nor symmetrical: a picture does not depict itself, and a picture is not depicted by what it depicts. Moreover, there are many things that look like one another without any one of them being a picture of any other. Hence the concept of a picture cannot be analysed as the concept of an item that looks like another. Although this argument is both valid and sound, it inflicts no harm on the idea that it is of the essence of a picture that it looks like what it depicts, since it shows only that *looking like* is not fully constitutive of *depiction*, not that it is not a necessary condition of it. It follows that if the intuition that a picture looks like what it depicts is to be turned into an analysis of the concept of depiction, it must be supplemented. The obvious supplement is a criterion of correctness determined by the history of production of a picture: if the picture is drawn or painted it is designed, not only to look like what it depicts, but also with the intention that it should be seen to look like it (and, perhaps, that it should be recognized that this *is* the intention with which it has been designed); if it is a photograph, it must be a product of the interaction between the light-sensitive surface in the camera and a state of affairs of the kind depicted that transmitted light to the camera in the right way, and it is precisely the function of a camera to produce two-dimensional likenesses of the visible world it faces. Such a supplement renders the intuition proof against the dismissive argument.

But although a criterion of correctness must figure in a theory of depiction, the argument is in fact misdirected against the theory I propose.

theory in his *Deeper into Pictures* (Cambridge: Cambridge University Press, 1987); Christopher Peacocke's sensational property theory in his 'Depiction', *The Philosophical Review*, 46/3 (July 1987); and Kendall Walton's make-believe seeing theory in his *Mimesis as Make-Believe* (Cambridge, Mass. and London: Harvard University Press, 1990).

[3] See Goodman, *Languages of Art*, ch. 1, sect. 1.

For the crucial concept is not the bare *looking like*, but a form of the more specific *seeing one thing as looking like another*: to see a picture as a depiction of its subject is to *see it as* looking like it—looking like it in a specific manner I intend to define. Since it is not true that if you see *a* as looking like *b* you thereby see *b* as looking like *a*, nor that whenever you see an object you see it as looking like itself, the fact that whereas the relation *looking like* is both symmetrical and reflexive *depiction* is neither, counts not at all against an account of depiction based on the perception of a likeness. So much for a swift rejection of the idea.

3. Now a picture is essentially a two-dimensional representation of a three-dimensional world, in the sense that the picture's depicted scene is visible in its two-dimensional marked surface. The crucial issue is the nature of the spectator's visual awareness of the picture-surface when he sees what a picture depicts. I shall assume that when the beholder sees a picture as a depiction of its subject he is visually aware of the presence and character of a marked surface in front of him.[4] The picture-surface does not look *to be* three-dimensional: it does not seem to the viewer that he is seeing a three-dimensional state of affairs. It follows, I believe, that the only relevant sense in which a picture, seen as a depiction of its subject, can look like its subject is with respect to the two-dimensional aspect of the subject's visual appearance. But what is this conception of the two-dimensional aspect of the visual appearance of a state of affairs?

4. In elucidating this conception it will be helpful to make use of a distinction between my *visual world* and my *visual field*. The celebrated perceptual psychologist James J. Gibson made use of such a distinction in *The Perception of the Visual World* and other early works.[5] He there represents the distinction between visual field and visual world as a difference between two kinds of seeing or experience ('pictorial' and 'objective'), one of which

---

[4] This assumption would need to be reformulated if it were intended to cover all kinds of picture, e.g. projected pictures. When you see a projected picture *as a picture*—when you see it as a two-dimensional representation of a three-dimensional state of affairs—you may not be visually aware of the presence before you of an opaque surface, but you must be visually aware of seeing *a two-dimensional appearance* of a three-dimensional state of affairs. For my immediate purpose it is easier to operate with the assumption as it stands.

[5] James J. Gibson, *The Perception of the Visual World* (Cambridge, Massachusetts: The Riverside Press, 1950), ch. 3. See also his *The Ecological Approach to Visual Perception* (Hillside, NJ and London: Lawrence Erlbaum Associates, 1986), 206–7, 286, where Gibson expresses regret at the title of his *The Perception of the Visual World*.

involves the experience of a visual field, the other the experience of a visual world. The visual field, unlike the visual world, is defined by reference to what you are visually aware of when your eyes are fixated, so that the visual field has boundaries, roughly oval in shape, it changes when the eyes move from one fixation point to another, and it possesses a central-to-peripheral gradient of clarity, for example, whereas the visual world lacks boundaries, it is stable under eye movements, and it is everywhere clear and fully detailed. This is not how I shall understand the distinction between visual field and visual world. The distinction between visual field and visual world that I wish to draw is not based on any differences between, on the one hand, what I am aware of when my eyes are fixated and I adopt an unusual attitude to my visual experience and, on the other hand, what I am aware of when I look at the world in a normal manner. It is concerned only with how the world is represented as being no matter how I may be looking at the world, and what it proposes to do is to exploit a division within the class of so-called representational properties of my visual experience (intrinsic properties of my experience in virtue of which the world is represented to me as being a certain way). The division it highlights introduces a distinction between my visual field and my visual world that is quite different from the early Gibsonian conception, according to which the visual world is just the world (as we see it to be) and the visual field is never wholly depthless. I shall understand the distinction in such a way that my visual field is a proper part of my visual world and I shall extrude depth from the visual field and assign it a place only within the complete visual world.

My visual world at any time is the complete way the world is then represented to me by my visual experience. My visual field is a certain aspect of the way the world is represented to me by my visual experience. When I look at the world I see objects spread out in a three-dimensional space: this is how the world looks to me, this is how my visual experience represents it as being. Within my truncated cone of vision each part of any object I see is presented to me, clearly or indistinctly, as having a certain intrinsic character, as lying in a certain direction from me, and being at the same distance as, or nearer or further away than, other parts. All of this is included in my present visual world. If we abstract the apparent distance of anything I see we are left with my present visual field. So my visual field is just my visual world considered in abstraction from one of its three spatial dimensions, namely, distance outwards from my point of view.

This distinction between my visual world and my visual field can be illustrated in the following way. Suppose I am looking at a circular object which, as I can see, is tilted away from me. I see the object as being circular and as being tilted away from me. But if a characterization of how the world is presented to me by my visual experience is required to abstract from apparent distance from me, it must specify the appearance of the circular object without mentioning the fact that it seems to be tilted away from me, for this involves my seeing one part of it as being nearer to me than another part. It is clear in what terms such a description should be formulated. For when I look at the object I see the points along its rim as lying in certain directions and at various relative distances from me; if I am to observe the restriction imposed by the conception of my visual field I must omit any reference to outwards distance; and this leaves the apparent directions of the points along the rim as the form of the object in my visual field. Since these are directions in a two-dimensional space (up and down, right and left), if I were to indicate in which directions I see the points along its rim and were to keep my hand at the same distance in front of me, then, given the way the circular tilted object looks to me, my finger would trace an elliptical path: the angle apparently subtended at my eyes by diametrically opposed points on the rim varies in such a manner that it is greatest when the diameter is transverse to my line of sight and least when it lies along it. It is in this sense that the circular object, which I see *to be* circular, *looks* elliptical. It would be a misunderstanding of the distinction between visual field and world to conclude, as has frequently been done, that whereas my visual world contains a circular object, my visual field contains a different item, one that is elliptical. The distinction is between a complete and a partial account of how my visual experience represents the world as being, not between different items that I am visually aware of when I see the world, or when I attend to my experience in a certain manner. When I see the object I am *simultaneously* aware of the apparent directions and the apparent relative distances of the points along the rim, but whereas my visual world includes both factors my visual field includes only the first.

Consider two more examples. In the first I am looking along railway tracks, which are parallel but, as they recede into the distance, look to converge and meet; in the second I am looking at two men of similar height, one of whom is at a much greater distance than the other and so looks smaller. Although the tracks look *to be* parallel and the men *to be* about the same height, the tracks look to converge and the more distant man looks smaller than the nearer. The sense in which the tracks look to converge is that the angle apparently subtended at my eyes by the width of the tracks gets less as they recede; the sense in which the more distant man looks smaller than the nearer is that the height of the first man apparently subtends a smaller angle than the height of the second. This is the sense in which, in the first case, the representation of the tracks in my visual field can be said to consist of converging lines, and, in the second case, the representation in my visual field of the more distant man can be said to occupy less space than that of the nearer. But it is important to remember that my visual field is not a two-dimensional *entity* that I see and a representation in my visual field is not an item that mediates my perceptual access to the world; a representation in my visual field is the manner in which the world is in some way visually represented to me in two of the three spatial dimensions.[6]

5. We are now in a position to return to the claim that the relevant sense in which a picture, seen as a depiction of its subject, looks like the subject it depicts is with respect to the two-dimensional aspect of the subject's visual appearance. This can be re-expressed in the following way: a picture looks like what it depicts only with respect to properties of the spectator's visual field, not those confined to his visual world.[7] So when you look at

---

[6] By 'my visual field representation' or 'a representation in my visual field' I mean the visual field representational *content* of my visual experience, not the experience itself: my visual field representation is *how* the world, with respect to its visual field properties, is represented to me by my visual experience.

[7] Christopher Peacocke has also put forward a theory of depiction based upon experienced visual field similarity. (See his 'Depiction'.) But his account differs from mine in three important ways. First, he construes the visual field in terms of *non-representational* (sensational) properties of visual experience, whereas my conception captures it in representational terms. (See his *Sense and Content* (Oxford: Clarendon Press, 1983), ch. 1.) (I believe the arguments for sensational properties are unconvincing.) Second, Peacocke's account represents experienced visual field *shape* similarity as being fundamental to pictorial perception, whereas mine is based on the more general idea of a perceived isomorphism of visual field *structure*. Third, Peacocke's account of depiction does not involve the idea that a picture *looks like* what it depicts, whereas mine does. This difference follows from our different understandings of the visual field. After this essay was completed I discovered, in reading John Hyman's *The Imitation of Nature* (Oxford: Basil Blackwell, 1989), that Rhys Carpenter in his *Greek Sculpture* (Chicago and London: University of Chicago Press, 1960) makes use of a distinction between visual field and visual world to elucidate the difference between pictures and sculptures. But, as Hyman points out, Carpenter

Poussin's *Echo and Narcissus* it is not so much your visual world as your visual field that resembles the one you would have if you were to see from a certain point of view a handsome youth enraptured by his reflection.

The plausibility of this line of thought emerges forcefully if we consider this schematic drawing of a cube:

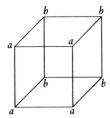

This schema of lines can be seen as depicting many different kinds of thing. Let us suppose you see it as a picture of, firstly a cubical wire framework, and secondly a transparent cubical block. In both cases you are visually aware of the presence of an opaque surface marked with straight lines. Now if you were to be looking at a real, rather than a depicted, wire framework from a similar point of view to the one from which it has been depicted in the drawing, the representation of the wires in your visual field would be isomorphic with the representation of the drawn lines in your visual field when you look at the picture. Similarly, if you were to look at a transparent cubical block, the representation of the edges of the block in your visual field would have the same form as the representation of the drawn lines in your visual field. It is for this reason that the same arrangement of lines can so easily be seen as a picture of either kind of object. Moreover, whichever of these two kinds of object it is seen as a picture of, there is more than one way in which it can be seen: face aaaa can be seen either as lying in front of or as lying beneath face bbbb. The reason is similar: the visual field representations of different orientations of the same cubical wire framework, or the same transparent cubical block, match in two-dimensional structure. So when you look at the schematic drawing, no matter which of these kinds of picture you see it as being, your visual experience contains the same two components: a visual awareness of

mistakenly conceives of the visual field as the two-dimensional projection of the world on to the retina. Moreover, Carpenter appears to conceive of the perception of a picture as an experience that involves the illusion of seeing depth and distance.

the lines as lying on the drawing surface and the same representation of the lines in your visual field.

It follows that this characterization of your experience fails to distinguish between your seeing the picture one way rather than another. But if we reflect on a case where you switch from seeing it one way to seeing it another way, it is clear what the distinguishing feature is. For the change in your way of seeing the picture cannot consist in the interpretation you are prepared to place on it, since you might already have been aware of the possibility of seeing it in different ways and have been prepared to interpret it accordingly. And it cannot consist in the fact that the representation of the lines in your visual field suddenly changes from being isomorphic with the visual field representation of one kind of thing to being isomorphic with that of another, since both before and after the change it is, as we have seen, isomorphic with them both. What happens when you switch from seeing the schematic cube as a picture of a wire framework to seeing it as a picture of a transparent block (or a wire framework oriented differently) is that *what you experience* your visual field representation as being isomorphic with changes: first you see the structure of lines as being isomorphic with the visual field representation of a wire framework and then as being isomorphic with the visual field representation of a transparent block (or a differently oriented wire framework). So the change does not consist in your suddenly realizing that the lines are isomorphic with the visual field representation of a transparent block (or a wire framework with a different orientation) or that they can be seen as isomorphic with it. It is a matter of your *seeing* the lines as looking to be isomorphic with it.

If we now generalize this description of seeing a schematic drawing of a cube, we obtain the following account of pictorial perception. When you see a picture and see what it depicts, two things must be true of your visual experience. First, your experience must involve a visual awareness of the presence before you of a marked surface. Secondly, you must see the structure of the surface as being isomorphic with the structure of the visual field representation of the picture's subject when seen from a certain point of view, namely, that from which it has been depicted. So when you see what is pictured in the surface you see a relation between it and objects of the kind depicted, in a similar sense to that in which you hear a relation between one theme and another when you hear one as a variation of the other; and neither in the pictorial nor in the musical case is the perception of this relation merely a matter of interpretation, rather than experience. For you to hear a musical passage as a variation on a certain theme you must experience the structure of the music as being isomorphic with that of the theme (and understand the composer's intention to be to design his music so): this is what your hearing the relation with the theme consists in. For a picture, the perception of this relation is, according to the account I have developed, an experienced isomorphism of representations in the visual field. When you see what is pictured in the marked surface you *see* the structure of the surface as being isomorphic with that of the visual field of the state of affairs depicted (as you *hear* the resemblance between the music and the theme); and this is not just a matter of realizing that this is the case, but a visual experience, a state of consciousness possessing what Wittgenstein called 'genuine duration', a state with a sharp beginning and end which endures continuously from one time to the other. Furthermore, just as the idea of the theme is intrinsic to the description of your experience of the music when you hear it as a variation on the theme, and an awareness of how the theme goes a precondition of undergoing the experience, so the idea of the state of affairs depicted is intrinsic to the description of your experience of the picture-surface when you see that state of affairs depicted in it, and an awareness of the look of that state of affairs a precondition of having the experience. For a perceived structural isomorphism with the visual field representation of a certain state of affairs is a perceived likeness with the visual field representation of that state of affairs *seen as* that state of affairs.

The significance of this last point can be brought out by considering a situation in which you are familiar with the look of one kind of thing, but have no idea what another kind of thing looks like. In fact, the two kinds of thing look just the same when seen from a certain point of view. Faced with a surface marked in such a way that the structure of its elements is isomorphic with that of the visual field representation of one or the other kinds of thing as seen from that point of view from which they look alike, the surface will look to you to be structurally isomorphic with the visual field representation of the familiar kind of thing, but not the unfamiliar kind—the surface will put you in mind only of the look *of the familiar object*.

The plausibility of this account of pictorial perception, and the importance of the idea of a *perceived* isomorphism of structure, is brought out by a consideration of Holbein's celebrated picture *The Ambassadors*. In the foreground of the picture there is a depiction of a skull, but the skull is represented anamorphically, so that if the picture is looked at from directly in front the depiction of the skull seems a strange yellow tilted smear, whereas seen from one side it assumes the form of a skull—the two men being transformed into blurs the more clearly the image of death enters the spectator's consciousness. Now the skull is represented anamorphically in the sense that its visual field form is grossly distorted when seen from the standard point of view that the spectator of a picture adopts: so much so that it is not seen as a distortion of the visual field of a skull seen normally. But although the depiction of the skull *is* isomorphic with the representation in the visual field of a skull in the sense that there is a one-to-one mapping between the points that compose the two, you *see* it *as* being structurally isomorphic only when you see it from the side, and, accordingly, you see it as a depiction of a skull only from that unusual, oblique point of view, not when looking at it from straight on.

The plausibility of this account of pictorial perception is reinforced by recalling the scene in the second half of Goethe's *Elective Affinities*[8] where members of the assembled company provide entertainment by representing well-known pictures by posing in the appropriate costumes on a lighted stage: they compose *tableaux vivants* of *tableaux morts*. There are two ways in which, when the audience admires the resemblance between the staged composition and the picture it represents, the audience might see the *tableau vivant*. On the one hand, it might see it as looking like the scene the picture depicts; on the other, it might see it as looking like the picture. But if—and this is the interesting case—the audience sees it as looking like the picture, there is one important respect in which it will not look like the picture: it will not look as if it is a flat surface. To be struck by the *tableau vivant's* likeness specifically to the picture—to see it as a representation of the picture, rather than the scene the picture depicts—the audience must bracket off the perceived third dimension and see it as if it were a flat surface: the perceived resemblance excludes the third dimension. Now this is just the converse of what I have called pictorial seeing: in the one case, a flat surface is seen as a depiction of a three-dimensional scene; in the other, a three-dimensional scene is seen as a representation of a picture. If the account I have given of seeing a *tableau vivant* as a

---

[8] Johann Wolfgang Goethe, *Wahlverwandschaften*, pt. II, ch. 5.

representation of a picture is along the right lines, so is my account of pictorial perception.

6. But if this account is to provide the foundation of a theory of depiction it must be refined and developed. First, we must face up to the fact that for many, perhaps most, pictures the visual field representation of the picture-surface is strikingly unlike that of the state of affairs depicted. In itself this creates little difficulty for the proposed account. In the first place, an acknowledgement of the possible disparity between the two visual-field representations is already implicit in the account, since the isomorphism it highlights concerns the *relations* between the elements of the two visual fields, which is compatible with great differences between the corresponding elements. Secondly, an obvious replacement for the idea that the spectator sees the picture-surface as having a structure which is isomorphic with the structure of the relevant representation in the visual field will be the idea that he sees the one as being like the other. The account can therefore easily accommodate noticeable dissimilarities in structure of visual field representations, since dissimilarities do not preclude a perceived resemblance.

But this response is uninformative about the pictorial significance of such perceived dissimilarities. There are two ways in which features of the visual field representation of the picture-surface can diverge from those of the state of affairs depicted and result in perceived differences. On the one hand, the visual field representation of the picture-surface can (and usually does) lack features possessed by the visual field representation of what is depicted; on the other hand, it can (and often does) possess additional features. How do such differences show up in what the spectator sees depicted?

It would be wrong to represent the absence of features, or the presence of additional features, in the representation in the visual field of the picture-surface as implying that the spectator sees what is depicted as lacking the absent features and as possessing the additional features. For this would overlook two distinctions, the distinction between something's not being depicted as possessing a certain feature and its being depicted as not possessing it, and the distinction between a perceived feature of the picture-surface that has pictorial significance and one that does not. To illustrate the first distinction: a black and white line drawing does not thereby depict its subject as lacking colour and a spectator who understands it does not see it as depicting a colourless state of affairs. The absence of colour in the picture is understood by the spectator, not as indicating a lack of colour in what is depicted, but only as not indicating any colour: the object, as depicted, has an indefinite appearance in the dimension of colour. The artist's intention is not to depict a black and white state of affairs, or a coloured state of affairs as being black and white; it is to depict only the spatial structure of a state of affairs and the comparative brightness of its parts, perhaps, not the colours of its constituent objects. To illustrate the second distinction: the individual lines or dots when cross-hatching or stipple is used to represent variations in tone lack pictorial significance and contribute to the depiction of light and shade only through the relative density of their combination with other lines or points. The spectator who understands these pictorial devices does not read their specific features into the objects depicted by means of them. As these examples show, to see the pictorial content of a picture it is often necessary to abstract from various details of the picture-surface, ignoring those aspects of the marks that are not representatives of depicted features of the depicted state of affairs. The fact of the matter is that, whereas every depicted feature of the object must have a perceptible feature of the picture which is representative of it, a perceptible feature of the picture need not be representative of any feature of the depicted object. The multiplicity of perceptible features of the picture can exceed the multiplicity of depicted features.[9]

It is important to recognize that perceived resemblances between representations in the visual field can involve very little of the detail of one or the other of the representations, as the examples I have used to illustrate the second distinction show. Consider another example, Picasso's 1946 pencil drawing *Head of a Girl*. The looping, spiralling lines with which Picasso has drawn the girl's hair do not look much like the visual field representation of any girl's hair you are likely to see. But if we abstract from most of the details of any such visual field representation, retaining only the feature of curling surroundings of a face, there is sufficient left to found a perceived resemblance with the picture. Hence it is easy to see how there can be pictures that are abstract representations of their subjects, or, more accurately, more abstract in their representation of some or all features of their subjects

---

[9] It is not always clear whether a perceived feature of the picture-surface possesses or lacks pictorial significance. Does Mondrian's stylized triangular and lozenge-shaped rendering of the nipples and navels in his triptych *Evolution* lack pictorial significance or depict the nipples and navels as so shaped?

than other pictures. Schematic depictions of objects do not depict their objects' structure in detail and usually omit such features as the play of light. Accordingly, they are seen as being like the visual field representations of their objects only with respect to the structural features they depict. The less the detail of the visible structure of a state of affairs is depicted, the greater the abstract nature of the picture: the greater the level of abstraction, the less definite the nature of the subject *as depicted*.[10] Moreover, it should now be clear that the account of pictorial seeing in terms of an experienced isomorphism of structure does not need to be watered down by being reformulated as a perceived *similarity* of structure. For it is built into the requirement of isomorphism that its demands are limited: the perceived isomorphism of structure that is constitutive of pictorial seeing refers to structure *at a certain level of detail*, so that a perceived similarity (but not identity) of structure at one level just is a perceived isomorphism of structure at a higher level. The combination of this point with one I have previously made—perceived features of the picture-surface can lack pictorial significance—renders this account of pictorial seeing immune to what would otherwise be obvious counter-examples.

Nevertheless the account is likely to be met with the objection that, if it applies at all, it applies only to certain styles of depiction, namely, those that are fairly close relations of optical perspective. Now it is in fact clearly unproblematic to apply the theory to pictures that are not designed to give a naturalistic effect of spatial recession, and even to pictures that are not constructed in accordance with a consistent mode of projection but depict some constituents of the depicted scene in plan and others in side elevation, say, as is often the case in Egyptian painting, or to pictures that are combinations of different views of a single thing or views from different points of view of parts of a single thing, as in Braque's *Pitcher and Violin*.[11] But, so it might be thought, there are kinds of projection, such

[10] A limiting case of abstraction in depiction would be a schematic picture intended to be seen as depicting a cube, but not any particular kind of cubical object (e.g. a cubical wire framework or a transparent cubical block). If you see the picture as intended, you see the structure of lines as being isomorphic with the structure of the visual field representation of a cube, but not, more specifically, a cubical object of a certain kind.

[11] The extraction of pictorial content by pictorial perception should not be thought of in a simplistic way as an instantaneous occurrence. In the first place, even if each part of the depicted scene has been depicted from the same point of view, it is rarely the case that the full depicted scene can be recognized in a single look; on the contrary, it is usually necessary to scan the picture. Second, many pictures depict elements of their content from different points of view in such a manner that it is necessary to

as reverse perspective, which are not concerned to represent how things look from any point of view, and when we look at pictures that use such modes of projection we do not see their structures as being isomorphic with those of the visual field representations of the objects they depict. It would be a mistake, however, to object to the theory of pictorial seeing I have put forward on these grounds. For the objection relies on a failure to distinguish between seeing a picture as a depiction of an object which has a certain form and seeing a picture as a depiction of an object which is depicted as having that form. When we look at a picture in reverse perspective of an object of a certain kind (a table with a rectangular top, for example), we can see it as a depiction of such an object, if we understand the mode of projection; and the information conveyed to us about the object's structure can be the same as, or even greater than, that which we obtain from a picture in normal perspective. But in such a case we see the form of the object depicted as being distorted, and so can be said to see the picture as a distorted depiction of the object. (A picture that is in this sense a distorted depiction of an object of a certain kind is not an [undistorted] depiction of a misshapen object of that kind, even though a picture of one sort could look exactly like, and so be mistaken for, a picture of the other sort.) Of course, since distortion is a matter of degree and it can be applied to many aspects of the form of an object, a mode of projection that distorts an object's form may result not in a configuration that is seen as a distorted depiction of the object, but in one that is not seen as a depiction of it at all—as with Holbein's anamorphic representation of a skull.

This account of pictorial seeing applies as easily to pictures of mythical or fictional kinds as to pictures of actual kinds. For although you cannot see a winged horse, you know how something that looks like a horse with wings would look like, and can therefore perceive the resemblance the account requires. But a merely fictional kind is not the only type of non-existent object that can, so it might seem, be depicted. There are also pictures of 'impossible objects', such as the three-pronged tuning fork, which consists of two rectangular bars at one end and three cylindrical bars at the other. There are even pictures of 'impossible worlds', such as Escher's *Autre Monde*. In these cases, not only can you never see anything

---

apply pictorial perception piecemeal, to one then another part of the picture, in order to generate the right interpretation.

of the kind depicted, you cannot coherently imagine seeing something which has the look of that kind of thing, since there can be no such look. But the impossibility of visual field representations of impossible objects, or of possible objects that look how impossible objects supposedly look when their impossibility is apparent to the eye, does not count against the idea that pictorial seeing is founded on a perceived structural isomorphism of visual field representations—as is clear if we examine how we see depictions of impossible objects and worlds. The picture of the impossible tuning fork is designed in such a manner that if we direct our gaze at one end of the configuration of lines we see the structure of the lines as being isomorphic with that of the visual field representation of two rectangular bars, whereas if we look at the other end the lines look to be structurally isomorphic with the visual field representation of three cylindrical bars. But if we allow our eyes to run back and forth along the lines, or take them in as a whole, we cannot impose on them a stable, consistent interpretation. The picture is just a tease, holding out to us with one hand what it withholds with the other, and we are looking at a picture of an impossible object only in the sense that the picture tempts us to see parts of it in ways which assign incompatible roles to the picture's elements. Escher's *Autre Monde*, which relies mainly on perspectival ambiguities, works in a similar fashion, and is not seen in its entirety as a depiction of a state of affairs, even an impossible one. Pictures of impossible objects or worlds are merely configurations which are composed of elements so designed that the spectator is strongly encouraged to see different sets of marks as depictions, but which resist integration when the spectator attempts to take in the complete configuration of marks and see it as a depiction of an object or scene. Hence they cause no trouble for an account of pictorial perception in terms of a perceived structural isomorphism.

It is important to realize that the idea of a perceived structural isomorphism is not restricted to the spatial structure of a visible state of affairs, that is, to spatial relations amongst its elements. It would be necessary to impose this restriction if the aim were to capture only what is barely essential to depiction; but it would be wrong to do so if the aim is to capture the full pictorial content of any depicted scene. Whereas a picture must be designed to depict spatial relations, it need not be designed to depict anything else. But if, as is usually so, it attempts more and aims to depict comparative brightness, perceived textures or colours, for example, then the perception of its pictorial content requires more than a perceived likeness with the spatial structure of the depicted state of affairs. When an artist depicts colour—when he depicts not merely a state of affairs composed of objects of kinds that are coloured in reality, but a state of affairs composed of objects that are depicted *as* coloured—the chromatic aspect of the visual field assumes a crucial role in the spectator's visual awareness of what the picture depicts. In such a case, the objects in the depicted state of affairs are seen as looking coloured according as their representatives in the picture-surface are seen as coloured, so that there is not only a perceived isomorphism of spatial relations but a correspondence of perceived colour: the spectator sees the picture not merely as a structural spatial isomorph but also as a chromatic icon.[12]

7. A theory of depiction is incomplete without an account of naturalistic depiction, and it is a virtue of the theory I have developed that, as I shall show, it yields so easily a plausible account of naturalism. But the word 'naturalism', used to describe manners of depiction, is ambiguous, and a picture that is naturalistic in one sense may not be so in another. In the sense I am concerned with, a picture is naturalistic if, or to the extent that, the depicted state of affairs is depicted as it looks. So a naturalistic picture is one in which the subject's visual appearance is accurately depicted.

But this introduction of the idea of naturalistic depiction is not fully satisfactory: it must be improved by the acknowledgement of the relativity of the concept. For, in the first place, there is no such thing as *the* visual appearance of an object or scene. The appearance an object presents to the viewer is dependent upon the point of view from which it is seen, the manner in which it is illuminated, and the mental and visual apparatus of the viewer. It also depends on the nature and condition of the medium

---

[12] Conceiving of a picture as a structure of elements and of pictorial perception as requiring a perceived isomorphism of structure makes possible a unitary account of pictorial content and enables the limits of depiction to be drawn. The foundation of visual field representational content consists of (i) purely spatial relations, (ii) variations in lightness and darkness, and (iii) variations in hue. Structures of marks on a surface can depict these features in so far as aspects of the marks have the right logical multiplicity. So two-dimensional spatial relations can be depicted by the two-dimensional spatial relations of the marks, hue by the marks' colours, lightness and darkness by the relative densities of points or lines or by the degree of lightness or darkness of an area. Moreover, the fineness of the depicted detail is determined by the fineness of variations in the representative aspects: pictures in a medium that restricts the available variations in a representative aspect are thereby restricted in the subtlety with which they can depict the corresponding feature.

through which the object is seen, as is underlined by Hazlitt's comment that Turner's paintings had become 'representations not properly of the objects of Nature as of the medium through which they were seen'. Furthermore, an object's appearance is affected by how the viewer focuses his eyes, the distribution of his attention, and the conscious or unconscious way in which he scans the environment; and since every artist sees the world he depicts, the manner in which he looks at the world will determine the appearance in his picture of the objects whose look he attempts to capture. It is characteristic of Cezanne's still lifes to contain apparent distortions of the forms of the objects depicted, and the objects, as depicted, are normally seen by the spectator as distorted. But, as Anton Ehrenzweig has argued, Cezanne's so-called distortions:

make sense if they are experienced as part of the total (undifferentiated) visual field rather than a wandering pinpoint of precise focal vision. Peripheral vision that fills far the greater part of the field of vision can easily distort the stable gestalt shapes of our ordinary awareness much in the way in which Cezanne made his apples bulge and his table tops topple, and fractured the edges of a table. Seen in this way Cezanne painted realistically.[13]

In addition to these reasons for admitting relativity, a picture can be naturalistic in its rendering of one aspect or feature of the world and not in another, and a picture that is overall more naturalistic than another can be less naturalistic in its treatment of some particular aspect of its subject matter. The use by Western artists of chiaroscuro and linear perspective to give the verisimilitude of solidity in natural objects and their recession in space makes their pictures *in these respects* more naturalistic depictions of the visible world than the works of, say, Japanese artists. Our judgements about the naturalism of pictures should be, therefore, not just comparative, but relative—relative to specific features of the world which are either not depicted or depicted more or less accurately.

Given this understanding of naturalism, what account should be given of the experience of seeing a picture as a naturalistic depiction? I have elucidated the experience of seeing what a picture depicts in terms of a perceived resemblance between the structures of two visual fields: the structure of the elements (drawn lines, for example) in one visual field is

[13] Anton Ehrenzweig, *The Hidden Order of Art* (London: Weidenfeld and Nicolson, 1968), 113.

seen as looking like the structure of the elements (edges, say) in another visual field. Now the points of perceived resemblance between the one and the other can be more or less numerous. For a schematic picture they will be few, and for a more detailed picture many. If we consider some visible feature (colour, for example) that the state of affairs depicted possesses in reality, either some corresponding aspect of the representation in the visual field of the depiction is experienced as more or less closely resembling the representation of that feature in the relevant visual field of that state of affairs or not. If the spectator is aware of the appearance of that feature in the state of affairs, to the degree that there is an experienced match, to that degree the spectator experiences the picture as depicting that feature naturalistically. This account applies to all features of the representation of the state of affairs in the visual field, and this includes distance 'cues', such as aerial perspective. But it does not apply to represented distance itself, which belongs not to the visual field but to the visual world. I believe that this is the point at which the idea of an imagined visual awareness of the third dimension should be introduced. A spectator experiences a picture that accurately depicts the spatial relations obtaining in a state of affairs as naturalistic in its depiction of distance not only to the degree that there is an experienced match of distance cues, but also (or alternatively) in so far as it encourages him to imagine the represented distances in the state of affairs depicted: the more vividly the spectator imagines the missing third dimension, the more intensely naturalistic he finds the picture's depiction of distance. The greater 'sense' of distance that some pictures give us arises from their strongly encouraging us to reverse in our imagination the activity of the artist, overcoming the loss of the third dimension intrinsic to a two-dimensional pictorial representation by its imagined reconstruction beyond (and perhaps in front of) the plane of the picture. The imaginative projection of the third dimension into the marks on the picture's surface, when strongly supported by the nature of the picture, makes the spectator's awareness of distance in the depicted state of affairs especially vivid and in that respect enhances the picture's naturalism.

8. A theory of depiction derives its support from its ability to explain salient facts about pictures and to make sense of pre-theoretical intuitions. The account I have developed accommodates the basic pre-theoretical intuition that a picture is designed to look like what it depicts by giving this intuition

a definite form. The sense in which, for a spectator who sees a picture as a depiction of a certain state of affairs, the picture looks like what it depicts is that the spectator sees the structure of the picture as being isomorphic with that of the (appropriate) visual field of the state of affairs depicted: the picture must look like what it depicts, but only in respect of the perceived structure of the picture and the visual field structure of what is depicted.

The power of the theory I have put forward is demonstrated by the ease with which it accounts for many of the most significant and distinctive features of pictorial representation:

(i) The force of the consideration that a picture depicts its subject from a point of view is in no way weakened by the existence of pictures that combine depictions of an object, or parts of an object, from different points of view, as in Cubist works, nor by the existence of pictures that appear not to have a fixed point of view, as in certain of Cezanne's water-colours, or for which there is an indefiniteness in the location of the point of view with respect to the depicted world, as in a panoramic landscape by Ruisdael, nor, finally, by the existence of pictures for which the nature of the point of view is minimally determined, as in a typical schematic picture by a young child. The reason why depiction must always be from a point of view is that a picture is seen as depicting its subject only if it is seen as being isomorphic with the relevant visual field of that subject, and a visual field of that subject has to be a visual field of it *as seen from* a point of view.[14]
(ii) A spectator who has no idea what a certain state of affairs would look like (or—to cover fictional kinds—is supposed to look) cannot see a picture as a depiction of that state of affairs because the kind of seeing this requires involves a perceived isomorphism of structure between the picture and the visual field of the state of affairs depicted—something that is denied to a spectator who is unaware of the look of that state of affairs.[15]

[14] What it is for a picture to depict its subject from a certain point of view is for the picture to be correctly seen as being structurally isomorphic with the visual field representation of that subject *as seen from* that point of view. The fact that a visual field representation of an object is always of the object as seen from a point of view is compatible with the existence of objects that look exactly the same from different points of view at equal distances, as in the case of a uniformly illuminated, uniformly coloured, and textured spherical object.

[15] The requirement is not that the viewer should be *familiar* with the look of the state of affairs, which would rule out the possibility of learning what a certain kind of thing looks like from a depiction of something of that kind. When an observer sees a depiction and learns from it what something of kind K (an ibex, say) looks like, what happens is that his prior knowledge of what a certain kind of

(iii) This theory of pictorial perception easily explains what Richard Wollheim has called the fact of 'transfer'[16]—the fact that if I can recognize a picture in a certain style of one kind of thing (a cat, say), and I know what another kind of thing (a dog, say) looks like, I am thereby endowed with the ability to recognize a picture in that style of that other kind. For pictorial perception is founded on the capacity to see a surface as structurally isomorphic with a representation in the visual field, and the possession of this capacity for one kind of thing demands no more than for another kind. It also demands no less—an awareness of how the thing looks. Hence, if this requirement is satisfied, the capacity generalizes from one kind of thing to another.

(iv) The reason why pictorial perception must satisfy 'the requirement of localization'[17]—for each depicted part of a depicted object, if a spectator sees that part depicted there must be an answer to the question of whereabouts in the picture he sees it depicted—is that seeing the structure of a surface as being isomorphic with the visual field structure of a state of affairs requires seeing elements of the surface as being representatives of elements in the state of affairs depicted.

(v) The (murky) intuition that depiction is based on a 'natural', rather than a purely 'conventional', relation can easily be preserved in the face of the obvious fact that, even given constancy of point of view and prevailing conditions, there are indefinitely many ways or styles of depicting any particular kind of thing. For a perceived structural isomorphism between each of the various members of a set and a certain state of affairs allows of differences in the representative elements of the structures of the members, differences in non-pictorial elements, differences in levels of abstraction at which the isomorphism is experienced, differences in the kind or number of features (colour, texture, play of light, etc.) of the state of affairs which

---

thing (a powerful goat-like creature, with huge sweeping horns) looks like enables him to see the picture as a depiction of that kind of thing and he learns (from a title, say) that something of kind K looks like that. The fact that you *can* learn what a certain kind of thing looks like by seeing what a picture depicts is most naturally explained by the account of pictorial perception I have offered. Briefly: you learn what something of kind K looks like by seeing a picture as an L-depicting-picture (in Nelson Goodman's sense) and by being informed that the picture is a K-depicting-picture. This combination of factors generates the knowledge of how something of kind K looks only because to see a picture as an L-depicting-picture is to see it as being structurally isomorphic with the (relevant) two-dimensional appearance of something of kind L, and in that sense to see it as looking like an L.

[16] Wollheim, *Painting as an Art*, 77. Cf. Schier, *Deeper into Pictures*, 44.
[17] See Wollheim, 'Seeing-as, Seeing-in, and Pictorial Representation'.

figure in the perceived resemblance, and, finally, allows for distortion of various aspects of the state of affairs.

(vi) The state of affairs depicted by a picture is often, as depicted, indefinite, so that it is neither depicted as possessing a particular visual feature nor depicted as not possessing it, and the spectator sees the picture accordingly. He is able to do this because the species of seeing that a picture demands does not require that for each visual feature of the state of affairs seen to be depicted some element of the picture must be seen as representative of it: it demands only a seen isomorphism of structure (at some level).

(vii) The naturalistic artist's attempt to 'copy' or produce a (two-dimensional) 'likeness' of the visible world—to be true to the world's visual appearance—receives its most unforced explanation by the account I have offered: within the limits of his medium, this is *exactly* what he tries to do. His work is a simulacrum of a visible state of affairs: it depicts a visual world state of affairs by being designed as a structural isomorph of a relevant visual field state of affairs.

(viii) Some pictures are much less easily recognizable as depictions of their subjects than are others; and parts or aspects of a depicted state of affairs can easily be overlooked and require careful scrutiny of the picture if they are to be discerned. Corresponding to this, in the first place, is the fact that a spectator may experience difficulty in seeing the structure of a picture as being isomorphic with that of the visual field of a state of affairs if much detail of the picture-surface lacks pictorial significance (as in certain puzzle-pictures) or the depiction is sketchy, or the relevant visual field is that of the state of affairs as seen from an unusual point of view or in circumstances that distort its normal appearance. Secondly, the fact that an object in a scene can be overlooked is mirrored by the fact that characteristics of the picture-surface can go unnoticed, and the difficulty in discerning the nature of an object when looked at from a certain point of view is likely to be matched by the difficulty in seeing its depiction from that point of view as being isomorphic with its visual field representation from that point of view.

(ix) A perceived isomorphism of structure provides the appropriate found-ation for the activity of imagining of one's seeing a picture that it is an instance of seeing face to face what is depicted—a mode of engagement with pictures that is familiar, although not mandatory. For the activity of imagined seeing must be disciplined if its content is not to diverge from that of the scene depicted, and the nature and specificity of what a spectator, who imagines of his seeing the picture-surface that it is an instance of seeing something else, imagines himself to be seeing is given by the respects in which the surface is perceived as structurally isomorphic with a visual field representation of a state of affairs—unless the spectator's imagination is not securely anchored in the pictorial content of the picture.

(x) The fact that a picture looks like what it depicts (in the sense I have indicated) forms the necessary bridge between our interest in looking at pictures and our interest in looking at the world, and it explains a picture's ability to induce in us responses similar to those induced by what it depicts, as when a schematic depiction of a smiling face causes us to smile. In particular, the fact that our visual interest in the world around us is enhanced and transformed by the contemplation of appearances afforded by pictures, and that we naturally delight in seeing accurately depicted what we delight in looking at face to face, receives its most natural explanation from a theory of pictorial perception that, while doing justice to the spectator's visual awareness of a two-dimensional marked surface before him, links that awareness as firmly as possible with the appearance of the world when it is looked at directly.[18]

---

[18] I am grateful to my former colleague W. D. Hart for his detailed comments and trenchant criticisms (which, for better or worse, I have sometimes resisted) on a typescript of which the material in this essay formed part of the second half. [2007: A great deal of work on pictorial representation has been published since I wrote this essay. By far the best defence of an experienced-resemblance approach to depiction is Robert Hopkins's *Picture, Image and Experience* (Cambridge: Cambridge University Press, 1998).]

12

Wollheim on Correspondence, Projective Properties, and Expressive Perception

> Il est des parfums frais comme des chairs d'enfants,
> Doux comme des hautbois, verts comme des prairies,
> —Et d'autres, corrompus, riches et triomphants.
>
> (Charles Baudelaire, *Correspondances*)

From his earliest writings about the topic, the paper 'Expression', for example, through *Art and Its Objects* (*AO*), 'The Sheep and the Ceremony' (SC), and *Painting as an Art* (*PA*), to 'Correspondence, Projective Properties, and Expression in the Arts' (CPE),[1] Richard Wollheim founded his conception of artistic expression on the notion of correspondence—correspondence between the internal and the external, a psychological or mental condition, on the one hand, and an item in the environment, a portion of nature or an artefact, on the other. It seems likely that throughout this time he also thought of artistic expression as being a function of projection—the projection of a psychological state

---

[1] Richard Wollheim, 'Expression' in G. N. A. Vesey (ed.), *Royal Institute of Philosophy Lectures 1966–67*, i: *The Human Agent*, (London: Macmillan, 1968), reprinted in Richard Wollheim, *On Art and the Mind* (London: Allen Lane, 1973); *Art and its Objects* (New York: Harper & Row, 1968); 'The Sheep and the Ceremony', The Leslie Stephen Lecture, University of Cambridge, 1979 (Cambridge: Cambridge University Press, 1979), reprinted in Richard Wollheim, *The Mind and its Depths* (Cambridge, Mass. and London: Harvard University Press, 1993); *Painting as an Art* (London: Thames and Hudson, 1987); 'Correspondence, Projective Properties, and Expression in the Arts', in Ivan Gaskell and Salim Kemal (eds.), *The Language of Art History* (Cambridge: Cambridge University Press, 1991), reprinted in Richard Wollheim, *The Mind and its Depths*. Where an article has been reprinted in a collection of Wollheim's essays, the page references in the text refer to that collection.

onto an object. But it is only in his later writings that projection emerged as the underlying motor of correspondence, and in these writings he has articulated a theory of expression in art that combines the phenomena of correspondence and projection. To examine this subtle and complex theory—as given in *PA* and further developed in 'CPE' (supplemented by *AO* and SC)—it is necessary to extract it from the marvellously rich tapestries into which it is woven. When the theory is isolated from the competing attractions of its surroundings, certain defects in the design, gaps or uncertain transitions and an unwanted tension, become visible—at least, to my eyes. But the threads that compose the theory appear to entwine in somewhat different ways and to vary in salience across the different works, and in disentangling the threads and weaving them into a self-standing design it is possible that my reconstruction will present only a distorted image of Wollheim's creation—or, at least, of his vision. If, however, my reconstruction is accurate,[2] the theory must, I shall argue, be both amended and amplified: one feature must be discarded, one explicated, a certain argument must be provided and the tension I identify needs to be resolved.

In a nutshell, the theory is as follows. Correspondence is the core of artistic expression: a work of art expresses a psychological condition by corresponding to it; it corresponds to the psychological condition in virtue of possessing a certain perceptible property; the work possesses this perceptible property because the artist gave it this property in order that it would correspond to the condition; and a properly sensitive and cognitively endowed spectator is aware of the correspondence by undergoing an experience of a certain kind when confronting the work—an experience of the work as corresponding to the condition.

But the phenomenon of correspondence is not restricted to works of art. It pertains equally to the natural world. The judgement of a work of art and the judgement of some part of nature that it corresponds to a certain psychological condition have exactly the same content (CPE 155). The difference between the two judgements is just that, in virtue of there being a standard of correctness for the first judgement, given by the achieved intention of the artist (SC 7, *PA* 85–6, CPE 155–7), the first kind of judgement requires a larger cognitive stock than the second, if it is to be

---

[2] This essay was read as a paper to a conference on Richard Wollheim's Aesthetics at Utrecht in May 1997. In the discussion that followed Wollheim acknowledged the accuracy of this reconstruction.

soundly based. This means that it is unnecessary to focus on works of art, rather than nature, in order to grasp the key element of Wollheim's theory of expression, correspondence, and its connection with the phenomenon of projection. Since this is my concern, I shall ignore the question whether the achieved intention of the artist is the appropriate standard of correctness for a judgement of correspondence about a work of art; I shall leave aside the question whether the theory identifies the most central or significant phenomenon of expressiveness in the appreciation of art, or of paintings in particular; and for the most part it will be a matter of indifference whether the item in the environment that corresponds to a psychological condition is thought of as a work of art or a portion of nature.

The fundamental question is: what is correspondence? Wollheim's answer is that correspondence is a relation between some part of the external world and an emotion, mood, or feeling that the part of the external world is capable of invoking in virtue of how it looks (*PA* 82): the world seems to a spectator who perceives the correspondence to match or be of a piece with the emotion, and this experienced correspondence is liable to induce the emotion in the spectator under certain conditions. More perspicuously, for nature or anything else to correspond to happiness, melancholy, depression, or terror, is for it to possess certain (relational) *properties*, properties of an unusual kind, namely *projective* properties. These projective properties are the previously mentioned perceptible properties in virtue of which an item that possesses them corresponds to a mood, emotion, or feeling.

So the question becomes: what is a projective property? Wollheim's answer is that a projective property is a property that is identified through a distinctive, triple-aspect experience (CPE 149),[3] an experience that exemplifies a particular species of seeing, 'expressive perception', a species that presupposes a certain psychological mechanism for dealing with emotions, feelings, and moods (emotions, in short).

This psychological mechanism is so-called complex projection.[4] But Wollheim's theory exploits, not the nature of the fundamentally

---

[3] The experience is both *caused* by and *of* the projective property, as with other kinds of veridical perception (CPE 149).

[4] For the distinction between simple and complex projection, see *The Thread of Life*, 214–15, *PA* 82–3, and CPE 150–2. It should be noted that Wollheim introduced this distinction into psychoanalytic theory.

242 WOLLHEIM ON CORRESPONDENCE AND EXPRESSIVE PERCEPTION

unconscious (*PA* 84) process of projection, but one—at least one—of its consequences. The consequence of the complex projection of an emotion E onto the natural world exploited by the theory is that some part of nature (N) is experienced as having a property (P), a property different from the emotion E projected, the two properties being related in this way: nature is felt to be of a piece with the subject's emotion. That is: to experience N as possessing P in virtue of projecting E onto it is to feel it to be of a piece with one's E; and, more generally, to experience N as possessing P (whether or not as a result of projecting E onto it) is to feel it to be of a piece with E. And this requires an affinity between N and E, i.e. features of N that make it a suitable object for the projection of E—ones that encourage and sustain such a projection.

The idea of expressive perception is therefore the key to the idea of a projective property, and so to the idea of correspondence. But what kind of perception is expressive perception? Expressive perception, the experience through which a projective property is identified—the form of seeing in which projective properties are experienced (*PA* 85)—is characterized, first, as being partly perceptual, partly affective: these constitute the first two aspects of the experience. Now, as a perception of the world this experience will have a representational content—it will represent the world as being a certain way—and as an affect it will be of a certain affective kind. So three questions need to be answered if we are to grasp the character of this experience (and so the character of a projective property): what is the representational content of its perceptual aspect, what is the nature of its affective aspect, and how are the two aspects related to one another?

I take the theory's answers to these questions to be as follows. First, the essential representational content of the perceptual aspect—that component of its representational content in virtue of which it is the perception of a projective property—is that the perceived world corresponds to an affective psychological condition—an emotion, feeling, or mood. Second, the affect is of the same nature as that of the corresponding psychological condition: if the corresponding psychological condition is melancholy, the affect is one of melancholy. And third, the affect has a twofold relation to the appearance (or appearances) of the object it is directed towards:[5] (a) it is

---

[5] This affect is directed, we are told, not just towards the property itself, but towards 'older or more dominant objects' (CPE 149).

caused by the look of the object that possesses the projective property and (b) it affects the look of the object, it colours what is seen, it affects how what is perceived is perceived, so that expressed emotion and perception are fused or integrated (*PA* 82, SC 5). This second relation between affect and appearance implies that a part of the world has a different look when it is perceived with or through this affect from what it has when it is not so perceived: when it is not so perceived it does not seem to match the psychological condition. So its bare appearance differs from its appearance as clothed by or dyed with the spectator's affect: projective properties are laid over various features of the perceived scene or object—features that are such as to encourage and sustain the projection of the corresponding emotion.[6]

But there is also a further characterization of the distinctive experience definitive of a projective property: it reveals or intimates a history or origin, either that of the kind to which it belongs—how the kind of experience it exemplifies comes about—or its own, namely an origin in complex projection. This feature is the third of its three aspects.

At this point it is necessary to take notice of a crucial difference in the nature of the theory as displayed in its various manifestations. In fact, on the evidence of the texts alone, an apparent shift in Wollheim's thinking about the connection between projection and correspondence might well be detected. Whereas SC represents expressive perception as, or as a result of, the projection of the subject's inner emotional state (or, rather, a constellation of such states) onto the object of perception, and maintains that the artist creates his work with the intention of exciting the spectator to project certain mental states onto the work, and *PA* represents correspondences as being formed in projection, CPE acknowledges that in general the perception of correspondence is not a consequence of an immediately preceding act of projection. The apparently abandoned

---

[6] Wollheim maintains that it is impossible to elucidate the required affinity between a part of nature and the corresponding psychological state, to spell out how nature must look if it is to be apt for the projection of that state onto it (CPE 154). But in general there is no insuperable difficulty in specifying the features that an item must possess if it is to be a suitable object of a certain kind of activity, and the reason Wollheim advances in support of his claim—that any convincing description of what it is about some aspect of nature that makes it suitable for the projection of a particular emotion would have to 'upgrade' the mere affinity into the projective properties of which it is 'the mere substrate'—is, I believe, not a compelling consideration. Nevertheless, items that possess projective property P might do so, it seems, not because each possesses the same set of features, but in virtue of indefinitely many differently composed sets of features.

position, seemingly occupied by SC (and also, perhaps, *PA*), represents the expressive perception of N as corresponding to E in this fashion: the look of N causes the subject (i) to experience E and (ii) to project E onto N, as a result of which N is experienced as corresponding to E. In other words, it presents the experience of correspondence that is integral to expressive perception as being the upshot of an act of projection carried out by the subject in front of the perceived scene.[7] But whether this position was abandoned or whether it was never truly embraced, it is certainly not Wollheim's considered view, which is my concern.

With this clarification the supposed third aspect of the experience definitive of a projective property is now ready for examination. In fact, the idea that the experience of expressive perception intimates an origin in complex projection is crucial to Wollheim's theory, for without this idea the theory, as it stands, would not wed expression to projection: the notion of correspondence, explicable independently of the concept of projection, would bear all the weight and would be self-supporting. To see this, consider what the rationale might be for the introduction of the concept of projection into an account of expression. For Wollheim, the rationale could not be that it is intrinsic to expressive perception that the activity of projection is actually operative in it, for, as I have already indicated, Wollheim's theory (in its most recent incarnation) is *not* that the perception of expression or correspondence is itself a matter of the projection of a psychological state that the spectator is in when she encounters, or as a result of encountering, the perceived scene or object. On the contrary, most experiences of expressive perception do not themselves originate in projection—in the projection of a currently experienced emotion (CPE 149). And although a consequence of complex projection is the perception of something in the environment as corresponding to a psychological state, it does not follow that it is intrinsic to such a perception that it, or the kind to which it belongs, originates in complex projection—this would follow only if the perception of correspondence *must* derive from projection. But it is often the case that a certain type of event that is a consequence of one

---

[7] In the discussion that followed the presentation of this paper Wollheim—I believe rightly—dismissed this position as absurd, implying that (despite the appearances) he had never embraced it. Note that the account of complex projection in *The Thread of Life* (Cambridge: Cambridge University Press, 1984), 214–15, reverses the relation between act of projection and experience of correspondence, presenting complex projection as being *triggered* by seeing or thinking of a part of the external world as matching or corresponding to an emotion.

kind of phenomenon can just as well be a consequence of another kind of phenomenon: although one result of the consumption of too much alcohol is a headache, the occurrence of headaches is not tied to the consumption of alcohol. So the concept of projection does not qualify for an essential role in an account of expressive projection merely because one way in which expressive perception can occur is in the aftermath of and as a result of complex projection. Another way of bringing out this point is to question what is meant by 'the sort of experience they [expressive perceptions] exemplify'. For as yet—in the light of any considerations actually brought forward by Wollheim in his writings—there is no reason to concede anything more in general than that an experience of expressive perception is an experience of a kind similar in one respect to the kind of experience immediately brought about by complex projection: it is a perception of correspondence. In the absence of a compelling argument for the claim that the perception of an external item as matching a psychological condition is possible *only because and in virtue of* prior projection, the recognition of projection as an essential constituent of the analysis of expression is entirely dependent upon the intimation thesis. In sum: the rejection of the idea that the activity of projection must take place in or immediately prior to expressive perception, and the failure to eliminate the possibility that the perception of correspondence might be rooted, not just in projection, but in some other, independent psychological phenomenon, requires the introduction of the intimation thesis to bind expressive perception to projection.

But the thesis is problematic. It will be simpler to concentrate on the standard case, in which the intimated origin is, not the experience's own, but (supposedly) that of the kind to which it belongs. First: in what sense is it supposed to intimate that the origin of the kind of experience it exemplifies is the activity of complex projection? Presumably, for an experience to intimate something about itself the intimation must be an aspect of its phenomenology. But what form does the intimation assume? I take it that the answer to this question is that the intimation helps to compose the experience's intentionality: it is part of its thought-content or it is at least contained in the experience as a thought.[8] But if this is so, what is the precise content of the intimating thought? Perhaps

---

[8] For this distinction, see *The Thread of Life*, 38, 118.

the natural interpretation would be to construe it as something like this: 'Experiences of this sort in general originate in complex projection'. But it is worth noticing that the comparison with bodily pain that Wollheim brings forward to clarify the intimation claim (CPE 150) invites a different interpretation. A bodily pain that does not originate in damage to the part of the body in which it is felt is held to intimate, not how it came about, but how pain in general arises, namely from damage to the body. But if it does carry the general intimation it does so only by falsely intimating its own origin in damage to the bodily part in which it is felt: the difference between a pain that does and one that does not originate in damage to the part of the body in which it is felt concerns, not the nature of the intimation carried by the pain, but only the intimation's truth-value. So another interpretation of the intimating thought—an interpretation that would render the thought generally false—would be this: 'This experience originated in (is an immediate upshot of) complex projection'. In fact, Wollheim's own suggestion is that the intimation is a matter of recognizing that the object of perception is something onto which we might have, or could have, projected the corresponding inner state (CPE 153–4).[9]

Whichever interpretation is preferred, if the intimation is supposed to be contained in the experience as a thought, it seems untrue that it really is a characteristic of the experience of expressive perception that the experience intimates the origin of the kind it exemplifies—an origin in complex projection, according to the theory. For this would require not only that anyone capable of expressive perception possesses the concept of complex projection—a requirement that many would regard as sufficient to render the characterization untenable, but that Wollheim himself might embrace, given his commitment to some knowledge of psychoanalytic theory being inherent or innate[10]—but also that this concept is drawn upon by the subject and enters into her experience of correspondence between inner and outer. And this certainly seems contrary to the facts, at least on the supposition that if an experience intimates something about itself this intimation must announce itself to us when we reflect on the experience in order to determine if it tells us this about itself. For reflection

---

[9] Wollheim sometimes seems to equate the experience of N as being of a piece with E with the perceptual recognition of N as being apt for the projection of E.

[10] In the discussion at Utrecht Wollheim confirmed what I had taken to be his belief that anyone capable of expressive perception possesses the concept of complex projection.

on the experience of expressive perception—at least, reflection on my own experience of the expressive perception of nature or the perception of the expressive properties of works of art—fails to reveal a thought concerning complex projection.

A final point about the intimation thesis: even if there is a kind of perceptual experience that possesses the intimation-of-origin-in-projection-aspect, it seems clear that there could be experiences otherwise intrinsically indistinguishable that lack the intimation-of-origin-in-projection-aspect. And an experience lacking the intimation-aspect would appear to be just as good a candidate for the role of the experience definitive of expressive perception as one that possesses it. In other words, there seems to be no good reason why only a perception that possesses the intimation-aspect should be held to constitute a perception of correspondence. For it to be essential to a perception of correspondence that it possesses the intimation-aspect, the possession of this aspect would, it seems, need to play a significant role in expressive perception—a role not in fact assigned to it by the theory and, moreover, one that expressive perception appears not to require.

For these reasons, the characterization in terms of intimation appears to me to be wide of the mark.[11]

But the subtraction of the intimation-aspect from Wollheim's characterization of the experience of expressive perception would render it too thin to be enlightening. For any illumination of the experience would be entirely dependent on the specification of, first, its affective aspect and, second, the way in which this affect transforms the affectless perception, because the essential representational content of the perceptual aspect of the experience—that the perceived object corresponds to, matches, is of a piece with, a particular psychological state—is specified in terms of an unelucidated notion of correspondence or match.[12] Moreover, the transformation effected by the affect appears to be precisely that the perception becomes the perception of a correspondence between outer and inner.[13]

---

[11] It is notable that the intimation-thesis is introduced into the theory only in CPE: there is no suggestion of it in any previous formulation.

[12] As it stands, this might well not do justice to Wollheim's position, for he sometimes appears to construe 'N corresponds to E' as being equivalent to 'N is suitable for E to be projected on to it'. But this equivalence would not be an equivalence of concepts, and the kind of argument necessary to support the equivalence is missing from every presentation of his theory.

[13] Wollheim never attempts to make clear why the perception of correspondence should be made possible only through an affect attached to, integrated into, the perception, or how exactly the affect

Accordingly, any light thrown upon the experience derives solely from the characterization of the affect integral to it.

In fact, there is also a question mark over the affective aspect.[14] For there is an important feature of Wollheim's theory that I have not yet mentioned which stands in a somewhat problematic relation to a feature of his account already introduced. The additional feature is this. In his mature thought Wollheim insists that it is unnecessary that the artist, in creating a work as an expression of an emotion, or the spectator, in appreciating it as an expression of an emotion—the artist being the original spectator of the work—should actually feel the emotion that the work expresses: it is perfectly possible for the artist not to be in the emotional condition expressed by the work or for the spectator not to be excited to that emotion; it is sufficient that each should be able to draw upon the emotion or upon memory of it (CPE 157, AO, §17). Rather than being expressive of an emotion in virtue of having been produced in that condition and/or being productive of it, a work of art is expressive of an emotion because it is the sort of thing that one would make if one were feeling the emotion and/or something that would elicit the emotion in one in certain circumstances.[15] (Compare the idea that to experience a part of nature as being of a piece with an emotion requires the recognition that one might or could have projected that emotion onto that part.) But this means that the theory is faced with a dilemma. For either the affective element of the distinctive experience of a projective property is an actual feeling of the expressed or corresponding emotion, or it is not. But if it is, this contradicts the concession that the spectator who perceives a projective property need

manages to transform a perception of something in the environment into one in which the item is seen to correspond to the psychological state the affect exemplifies.

[14] In addition to the consistency problem identified below, there is a question about the rationale for insisting on an affective aspect to the experience of expressive perception. The rationale could not be that the suitability of an item to have E projected onto it can be recognized only by the item's encouraging the spectator actually to project E onto it, given Wollheim's position that recognition of that suitability does not itself essentially involve that projection. Perhaps the intended rationale is that the suitability of an item to have E projected onto it is recognizable only through the item's inducing in the spectator an affect of the same nature as E.

[15] In AO (§16) there is the suggestion that a spectator, who appreciates what a work expresses but who does not think of the work as being produced in that emotional condition or is not moved to that emotion, will think one or both of two thoughts: in lieu of attributing the emotion expressed to the artist, the spectator will see the work as being the sort of thing that she would make if she were feeling the emotion; and if the work does not cause the spectator to feel the emotion expressed, she will regard the work as something that would elicit the emotion in her in other circumstances.

not actually feel the emotion expressed. So if the characterization of the distinctive experience of a projective property is to be preserved, the second horn of the dilemma must be embraced. But if the affective aspect of the distinctive experience of a projective property is not an actual feeling of the emotion expressed, what is this affective element and how can it fuse with the perception and colour what is seen?

What Wollheim's theory needs is a sense in which an emotion can be present in a person—present in a non-dispositional sense—without the person actually feeling that emotion. Although he believed that there is such a sense, in the absence of an elucidation of it a resolution of the tension in the theory by reference to it would be merely programmatic. Furthermore, even if an emotion can be non-dispositionally present in a person without her actually feeling the emotion, this would not be enough to reconcile Wollheim's commitments. For his theory requires the affective aspect of the experience of expressive perception to transform the perception from what it would be if stripped of the affect. It would therefore not be sufficient to identify a sense in which someone who does not actually feel the emotion might nevertheless have the emotion present in her in a non-dispositional sense—by thinking about or imagining undergoing the emotion, for example. What is needed is a conception of an emotion that someone does not actually feel on a certain occasion yet is present in the person in an occurrent sense that enables it to modify a perception from not being a perception of correspondence to being such a perception. And the difficulty in specifying the required conception—in explicating the idea of the occurrent realization of an emotion not actually felt and in establishing that it is suited to the required transformation of an affectless perception—is magnified by the indefiniteness in which the concept of correspondence is shrouded.

Part of the difficulty for Wollheim's theory presented by the tension within it derives from his attempt to construct a monolithic concept of expressive perception, applicable to both nature and art. In my view not only is the perception of nature as the bearer of affective properties a different form of perception from the perception of works of art as being expressive of emotion, but there is no form of perception that is correlative with a significant conception of the artistic expression of emotion applicable uniformly across the arts: the variety of the artistic expression of emotion—the variety of the phenomena included under that umbrella notion—precludes this. However, even if the issue of a unitary conception of the artistic expression of emotion is left aside, the experience of, and response to, nature *as nature*, which includes the perception of nature as the bearer of affective properties, is markedly different from the appreciation of art—central cases of the perception of paintings as expressive of emotion, in particular—which is saturated with the understanding of works of art as products of the human mind. A partial resolution of the tension that threatens to tear the theory asunder would therefore be possible, at the expense of a principled bifurcation of the theory, by recognizing that the expressive perception of nature requires the beholder actually to feel the emotion she sees nature to correspond to; for it is only in the case of art that Wollheim has insisted that someone who perceives an external item as corresponding to an emotion need not actually feel that emotion. And this would not be a merely *ad hoc* manoeuvre, for an actual feeling of melancholy or happiness is, it seems, a constituent of the kind of perception of a landscape as being melancholy or happy that Wollheim had in mind. Furthermore, Wollheim himself appears to recognize that this is so. For, first, on at least two occasions where he introduces the notions of expressive perception and correspondence, each time in application not to art but to the natural world, Wollheim builds into his characterization of the expressive perception of some portion of nature the condition that the subject undergoes an emotional experience evoked by what lies before her: the position of both SC and *PA* is that a landscape that is perceived as corresponding to happiness, melancholy, loneliness, or despair is one that induces the emotion, an actual feeling, in the spectator, which feeling transforms the look of the landscape. And, second, Wollheim nowhere departs from this account of the expressive perception of nature by acknowledging the possibility of an appreciation of nature's affective qualities that is not founded on what a spectator actually feels in front of nature.

In conclusion, if the theory is to be viable, whether as an account of artistic expression or the perception of nature as the bearer of emotional properties (i) the characterization of any instance of expressive perception as intimating the origin of the kind of perception it exemplifies in complex projection must be jettisoned, (ii) an argument must be provided that establishes that the perception of correspondence is possible only in virtue of the perceiver having the capacity for complex projection (on pain of expressive perception not being tied to complex projection), (iii) the notion of correspondence needs to be rendered definite by an elucidation of what it is for someone to experience an external item as corresponding to a psychological condition, and this elucidation must further an understanding of why an affect is an integral part of the perception of correspondence and of the affect's capacity to endow the perception with a representational content that it would otherwise lack. In addition, if the theory seeks to capture a central phenomenon of artistic expression, at least within the field of painting, and it remains true to the idea that one who perceives a work's expressive properties does not need actually to feel the emotions expressed by the work, the precise sense in which the experience of expressive perception has an affective aspect—one that does not consist in an actual feeling of the affect—must be clarified.[16]

---

[16] I have had to make small changes to the text to accommodate the fact that the paper was written and delivered while Wollheim was still alive. For Wollheim's response to my assessment of his theory, see Rob van Gerwen (ed.), *Richard Wollheim on the Art of Painting* (Cambridge: Cambridge University Press, 2001), 254–5.

13

Wittgenstein on Aesthetics

1. Wittgenstein had a deep and enduring interest in at least two of the major art forms, literature and music; practised, if only briefly, two others, architecture and sculpture;[1] was an artistic benefactor, leaving part of the fortune he inherited from his father, all of which he gave away, to be distributed to Austrian artists who needed financial support; and towards the end of his life acknowledged aesthetic along with conceptual questions as the only ones that really gripped him (*CV*, p. 91, 1949).[2] But in his first masterpiece his conception of the nature of propositions precluded him from saying anything about art, and art makes only a rare intrusion into his second. In truth, art did not lie at the centre of his philosophical concerns. Nevertheless, it is precisely because he held the finest art in such high esteem, assigning to it an absolute value, that it eludes the net of language as articulated in the *Tractatus*, and he confessed that because it was impossible for him to say in *Philosophical Investigations* one word about all that music had meant in his life, it would be difficult for him to be understood.

2. The *Tractatus* has only a single gnomic remark about aesthetics: 'Ethics and aesthetics are one' (6.421).[3] One, but not the only, meaning of this is clear. Both ethics and aesthetics are concerned with judgements, not of relative but of absolute value. But absolute value lies outside the world (of facts), so that it cannot be expressed in propositions. Accordingly, ethics

---

[1] Wittgenstein is also assumed to have written the poem he gave to Hofrat Ludwig Hänsel, which is appended to the notes taken from his writings as published in the revised edition of *CV*. If this composition, which suffers from a number of defects, really is by Wittgenstein, it provides some confirmation of his own opinion that he would be unable to write a poem (*CV*, p. 67, 1947). According to Paul Engelmann, 'Wittgenstein certainly never wrote a poem in his life' (*LWM*, p. 89).

[2] I use abbreviations for volumes containing Wittgenstein's works or letters or notes taken from his lectures. See end of essay.

[3] This derives from *N*, 24.7.16.

and aesthetics are in this sense one: neither can be put into words. Hence the silence of the *Tractatus* about aesthetics.

It follows that Wittgenstein's early aesthetics, in so far as it can be recovered, must be pieced together from a handful of somewhat scattered remarks that he wrote in the second half of 1916 and which are recorded in the *Notebooks 1914–16* (which, happily, are not so strictly governed by the self-denying ordinance more or less observed in the *Tractatus*). But these remarks are expressed either in an oracular manner, and so stand in need of interpretation, or in a tentative, questioning form, in which case, if they are to be of use, they must be taken as definite indications of Wittgenstein's thoughts. Some of the pieces required to build a picture of Wittgenstein's aesthetics fit fairly easily together; some that are needed to complete the picture are missing. So any reconstruction must be in some respects conjectural. While it is clear that the roots of his aesthetics lie in that of Schopenhauer, for whom the aesthetic attitude was one of pure will-less contemplation in which the subject's entire consciousness is filled by a single perceptual image, so that the object contemplated becomes for the duration of the contemplation the subject's whole world, Schopenhauer quoting Spinoza's 'Mens aeterna est, quatenus res sub aeternitatis specie concipit' in support of his idea that in aesthetic contemplation a person becomes timeless, Wittgenstein's aesthetics diverges from Schopenhauer's in important respects.

According to the *Notebooks*, the connection between art and ethics is that 'The work of art is the object seen *sub specie aeternitatis*; and the good life is the world seen *sub specie aeternitatis*' (7.10.16). Focusing exclusively on art, what this means is that the work of art is the object seen from the point of view of one who is living eternally (in the sense of timelessly) in that she is living in the present (N 8.7.16, T 6.4311). More precisely, the work of art is the representation of the object as the object is seen from the point of view of such a person. The point of view of one living in the present is such that the perceived object is seen without concern for what might happen in the world: it is seen as by one for whom life is unproblematic, one who, being in agreement with the world, experiencing neither fear nor hope (N 14.7.16), is living a good, a happy life, one whose world is happy (N 8.7.16). Accordingly, 'the essence of the artistic way of looking at things [is] that it looks at the world with a happy eye'

(*N* 20.10.16). Correlatively—since 'Art is a kind of expression. Good art is complete expression.' (*N* 19.9.16), and 'There is certainly something in the conception that the end of art is the beautiful. / And the beautiful *is* what makes happy.' (*N* 21.10.16)—the imaginative adoption of this point of view in the engagement with a beautiful work of art—one in which the artist has completely expressed the manner in which the represented object has been seen—renders one happy.

This is an incomplete picture for more than one reason. Most importantly, it omits the unusual form of mysticism that formed the foundation of Wittgenstein's attitude to human life. To fill this gap it is necessary to add a number of ideas. The first is that, in contemplating an object the object becomes one's world, each thing, as a world, being equally significant (*N* 8.10.16). The second is that for a person who experiences wonder at the existence of the world, the experience is one of absolute value (*LE*).[4] The third is that what is mystical is *that* the world exists (*T* § 6.44). The fourth is that 'aesthetically ['künstlerische', literally 'artistically'] the miracle is that the world exists' (*N* 20.10.16). The fifth is that to view the world *sub specie aeternitatis* is to view the world as a limited whole, the feeling of which is the mystical feeling (*T* §6.45). The final idea is that things that cannot be put into words *make themselves manifest* and are what is mystical (*T* §6.522). From these, sympathetically interpreted, it is possible to derive the conclusion that in the appreciation of a work of art, which involves the contemplation of the object as represented by the artist, the object as represented being for the duration of the contemplation one's world, one undergoes an experience of wonder at the existence of the object, an experience encouraged by the artist, a mystical experience of intrinsic, absolute value in which the wonderfulness of the object (as represented)—something that cannot be expressed in propositions—is made manifest to one.[5] And this involves the idea that although the most important aspect of human life, the ethical, cannot be put into words, it makes itself manifest in good art, as, for example, Uhland's poem 'Count

---

[4] 'A Lecture on Ethics' [*LE*], in James Klagge and Alfred Nordmann, *Ludwig Wittgenstein: Philosophical Occasions 1912–1951* [*PO*] (Indianapolis and Cambridge: Hackett, 1993), 41.

[5] For a greatly more detailed construction of Wittgenstein's early aesthetics along these lines, enriched by both an outline of Wittgenstein's early ethics and an account of those aspects of his early aesthetics that he rejected in his mature thought, see R. K. Elliott's outstanding 'Wittgenstein's Speculative Aesthetics in its Ethical Context', in Robin Barrow and Patricia White (eds.), *Beyond Liberal Education: Essays in Honour of Paul H. Hirst* (London: Routledge & Kegan Paul, 1993).

Eberhard's Hawthorn', which Paul Engelmann, who described it as being rare in not attempting to express the inexpressible, and so achieving it, sent to Wittgenstein and which Wittgenstein responded to by writing:

The poem by Uhland is really magnificent. And this is how it is: if only you do not try to utter what is unutterable then *nothing* gets lost. But the unutterable will be—unutterably—*contained* in what has been uttered![6]

Assuming that this is a fairly accurate sketch of Wittgenstein's early aesthetic, and abstaining from any direct criticism of the mysticism of which it is an expression, whatever merits it might have as an account of a certain kind of experience of contemplating an object—one that can also be obtained from a beautiful artistic representation of the object—as a philosophy of art it suffers from a number of manifest weaknesses, of which I shall mention three. First, as it stands it is applicable only to those art forms, such as representational painting, fiction, and poetry, in which works can properly be thought of as representing objects—objects that, as represented, are available for contemplation. Second, it appears blind to the many valuable works of art that, in the sense at issue, can be said to present an object for contemplation, but which are not experienced as beautiful, before which one does not undergo an experience of wonder at the existence of the object, which are not seen from the point of view of one who is, even temporarily, living in the present, and which do not render one happy (in Wittgenstein's or any other sense of the word). Third, it fails to do justice to the way in which the manner of representation of the object figures in the aesthetic appreciation of a work of art. For it assigns to the manner of representation only an enabling function—the function of enabling the spectator or reader to duplicate the way in which the artist viewed the object with wonder—rather than recognizing it as itself a constituent of the work's aesthetic appeal.

3. If we turn to Wittgenstein's later thoughts about art, although there is no extended treatment of aesthetics in his own writings, the resources are not so meagre. In addition to remarks scattered across his published writings, there are notes, more or less reliable, more or less fragmentary, of what he is supposed to have said about aesthetics in various informal 'lectures' that he gave in Cambridge in 1932–3 and in the summer of 1938,

[6] Engelmann, *LWM*, p. 7.

taken by some of those who attended his classes. The lecture notes confirm that he had strong opinions about aesthetics; it should be remembered, however, that many of the recorded thoughts were not considered and carefully articulated opinions but spontaneous remarks.

4. In his lectures Wittgenstein makes a number of claims about the concept of beauty, some of which appear also in his published writings. In the first place, he distinguishes two uses of the word 'beautiful', the first as an expression of approval, the second as giving an item a character, comparable to describing a melody as 'youthful' or a piece of music as 'springy', 'pompous', 'stately', or 'melancholy'. One claim is that such adjectives as 'beautiful' and 'lovely', used as words of approval, play little role in real life when aesthetic judgements are made or in aesthetic controversies—except by those who cannot express themselves well and who use them as interjections. But this claim is of little importance, being compatible with the fundamental status in aesthetic or artistic appreciation of the idea of aesthetic or artistic value, which has often been designated, rightly or wrongly, as beauty. A second claim is that 'beautiful' does not mean the same as 'agreeable'. It does not, Wittgenstein argues, since, for example, we might choose not to attend a performance of a particular work precisely because we cannot stand its greatness and we might prefer one work to another that we think is much finer. Here, it is clear, the notion of beauty is going proxy for that of artistic value and this second claim, understood in this way, is now widely recognized. A third, which might best be considered as a conjunction of propositions, can be expressed like this: the word 'beautiful' is a 'family resemblance term', being applied to its instances in virtue, not of something common and peculiar to them, but of 'a complicated network of similarities overlapping and criss-crossing'; it has different meanings when applied to things of different kinds; the beauty of a face is something different from the beauty of a chair or a flower or the binding of a book; the fact that more can be said about whether the arrangement of flowers in a bed is beautiful than about whether the smell of lilac is beautiful shows that 'beautiful' differs in meaning in the two cases. Now it is unsurprising to find Wittgenstein applying one of the leading ideas of his later thought to the concept of beauty, denying that beautiful things fall under the concept of beauty in virtue of sharing a property common to and distinctive of them. But it might be thought

that this is not tantamount to asserting that it has a multiplicity of different meanings. However, Wittgenstein was in fact happy to present his insight in this fashion, as his representing the word 'good', as used in ethics or aesthetics, as having 'a family of meanings' shows (*PI*, §77). Moreover, for any family resemblance term in our language, it would be possible for there to be a language in which the range of the term in our language is divided up amongst a number of terms in the foreign language, and yet for it to be possible, on a certain occasion, in application to particular things, for us to lose nothing of the sense of what we want to say in using our term by using instead the more specialized word (see *CV*, pp. 27–8); and Wittgenstein himself, with the idea of family resemblances in mind, advocated approaching the melodies of different composers 'by applying the principle: every species of tree is a "tree" in a different sense of the word' (*CV*, p. 54). But it might well be better to express the reason why the beauty of one kind of thing (a person's eyes, say) is very different from the beauty of another kind (a Gothic church, for example) is because 'beautiful', like 'good', is often used as an attributive, rather than a predicative adjective, needing to be taken together with the substantive it qualifies, so that what makes an instance of one kind of thing beautiful (as something of that kind) differs from what makes an instance of another kind a beautiful thing of that kind.[7]

In aesthetic judgements, about music or poetry or clothes, for example, the words used are not such aesthetic adjectives as 'beautiful' but, Wittgenstein maintains, words akin to 'right' and 'wrong', 'correct' and 'incorrect'. A certain kind of sensitive, discriminating person who is adept at distinguishing what is correct from what is incorrect in a particular area, who experiences aspects of objects within that domain as in accordance with or as transgressing the rules (of harmony and counterpoint, or of the measurements of a coat, for example), or as close to or distant from an ideal, is said to appreciate items of that kind. This normative element in the appreciation of a work of art or non-artistic artefact is misrepresented if artistic or aesthetic appreciation is thought of as merely a matter of

---

[7] Alice Ambrose's notes of Wittgenstein's lectures 1932–3 represent Wittgenstein as saying 'The words "beautiful" and "ugly" are bound up with the words they modify, and when applied to a face are not the same as when applied to flowers and trees' (*AWL*, p. 35), which might perhaps be interpreted as in a rough way making the point that 'beautiful' is often used as an attributive adjective.

what gives pleasure to the listener, reader, or viewer. In fact, Wittgenstein maintains, it is impossible to describe properly what aesthetic appreciation consists in; it can be made sense of only by locating it in the cultural context to which it belongs and from which it derives its distinctive shape; different cultures determine different forms of artistic and aesthetic appreciation; the character and scope of appreciation vary from person to person; and any description of a culture that illuminates the nature of aesthetic judgements within that culture will be a description of a complicated set of activities from which the words used to express those judgements draw their life.[8]

Wittgenstein has been criticized for making a grasp of rules an integral element of the notion of aesthetic appreciation.[9] For although aesthetic judgement and artistic criticism are certainly directed towards the evaluation of an object or work of art and the identification of its merits or demerits, the reasons available for judgements of these kinds are not restricted to what agrees with or flouts a rule, or—to take up the other element Wittgenstein acknowledges—in what way or to what degree something is distant from or near to an ideal. Moreover, there are no established rules that many poor or mediocre works of art violate or to which many fine works conform. But, as far as rules are concerned, Wittgenstein's view appears to be no more than that a knowledge of rules is essential in certain areas for the formation and refinement of aesthetic appreciation, not that criticism is confined to or in the main consists of appreciation of rule-following or rule-transgression. It is true, however, that the idea of something's being correct or incorrect has little relevance to what is usually understood by aesthetic appreciation, and unless the notion of an ideal is understood to cover every aesthetic merit, the elements explicitly acknowledged in Wittgenstein's account of aesthetic judgement fail to recognize the variety of resources available to the critic in praising or criticizing a work. Wittgenstein excludes 'the *tremendous* things in Art' from the domain of appreciation, for in these cases it is not a matter of finding them correct. But since, as I have already indicated, the notion of correctness lacks an important place in the ordinary notion of aesthetic appreciation, the fact that the 'entirely different things' that come into play with the tremendous are not specified need not concern us.

    [8] Michael Tanner's highly sympathetic and intelligent 'Wittgenstein and Aesthetics' (*The Oxford Review*, no.3 (Michaelmas 1966), 14–24) contains the best elucidation of this view.
    [9] See, for example, H. Osborne, 'Wittgenstein on Aesthetics', *The British Journal of Aesthetics*, 6/4 (October 1966), 385–90.

This is underlined by the fact that Wittgenstein's account of aesthetic judgement outlined above is restricted to a single kind of aesthetic judgement, one that explicitly evaluates the object judged, deeming it admirable, wonderful, well done, defective, lacking in some desirable quality, or whatever. But the language of criticism encompasses more than one sort of aesthetic judgement, and this range is implicitly recognized by Wittgenstein in his remark 'It is possible—and this is important—to say a *great deal* about a fine aesthetic difference' (*LWI*, §688, *PI*, p. 219)[10] and is manifest in his concern with the enhancement of the understanding of art through appropriate characterization of a work, a topic I consider later. However, what can be said here is that, at least as far as the individual appeal of a work is concerned, if not the work's artistic value, Wittgenstein held that if you get another to perceive a work as having the same aesthetic character as you do but it does not appeal to them, then that is the end of the discussion; and he pointed a parallel with a discussion in a court of law, where, reaching agreement on the circumstances of some action, you hope that what you say will appeal to the judge.[11]

5. Although Wittgenstein on one occasion practised architecture, assuming control of the project to design a house in Vienna for his sister Gretl, applying himself to the task with characteristic fanatical zeal, he believed that he possessed only artistic taste, understanding, and good manners, rather than creative power, and thought of his architectural work as merely the rendering of an old style into a language appropriate to the modern world. Nevertheless, in light of his strong feelings about architecture it is disappointing to find virtually nothing in his published writings about architectural aesthetics. In fact, there is little more than these remarks:

Remember the impression made by good architecture, that it expresses a thought. One would like to respond to it too with a gesture.

(*CV*, p. 26)

Architecture is a *gesture*. Not every purposive movement of the human body is a gesture. Just as little as every functional building is architecture.

(*CV*, p. 49)

---

[10] See also *RPPI*, §357.
[11] See *AWL*, p. 39 and G. E. Moore, 'Wittgenstein's Lectures in 1930–33', *PO*, p. 106.

Architecture glorifies something [its purpose] (because it endures). Hence there can be no architecture where there is nothing to glorify.[12]

(*CV*, p. 74)

The principal thought is that a building is properly thought of as architecture only if it is a gesture, and good architecture, through its endurance, glorifies the function of the building—as palace, church, or house, for example—and inclines one to respond to it with a gesture of one's own (a response that I seem to be immune to). Wittgenstein does not explain his characterization of architecture as being a gesture and there is no indication of what the connection might be between architecture's being a gesture and good architecture's glorifying something. If we leave aside the idea of glorification, two linked questions arise. The first is what exactly the characterization of a work of architecture as a gesture comes to: can a building be communicative or expressive in the sense that a gesture is, and, if so, how large a range of psychological states can buildings encompass? The second is whether this characterization, properly understood, is an appropriate indication of the kind of aesthetic significance architecture possesses.

Perhaps it will be thought that to pose these questions is to take too seriously an isolated remark or two from writings that Wittgenstein had no intention of publishing. But this is not so. For Wittgenstein's notion of a gesture informs his thoughts about another art—one that was especially dear to him. Wittgenstein had an exceptionally good musical memory and an acute ear, and frequently—'every day & often' (*CV*, p. 32)—heard music in his imagination; he played the clarinet very well and was unusually adept at whistling music, sometimes performing complete works. Music was, perhaps, his favourite art, and he regarded it as being in a certain sense 'the most sophisticated art of all' (*CV*, p. 11). So it is unsurprising that by far the greatest number of remarks on aesthetics in his published writings are on music; and he is fond of representing a musical theme that impresses him as being a gesture. To understand Wittgenstein's aesthetics of music it is necessary to understand this characterization, and a correct interpretation of it will make clear whether the idea of architecture as being a gesture identifies architecture's principal aesthetic character.

---

[12] I have chosen one of Wittgenstein's formulations and inserted the words in square brackets from another of the variations he rings on this theme.

6. The main issue that occupies Wittgenstein is: what is it to listen to or to play a piece of music with understanding?

As in the familiar case of understanding language, Wittgenstein argues that it is wrong to think of understanding a piece of music—one you are playing or are merely listening to—as consisting in a process of some kind accompanying the playing or listening: no accompanying process is either necessary or sufficient for understanding.[13] But he goes further and likens understanding a sentence to understanding a theme in music:

> Understanding a sentence is much more akin to understanding a theme in music than one may think. What I mean is that understanding a sentence lies nearer than one thinks to what is ordinarily called understanding a musical theme.
>
> (PI, §527)[14]

To see more clearly what this comes to it is necessary to look at Wittgenstein's thoughts about understanding and failing to understand a musical theme.

What Wittgenstein writes about understanding a picture, applies equally to understanding music:

> Here too there is understanding and failure to understand. And here too these expressions may mean various kinds of thing.
>
> (PI, §526)

The principal form of lack of understanding is, of course, not hearing (or playing) the music correctly. Wittgenstein rightly emphasizes the importance of phrasing, 'which can refer to hearing as well as to playing' (PI, p. 202), and other phenomena that are akin to perceiving an aspect, such as 'the reinterpretation of a chord in music, when we hear it as a modulation first into this, then into that key' (PI, §536), or understanding a Gregorian mode, where coming to understand it is a matter of hearing something new, in the same sense as that in which suddenly seeing grouping or seeing a flat pattern three-dimensionally is seeing something new (PR, §224).[15] A rather different case that Wittgenstein mentions is that of hearing

---

[13] See, for example, RPPII, §§466–9, §497, §§502–4 (= Z, §§162–5, §159, §§171–3).

[14] The previous version of this at BB, p. 167 elaborates a little. The entire PI, §527 puts together two passages, edited, from BB, pp. 167, 166.

[15] Hence Wittgenstein's characterization of lack of a 'musical ear' as being akin to aspect-blindness (PI, p. 214).

a movement of a Bruckner symphony not as so many little bits, which are always falling short, but as an organic whole (*LWI*, §677). All these cases (which could be added to indefinitely) are ones where music can be *heard* in different ways. It is therefore unsurprising that Wittgenstein should write:

The understanding of a theme is neither sensation nor a sum of sensations. Nevertheless it is correct to call it an experience inasmuch as *this* concept of understanding has some kinship with other concepts of experience. You say 'I experienced that passage quite differently this time'.

(*RPPI*, §469 = *Z*, §165)

Another case that Wittgenstein mentions is that of hearing a repeat or transition as correct or necessary. In *Remarks on the Foundations of Mathematics* there is the isolated enigmatic sentence 'The *exact* correspondence of a correct (convincing) transition in music and mathematics' (*RFM*, Part III, §63), which, happily, is illuminated by a much later remark:

Take a theme like that of Haydn's (St. Antony Chorale), take the part of one of Brahms's variations corresponding to the first part of the theme, and set the task of constructing the second part of the variation in the style of its first part. That is a problem of the same kind as mathematical problems are. If the solution is found, say as Brahms gives it, then one has no doubt;—that is the solution.

(*RFM*, Part VII, §11)

In *Philosophical Grammar* Wittgenstein distinguishes two kinds of musical understanding: (*a*) intransitive (or autonomous) understanding, as in understanding a melody in the sense of being able to follow the melody as a melody (*PG*, Part I, §§37,34), and (*b*) understanding a piece of music in the sense of understanding why it should be played in a certain manner, the understanding consisting in the ability to translate what is understood into another 'medium' or 'expression' (*PG*, Part I, §§4,37). Wittgenstein does not there explain what is meant by such a translation, but this becomes clear if we now consider another form of musical understanding, one to which Wittgenstein frequently returned, that of understanding what a musical phrase or theme 'says' or expresses, that is, what its character is, and this, for Wittgenstein, is equivalent to making sense of the impression the music makes on one, or, as he sometimes puts it, the special 'feeling' that a musical phrase gives us (*PI*, p. 182).[16] In fact, Wittgenstein passes freely between this issue and that of understanding how a theme should be played and why it should be played in this manner, and it is easy to see why: if a theme has a certain character then it should be played in such a manner that brings out or respects that character, and if it should be played in a certain manner this is precisely because of the character it possesses. The lack of understanding that Wittgenstein is concerned with is manifested when, being struck by the character of a theme, one finds that one does not know how to describe it. It is also manifested when one does not know how a theme should be played or feels unable to explain why it should be played in a certain manner. It is in response to this difficulty that a crucial aspect of Wittgenstein's thoughts about the aesthetics of music emerges—his emphasis on the importance of comparisons, an emphasis that is given additional significance when it is generalized across the arts in his opposition to the relevance of experimental psychology to aesthetics. For, Wittgenstein maintains, it is often the case that there is no better way, and sometimes there is no other way, of characterizing or making clear a theme's expression—'A theme has a facial expression just as much as a face does'[17] (*RPPI*, §434; *CV*, p. 59)—than by drawing a comparison between the theme and something else; and a person's understanding of a theme's character may consist in the ability to produce an apt comparison.

7. The comparisons one finds in Wittgenstein's writings are more or less restricted to comparisons of music with the same small set of linguistic, more specifically vocal, *actions*:

Here it's as if a conclusion were being drawn, here as if something were being confirmed, *this* is like an answer [reply] to what was said before.

(*Z*, §175)

---

[16] The treatment that Wittgenstein accords this issue of understanding a theme's character he also applies to certain other examples of musical understanding—understanding the necessity for the repeat of a theme or part of one (*CV*, p. 59), or the necessity with which one theme follows another (*CV*, p. 65), for example.

[17] *RPPI*, §434, *CV*, p. 59. Hence Wittgenstein's suggestion that following a musical phrase with understanding is comparable to observing a face and drinking in the expression on the face (*CV*, p. 58), and his other suggestion that just as suddenly understanding the expression on a face might consist in finding the word that sums it up, so suddenly understanding a musical theme might consist in finding a verbal counterpart of the theme (*BB*, pp. 166–7).

Why is just *this* the pattern of variation in loudness and tempo [of a certain musical theme]?... I should not be able to say [what it is all about]. In order to 'explain' I could only compare it with something else which has the same rhythm (I mean the same pattern). (One says 'Don't you see, this is as if a conclusion were being drawn' or 'This is as it were a parenthesis', etc. How does one justify such comparisons?—There are very different kinds of justification here.

(*PI*, §527)

But this gives a false impression of Wittgenstein's conception of the range of possible apt comparisons. For, as he notes:

There is a strongly musical element in verbal language. (A sigh, the intonation of voice in a question, in an announcement, in longing; all the innumerable *gestures* made with the voice.)

(*Z*, §161; cf. *RPPI*, §888)

And this, it seems clear, implies Wittgenstein's readiness to extend the range of appropriate examples to all aspects of the voice that can be mirrored in music. He himself refers to music 'that corresponds to the expression of bitter irony in speech' (*CV*, p. 63).[18] Moreover, he mentions at least one kind of comparison that is not with a linguistic act—the entry of a new character in a story or a poem (*CV*, p. 65). Furthermore, the following passage might perhaps be interpreted to license comparisons with more or less anything:

Does the theme point to nothing beyond itself? Oh yes! But that means:—The impression it makes on me is connected with things in its surroundings—e.g. with the existence of our language & of its intonation, but that means with the whole field of our language games.

If I say e.g.: It is as if a conclusion were being drawn here, or, as if here something were being confirmed, or, as if *this* were the answer to what went before—then the way I understand it clearly presupposes familiarity with conclusions, confirmations, replies, etc.

(See *CV*, p. 59 and the near identical *RPPI*, §§433 and *Z*, §175)

Even if this interpretation should be resisted, there is nothing in Wittgenstein's writings that rules out comparisons with many kinds of phenomena

---

[18] See also *CV*, p. 93. Wittgenstein is referring to the fugato in the first movement of Beethoven's ninth symphony.

other than vocal actions or expressive aspects of the voice.[19] He himself, referring to Labor's playing, writes:

What was it about this playing that was so reminiscent of speaking? And how remarkable that this similarity with speaking is not something we find incidental, but an important and big matter!—We should like to call music, & certainly *some* music, a language; *but* no doubt not *some* music.

(*CV*, p. 71)[20]

And if not all music is highly reminiscent of speech, as it certainly is not—Wittgenstein writes that 'Bach's music is more like language than Mozart's & Haydn's' (*CV*, p. 40)—comparisons with speech will not always be an appropriate way of inducing understanding. Sometimes comparisons with silent thought processes will be more apt. Furthermore, although music is, like speech, an audible phenomenon, it is, simply in virtue of its character as a process, open to characterization other than by reference to speech, and it is clear that comparisons with many kinds of non-linguistic phenomena—all the various modes of motion, fusion and fission, transformations, rising and falling, decline and regrowth, waxing and waning, outbursts of energy, feelings and emotions themselves (rather than their expressions in behaviour), to list but a few—are often more suitable than comparisons with anything specifically linguistic.

Now the ordinary idea of a gesture covers a variety of meaningful bodily actions—actions that express a psychological state or attitude, convey a greeting, request, assent or rejection, indicate an object, or are used as a device to impress, to intimidate, to enforce or to persuade—bound together by the fact that the meaning they possess is not determined by a vocabulary and syntactical conventions (as the meaning of sign language is). But it will have been noticed that Wittgenstein operates with a rather unusual notion of a gesture, for under the head of gestures he includes, not just expressive movements of the body, but all characteristics of the voice

[19] Wittgenstein used to recite with a shudder of awe Mörike's description of music: 'Coming as from remotest starry worlds, the sounds fall from the mouth of silver trombones, icy cold, cutting through marrow and soul; fall through the blueness of the night' (Engelmann, *LWM*, p. 86).

[20] This might be thought to be incompatible with Wittgenstein's remark 'Understanding a musical phrase may also be called understanding a *language*' (*RPPII*, §503 = *Z*, §172). But the point of Wittgenstein's remark is not that music is a language (or a set of languages) in the sense in which the English language is one, but that, like the understanding of a sentence, the understanding of a musical theme requires familiarity with and understanding of much more of the same kind.

that, considered in abstraction from any thought-content that an utterance may possess, are indications of either the kind of vocal action performed or the psychological state of the speaker. Accordingly, Wittgenstein uses 'gesture' and 'expression' more or less interchangeably, indicating that the item referred to has, in this wide sense, an expressive character, as when, speaking of a door that is slightly too large, he is reported as saying that 'it hasn't the right expression—it doesn't make the right gesture' (L&C, p. 31). And this use of the term 'gesture' renders Wittgenstein's characterization of architecture as a gesture relatively uninteresting, for its application to architecture is intended, not to imply that architecture's aesthetic character should be thought of in terms of kinds of linguistic actions, but only to indicate that the physiognomic perception of buildings, an oft-remarked phenomenon, is of prime importance in the aesthetic appreciation of architecture—a standard position (although one not above criticism).

Wittgenstein also characterizes music for which a gesture is an apt comparison as itself a gesture:

there *is* a paradigm outside the theme: namely the rhythm of our language, of our thinking and feeling. And the theme is also in its turn a *new* bit of our language, it is incorporated in it; we learn a new *gesture*.

The theme and the language are in reciprocal action.

(RPPI, §§435–6)

This musical phrase is a gesture for me. It creeps into my life. I make it my own.

(CV, pp. 83–4)

And although Wittgenstein does not elaborate, this must mean that by imagining, whistling, or playing a musical phrase, the character of which he finds expressive, he uses the phrase as an expression of that character.

Wittgenstein does not explain the connection between, on the one hand, a theme's being a gesture[21] and, on the other hand, its character or the manner in which it should be played being explicable by a comparison. But the explanation is obvious: if a theme can itself be thought of as a

---

[21] Wittgenstein nowhere maintains that every theme is a gesture or that a piece of music consists of a succession of gestures (although see CV, p. 84). Roger Scruton (The Aesthetics of Music (Oxford: Clarendon Press, 1997)) has placed the notion of gesture at the heart of his aesthetics of music but has developed it in a way which would not have gained Wittgenstein's approval, for he represents the very experience of music—of hearing sounds as music—as essentially involving the imagination of a bodily action, something that Wittgenstein never countenanced.

gesture then its character or the manner in which it should be played can be elucidated by comparing it with a gesture that has a similar expressive character. A musical theme which, as such, lacks a thought-content, cannot be a question; but it may nevertheless have the character of a question (a questioning character), and if it does, then bringing this to a person's consciousness endows him with the requisite understanding.

8. The elucidation of an object's character by means of comparisons plays a significant role in Wittgenstein's opposition to the relevance of psychological experiments or causal investigations to aesthetics.

Wittgenstein identifies aesthetic reactions that manifest admiration, distaste, or dissatisfaction, for example, as being of prime importance in aesthetics. The crucial feature of such aesthetic reactions is that they are 'directed', that is, intentional, having some item or some feature of an item as their object. Although not wrong, it is, he claims, misleading to think of an expression of discontent, such as 'The door is too low', as an expression of discomfort combined with knowledge of the cause of the discomfort, or to take the question 'What's wrong with this picture?' as announcing a certain discomfort and seeking its cause. For although the word 'cause' is sometimes used to refer to the object of a reaction, it also has other uses in which what is caused does not have an object it is directed to, which is its cause, and it is likely to suggest an analogy with such a use as, for example, when what is being referred to is a pain and its cause, so that an expression of discontent is thought of as an expression of an 'undirected' discomfort combined with knowledge of (or belief about) its cause. Such an expression of aesthetic discontent as 'The door is too low' is not a conjecture but a criticism. It is clear that psychological experiments designed to determine which musical or pictorial arrangement produces the more pleasing effect on a particular person or a set of people are irrelevant to aesthetics, for aesthetics is concerned, not with whether people like a work, but with what reason there may be for a work to be as it is or whether the work would be better if it were different in a particular way. More importantly, Wittgenstein maintains that a psychological investigation of an aesthetic reaction aimed at determining its cause is of no interest to aesthetics, for aesthetics is concerned with the reasons for a person's admiration, satisfaction, or discontent, and these reasons, which will be given by characterizations of the object of the reaction, will be correctly identified only if they command the assent of the person. In close connection with this, Wittgenstein maintains that the sort of explanation one wants when one is puzzled about an aesthetic impression—puzzled about the effect a work has upon one, as he sometimes puts it—is not a causal explanation (corroborated by experience, psychological experiments, etc.). Rather, the puzzlement can be dissolved only in another kind of way—by certain kinds of comparison:

The sort of explanation one is looking for when one is puzzled by an aesthetic impression is not a causal explanation . . .

(*L&C*, p. 21)

The puzzles which arise in aesthetics, which are puzzles arising from the effects the arts have, are not puzzles about how these things are caused.

(*L&C*, p. 28)

As far as one can see the puzzlement I am talking about can be cured only by peculiar kinds of comparisons . . .

(*L&C*, p. 20)

It has been thought that Wittgenstein moves directly from the fact that an aesthetic reaction is intentional to the conclusion that no investigation aimed at discovering the cause of the reaction is necessary to discover what it is directed to and that no causal investigation could show the subject's identification of its object to be mistaken—the subject's belief about the reaction's object has no causal implications and the subject cannot but be aware of what its object actually is.[22] But this fails to do justice to Wittgenstein, and it does not engage with Wittgenstein's principal concern, which is aesthetic puzzlement. Now Wittgenstein was well aware that the object of an aesthetic reaction can also be, in the sense at issue, its cause:

The cause, in the sense of the object it is directed to is also the cause in other senses. When you remove it, the discomfort ceases and what not.

(*L&C*, p. 15)

Moreover, one case that Wittgenstein mentions—looking at a picture and saying 'What's wrong with this?'—makes clear that an aesthetic reaction

[22] If Wittgenstein had made this move it would be vulnerable to the arguments brought against it by Frank Cioffi in his excellent 'Aesthetic Explanation and Aesthetic Perplexity', *Acta Philosophica Fennica*, 28/1–3 (1976), 417–49.

can be directed to an object in such a manner that leaves room for an uncertainty on the subject's part that could be removed by identifying the cause of dissatisfaction: the intentional object of the person's reaction is, for the subject at the time, nothing more specific than the picture, the subject being unaware of what feature of the picture mars it for him or her. Cases of this kind can be multiplied indefinitely. Most importantly, there are different kinds of aesthetic puzzlement, in some of which the puzzle is amenable to causal investigation and the puzzled subject might easily come to embrace a false solution to the puzzle; Wittgenstein's examples are something of a medley; and it is necessary to identify the real focus of his concern.

The principal forms of aesthetic puzzlement that Wittgenstein seems to have had in mind are ones which concern what it is about a work of art that makes it so impressive, or impressive in a particular way—where this means, not what elements of it are responsible for its being impressive, but what its impressiveness consists in, i.e. how it should be characterized—or what is wrong with a certain work or a performance of it—where this means what character has been given to it and why that is misplaced—or why a work has just the distribution of features that it does—where this means what character this distribution gives it and why it has been given this character. In such cases, what is needed to remove the puzzlement is, Wittgenstein claims, some means of focusing attention on the character of the work in such a manner as to enable us to perceive the work as having this character. One way in which this can be achieved is by placing side by side with the work other items that possess the character or by indicating an analogy between the work and something else, as with Wittgenstein's favourite kind of example, the comparison of the particular pattern of variation in loudness and tempo in a musical theme with various speech acts. Such an explanation, if accepted, is persuasive, rather than diagnostic, effecting a clarification or change in the perception of the work, the subject's formerly inchoate impression becoming definite; it differs from the causal diagnosis of a pain in the stomach, where the sufferer's acceptance of the diagnosis is unnecessary and leaves the pain unchanged. This makes it clear that the principal concern of Wittgenstein's interest in aesthetic puzzlement is the enhancement of artistic appreciation: the kind of explanation that dissolves the puzzlement must further the understanding and appreciation of the work of art. This explains his emphasis on comparisons, the requirement that the puzzled subject should agree with a proposed solution to his problem, if the proposed solution is to remove the puzzlement, and the resultant transformation of the subject's impression.

9. Wittgenstein's emphasis on the possibility of musical understanding being effected through the drawing of a comparison between a piece of music and a speech act or succession of speech acts (or 'gestures' of the voice) leaves a number of issues untouched or unresolved. He was, of course, well aware that someone's understanding of a piece of music can be transformed by means of an explanatory comparison even though the person has not been given compelling reasons for accepting the explanation, that is, for the aptness of the comparison, its suitability to indicate, by analogy, the music's character (*CV*, p. 79). He certainly believed that there are right and wrong ways in which a piece of music can be understood, and the appropriateness of any suggested comparison will be determined by what is a correct understanding of the piece. It is regrettable that although he asserts that there are different kinds of justification for explanatory comparisons (*PI*, §527), he nowhere indicates any of them, and he does not engage with the issue of the intersubjective validity of a description of the aesthetic character of a work of art. It is clear that for him a comparison that effects the understanding of the character of a piece of music explains how the piece 'fits into the world of our thoughts and feelings' (*CV*, p. 65),[23] which is certainly a desirable aim. But although he regarded the similarity of (some) music with speech as being 'a big and important matter' (*CV*, p. 71), he did not elucidate its importance; and there is no suggestion as to what the importance might be of similarities with other kinds of phenomena for the vast body of impressive music the character of which is not illuminated by comparison with vocal actions. In an insightful paper Jerrold Levinson, taking inspiration from some of Wittgenstein's remarks, in particular from Wittgenstein's emphasis on comparisons with speech acts, has explored the possibility of construing music, not just as revealing thought processes in the composer, but as itself, like speech, a vehicle of thought, thought embodied by the music.[24] Now similarities between music and speech acts of the kind that Wittgenstein specifies in his comparisons license only that pieces of music that sustain such comparisons have the *audible appearance*

---

[23] See also *RPPI*, §§34–6, 433–6.
[24] Jerrold Levinson, 'Musical Thinking', *Midwest Studies in Philosophy*, 27 (2003), 59–68.

of speech acts, acts which express thoughts. Levinson, who at one point clearly recognizes this limitation, makes a powerful case for the presence and importance of thinking in music, which goes a certain way towards vindicating Wittgenstein's conviction; but the strength of his argument is weakened, happily only minimally, by his flirtation with the view that just as the thought expressed by a stretch of discourse cannot be rendered into music, so the thought expressed by a musical passage cannot be rendered into words—a view that effectively equivocates on the notion of thought by severing the essential connection between the idea of thought and the content of a propositional attitude (something that can be doubted, believed, known).

10. Wittgenstein's elucidation of his claim, quoted above, that 'The puzzles which arise in aesthetics, which are puzzles arising from the effects the arts have, are not puzzles about how these things are caused' (*L&C*, p. 28), reveals that it is in fact directed at a certain conception of the aim of art, which in an unacceptable manner locates the value of a work in its effects. In his published writings Wittgenstein's greatest aesthetic concern is to enforce the autonomy of artistic value, and in particular musical value, against views that deny works of art a distinctive value. His principal target is those theories or tendencies of thought that fail to recognize the true character of artistic value by succumbing to a certain temptation. This temptation—one that Tolstoy fell victim to, as Wittgenstein was well aware (*CV*, p. 67)—arises in reflection upon the nature of art and consists in misrepresenting the appreciation of a work of art. Appreciation is construed as an effect of engaging with the work, but not as the perceptual or perceptual-cum-imaginative experience of the work itself, the 'impression' of the work. Rather, the experience of the work itself is thought of as inducing some other experience, rewarding if we find the work valuable, unrewarding if we do not, which is then conceived of in abstraction from the work that gives rise to it: it is not internally related to the work, and so in principle it could be produced by quite a different cause. The result is that the value of a work of art is thought of as residing in its effects, and these effects are thought of as possessing a nature independent of the work that causes them. So the value of a work of art stands to the work in much the same relation that the value of a medicine stands to the medicine: just as the valuable results of the

medicine can be fully characterized without mentioning the nature of the medicine that causes them, so the value of a work of art is located in an independently specifiable effect. But, as Wittgenstein insisted, this is certainly a misrepresentation of artistic value. For the experience of a work of art does not play a merely instrumental role in artistic appreciation. On the contrary, to appreciate the value of a work is to experience it with understanding—to read, listen to, imagine, look at, perform the work itself. When we admire a work without reservation, it is not replaceable for us by another that creates the same effect, for we admire the work itself, so that its value does not consist in its performing a function that another work could perform just as well. Wittgenstein emphasizes the autonomy of artistic value many times and in a variety of ways, usually with reference to music. For example:

There is a tendency to talk about the 'effect of a work of art'—feelings, images, etc. Then it is natural to ask: "Why do you hear this minuet?", and there is a tendency to answer: "To get this and that effect." And doesn't the minuet matter?—hearing *this*: would another have done as well?

(L&C, p. 29)

If I admire a minuet I can't say: "Take another. It does the same thing." What do you mean? It *is* not the same.

(L&C, p. 34)

There is *much* that could be learned from Tolstoy's false theorizing that the work of art conveys 'a feeling'.—And you really might call it, if not the expression of a feeling, an expression of feeling, or a felt expression. And you might say too that people who understand it to that extent 'resonate' with it, respond to it. You might say: The work of art does not seek to convey *something else*, just itself. As, if I pay someone a visit, I don't wish simply to produce such & such feelings in him, but above all to pay him a visit, & naturally I also want to be well received.

(CV, p. 67)

It has sometimes been said that what music conveys to us are feelings of joyfulness, melancholy, triumph, etc., etc. and what repels us in this account is that it seems to say that music is an instrument for producing in us sequences of feelings. And from this one might gather that any other means of producing such feelings would do for us instead of music.—To such an account we are tempted to reply 'Music conveys to us *itself*!'

(BB, p. 178)

11. At this point it is instructive to consider the distinction Wittgenstein draws in *The Brown Book* (*BB*, pp. 158f.) between a transitive and an intransitive use of the word 'particular'. It is used transitively when it is used as 'preliminary to a specification, description, or comparison', intransitively when it is used 'as what one might describe as an emphasis', where this covers two kinds of emphasis, on the one hand, using it to mean something like 'striking' or 'uncommon', on the other, as an expression of our state of attention when it is focused on the phenomenon to which we are referring. And Wittgenstein identifies a common illusion generated by such a double usage of a word, one that is liable to arise when we are contemplating something and giving ourselves up to the character of the object, allowing it to make its full impression on us. The illusion comes about because it seems to us as if we are attempting to describe the object, despite the fact that no description will satisfy us, the reason being that really we are using the word in the intransitive manner, as an emphasis of the second kind, our confusion leading us to express ourselves by means of a reflexive construction, something of the form 'This has *this* character', indicating the object in question both times, as it were comparing the object with itself. Wittgenstein illustrates this with an example of the particular expression on a pictured face, and later writes:

The same strange illusion which we are under when we seem to seek the something which a face expresses whereas, in reality, we are giving ourselves up to the features before us—that same illusion possesses us even more strongly if repeating a tune to ourselves and letting it make its full impression on us, we say 'This tune says *something*', and it is as though I had to find *what* it says. And yet I know that it doesn't say anything such that I might express in words or pictures what it says. And if, recognizing this, I resign myself to saying 'It just expresses a musical thought', this would mean no more than saying 'It expresses itself'.

(*BB*, p. 166)

And to say 'It expresses itself' would be to use 'express' intransitively, saying nothing about the music's character but being as it were hypnotized by it.

Now Wittgenstein rightly asserts that:

When a theme, a phrase, suddenly says something to you, you don't have to be able to explain it to yourself. Suddenly *this* gesture too is accessible to you.

(*RPPI*, §660; cf. *Z*, §158)

But the inability to describe the impression a theme (line of poetry, or whatever) makes on you, can, as Wittgenstein remarks, result in a reaction closely related to that of the intransitive pronouncement, namely the claim that the impression is indescribable. Of course, Wittgenstein does not concede this claim, for it might well be the case that some description is forthcoming which is accepted as fitting the impression perfectly. But he is more concerned to expose the inadequacy of an idea that might underlie the belief that the impression is indescribable, namely, that we lack the vocabulary or technique necessary for describing it,[25] and another idea, that the impression is separable from the theme, which he undermines with a wry question:

'The impression (made by this melody) is completely indescribable.'—That means: a description is no use (for my purpose); you have to hear the melody.

If art serves 'to arouse feelings', is, perhaps, perceiving it with the senses included amongst these feelings?

$(CV, \text{ p. } 42)^{26}$

12. It has been argued that Wittgenstein regards the intransitive notion of expression as being fundamental in aesthetics and does not allow that (some) music can properly be thought of as, in the transitive sense, the expression of a feeling.[27] But this is wide of the mark and betrays a lack of understanding of the transitive/intransitive distinction. The intransitive notion of expression, as Wittgenstein explains it, could not play a significant role in aesthetics, especially in connection with understanding the character of a piece of music; and for it to be illegitimate to apply the transitive notion to music it would have to be always false that a piece expresses a specifiable feeling. But, of course, Wittgenstein is happy to acknowledge that there is no impropriety in thinking of a piece of music as being an expression of a feeling (in the transitive sense); on the contrary, it is frequently correct to characterize it by reference to the feeling it expresses (LWI, §774). At the same time he wishes to enforce a point of a familiar kind, which can be illustrated best by a passage near the end of The Brown Book (BB, p. 184). Here Wittgenstein discusses an experience that, he writes, he would call a feeling of pastness, and which he roughly describes by saying that it is

---

[25] See L&C, pp. 37–40, PI, §610.   [26] See also PI, pp. 182–3 and LW, I §§373, 376, 380–2.
[27] Roger Scruton, 'Wittgenstein and the Understanding of Music', The British Journal of Aesthetics, 44/1 (January 2004).

the feeling of 'long, long ago', these words and the tone in which they are said being a 'gesture' of pastness, this feeling being specified further as that corresponding to the tune 'Wie aus weiter Ferne' from Schumann's *Davids Bündler Tänze*. This tune, played with the right expression, is, he writes, 'the most elaborate and exact expression of a feeling of pastness which I can imagine'. He then raises this question:

should I say that hearing this tune played with this expression is in itself that particular experience of pastness, or should I say that hearing the tune causes the feeling of pastness to arise and that this feeling accompanies the tune? I.e., can I separate what I call this experience of pastness from the experience of hearing the tune?

It is clear that Wittgenstein denies the separability. His point is that to experience the tune as the expression of the feeling is not to hear the music and to undergo a separable feeling. It is, rather, to hear the tune in a certain manner, as having a certain aesthetic character, comparable—in respect of the inseparability of the experience of pastness from the experience of the music—with hearing a musical phrase as if it were asking a question or drawing a conclusion (*PI*, pp. 182–3).

13. In his later philosophy Wittgenstein's thoughts about aesthetics appear to have been focused almost exclusively upon art, issues in the aesthetic appreciation of nature not appearing to engage him. But one late remark (1947), the interpretation of which is uncertain, appears to indicate that our aesthetic response to nature's most wonderful products played a fundamental role in his thought about art:

The miracles of nature.
   We might say: art *discloses* ['zeige' = 'shows', 'displays'] the miracles of nature to us. It is based on the *concept* of the miracles of nature. (The blossom, just opening out. What is *marvellous* about it?) We say: 'Look, how it's opening out!'

(*CV*, p. 64)

This is not a mere recrudescence of Wittgenstein's early aesthetic, for which the exclusive contemplation of any object whatsoever—Wittgenstein's example is a stove (*N* 8.10.16)—is, for the right person, an experience of wonder. Here the emphasis is on *natural* things and, specifically, those that are most likely to induce wonder, whether or not we live in the present; and the claim is that art is based, not on the miracles of nature, but on the concept of them. The concept of the miracles of nature is the concept of those natural objects (crystals) or phenomena (the opening of blossom) that are best suited to arouse wonder in human beings. If Wittgenstein's claim were that the *concept* of art is based on the concept of the miracles of nature it would, whatever its merits or defects, be easy to interpret it as an assertion about the logical priority of the two concepts. But that is not his claim. If 'art' is understood to cover all the main art forms, so that every art is supposed to be based on the concept of wonder-inducing natural things, I believe that there is no way in which the claim can be interpreted so as to render it both interesting and viable.[28]

ABBREVIATIONS AND REFERENCES

AWL   *Wittgenstein's Lectures, Cambridge, 1932–1935,* ed. Alice Ambrose (Oxford: Basil Blackwell, 1979)

BB   *The Blue and Brown Books,* 2nd edn. (Oxford: Basil Blackwell, 1960)

CV   *Culture and Value,* ed. Georg Henrik von Wright in Collaboration with Heikki Nyman, trans. Peter Winch (Oxford: Blackwell, 1998)

L&C   *Lectures and Conversations on Aesthetics, Psychology and Religious Belief,* ed. Cyril Barrett (Oxford: Basil Blackwell, 1966)

LE   'A Lecture on Ethics', as reprinted in *PO*

LWI   *Last Writings on the Philosophy of Psychology,* Volume I, ed. G. H. von Wright and Heikki Nyman, trans. C. G. Luckhardt and Maximilian A. E. Aue (Oxford: Basil Blackwell, 1982)

LWM   *Letters from Ludwig Wittgenstein with a Memoir,* trans. L. Furtmüller, ed. B. F. McGuinness (Oxford: Basil Blackwell, 1967)

N   *Notebooks 1914–1916,* 2nd edn. (Oxford: Basil Blackwell, 1979)

PG   *Philosophical Grammar,* ed. Rush Rhees, trans. Anthony Kenny (Oxford: Basil Blackwell, 1974)

---

[28] I here diverge from R. K. Elliott (see n. 5), who interprets Wittgenstein's 1947 remark as filling a gap in his early aesthetic, construing 'miracles of nature' to include, not specifically products of nature, but anything whatsoever, as long as it is seen from the right point of view.

PI	*Philosophical Investigations*, 2nd edn., trans G. E. M. Anscombe (Oxford: Basil Blackwell, 1958)
PO	*Philosophical Occasions 1912–1951*, ed. James Klagge and Alfred Nordmann (Indianapolis and Cambridge: Hackett Publishing Company, 1993)
PR	*Philosophical Remarks*, ed. Rush Rhees, trans. Raymond Hargreaves and Roger White (Oxford: Basil Blackwell, 1975)
RFM	*Remarks on the Foundations of Mathematics*, 3rd edn., ed. G. H. von Wright, R. Rhees and G. E. M. Anscombe (Oxford: Basil Blackwell, 1978)
RPPI	*Remarks on the Philosophy of Psychology*, i, ed. G. E. M. Anscombe and G. H. von Wright, trans. G. E. M. Anscombe (Oxford: Basil Blackwell, 1980)
RPPII	*Remarks on the Philosophy of Psychology*, ii, ed. G. H. von Wright and Heikki Nyman, trans. C. G. Luckhardt and M. A. E. Aue (Oxford: Basil Blackwell, 1980)
T	*Tractatus Logico-Philosophicus*, trans. D. F. Pears and B. F. McGuinness (London: Routledge & Kegan Paul, 1961)
Z	*Zettel*, 2nd edn., ed. G. E. M. Anscombe and G. H. von Wright, trans. G. E. M. Anscombe (Oxford: Basil Blackwell, 1981)

Sources and Acknowledgements

The places in which the essays originally appeared are listed below. I am grateful to the publishers for permission to reprint them.

1. 'Aesthetic Judgements, Aesthetic Principles and Aesthetic Properties', *European Journal of Philosophy*, 7/3 (December 1999), 295–311. This essay was read to the Aesthetic Justification conference held at University College London, 27–8 March 1999.

2. 'Aesthetic Essence', in Richard Shusterman and Adele Tomlin (eds.), *The Value of Aesthetic Experience* (Routledge, 2007), 17–30.

3. 'The Acquaintance Principle', *The British Journal of Aesthetics*, 43/4 (October 2003), 386–92. [There are some insertions plus a post-script.]

4. 'The Intersubjectivite Validity of Aesthetic Judgements', *The British Journal of Aesthetics*, 44/4 (October 2007), 333–71.

5. 'The Pure Judgement of Taste as an Aesthetic Reflective Judgement', *The British Journal of Aesthetics*, 41/3 (July 2001), 247–60.

6. 'Understanding Music', *The Aristotelian Society*, Supplementary Volume 59 (1985), 231–48 (reprinted by courtesy of the editor of the Aristotelian Society: © 1985); ' "Sibley's Aesthetics" ', Critical Study of Frank Sibley's *Approach to Aesthetics* and of *Aesthetic Concepts: Essays after Sibley*', ed. Emily Brady and Jerrold Levinson, *The Philosophical Quarterly*, 52/207 (April 2002), 237–46. [A small bunch of paragraphs has been cut from the first publication and a considerably greater amount of material has been incorporated from the second publication.]

7. 'The Characterisation of Aesthetic Qualities by Essential Metaphors and Quasi-Metaphors', *The British Journal of Aesthetics*, 46/2 (April 2006), 133–44.

8. 'Musical Movement and Aesthetic Metaphors', *The British Journal of Aesthetics*, 43/3 (July 2003), 209–23.

9. 'Aesthetic Realism and Emotional Qualities of Music', *The British Journal of Aesthetics*, 45/2 (April 2005), 111–22.

10. 'On Looking at a Picture', in Jim Hopkins and Anthony Savile (eds.), *Psychoanalysis, Mind, and Art: Perspectives on Richard Wollheim* (Basil Blackwell, 1992), 259–80. [There are small additions plus postscript.]

11. 'The Look of a Picture', in Dudley Knowles and John Skorupski (eds.), *Virtue and Taste: Essays on Politics, Ethics and Aesthetics* (Basil Blackwell, 1993), 154–75. A shorter version of this essay was delivered as an inaugural lecture on 3 December 1991 at University College London.

12. 'Wollheim on Correspondence, Projective Properties and Expressive Perception', in Rob van Gerwen (ed.), *Richard Wollheim on the Art of Painting: Art as Representation and Expression* (Cambridge University Press, 2001), 101–11. This essay was read to the conference on Richard Wollheim's Aesthetics entitled 'Art: Representation and Expression' held at Utrecht in May 1997.

13. 'Wittgenstein's Aesthetics', forthcoming in Marie McGinn (ed.), *The Oxford Handbook on Wittgenstein*.

Name Index